THE TURBULENT TRIANGLE

Isaac C. Rottenberg

THE TURBULENT TRIANGLE: CHRISTIANS-JEWS-ISRAEL is an insider's account of Christian-Jewish dialogue over the past four decades, focusing particularly on the role the State of Israel has played in recent relations between Jews and Christians.

The author offers critical insights on the inner workings of ecclesiastical and ecumenical bureaucracies. He discusses fundamentalism on the Right as well as the Left and deals frankly with such sensitive issues as Christian mission efforts directed at Jews and the phenomenon of "messianic churches."

This book tells the story of what the churches have said and done regarding the State of Israel. Knowing the past record of Christian attitudes toward Israel may prepare us for what lies ahead during the next critical stage of Middle East politics.

THE
TURBULENT
TRIANGLE

Christians-Jews-Israel

A Personal-Historical Account

Isaac C. Rottenberg

Excerpts from ISRAEL: AN ECHO OF ETERNITY
by Abraham Joshua Heschel. Copyrighted ©
1967, 1968, 1969 by Abraham Joshua Heschel.
Reprinted by permission of Farrar, Straus and Giroux, Inc.

Excerpts from OUTPLACE THOSE TERMINATORS
reprinted by permission of the Wall Street Journal.
© Dow Jones & Company 1987. All Rights Reserved.

Published by Red Mountain Associates, P. O. Box 2113,
Hawley, Pennsylvania 18428

ISBN 0-89962-746-3

Manufactured in the United States of America

Contents

To My Grandchildren,

Nicole
Carmen
Ian
Lowell
Rebecca
Sean
Devon
Elizabeth
Samuel
Daniel
Pieter
and any who may follow.

*"Life only demands from you the strength you possess.
Only one feat is possible . . . not to have run."*

Dag Hammerskjöld - MARKINGS

Introduction I

This book is about Christian-Jewish relations in the broadest sense of that term. More specifically, however, it deals with the dialogue between Christians and Jews that has developed over the past four decades or so. To be more specific yet, I have focused particularly on one factor that has influenced the dialogue at critical points, namely what might be called the "Israel dynamic."

The emergence of the state of Israel was a momentous event in Jewish history, like a national rebirth after the devastations of the holocaust, so nearly-fatal to European Jewry. On the other hand, the establishment of the state of Israel was a reality that many dialogue partners in the so-called "mainline" churches found hard to digest, while for some evangelical Christians it became a central theme in their theology of history. The often emotionally charged interaction between those views and sentiments is an important part of the plot in my story.

I have characterized this book as a personal-historical account. I purposely did not set out to write a scholarly study, featuring an extensive footnote apparatus. Rather, I wanted to present the point of view of a participant, an activist in the Christian pro-Israel community who happened to have a somewhat uncommon background. For instance, I have gone through an immigrant's experience, even though I came to this country with a U.S. passport after having lived under Nazi occupation in Holland. I was raised in the Dutch Calvinist tradition, but my paternal grandfather was a Hassidic Rabbi in Poland and my father a convert to Christianity. As a Pastor, I have come to know the life of Christians on the local church level, but as a denominational executive I have also become familiar with the world of ecclesiastical and ecumenical bureaucracies.

These are among the experiences that have had a formative influence on my life, reflected in the story of this book. Some sections are unabashedly autobiographical, but even in those parts my basic intent is to deal with issues. In other words, I have tried to place those elements of my life story that are shared here into a broader context: historical interrelationships, particularly the history of Christian anti-Judaism; the bureaucratic mind-set and church politics, especially the politics of Christian mission; the spirit of triumphalism on both the Left and Right; conversion and its complexities for Christians and Jews. These are some of the issues I seek to explore as I develop my central theme: Christians, Jews and Israel.

In the past I have written for publication while serving as a parish minister and also while lecturing at a theological school. This book was written while, as the executive director of the National Christian Leadership Conference for Israel, I was involved in the less sedate lifestyle of a political activist. As a result, it may bear some of the marks of a "tract for the times," a characterization, incidentally, with which I feel quite comfortable.

My scribblings on yellow pads were transformed by my wife, Malwina, into a word-processed manuscript that an editor could work with. For that and much else I owe her a debt of gratitude.

I.C.R.

Introduction II

The preceding introduction was written in the late Fall of 1987, with the publication date of October 1988 in mind. The 40th anniversary of Israel's independence, as well as of the founding of the World Council of Churches, seemed an appropriate time to focus on the issues discussed in this book.

Unfortunately, I entrusted the manuscript into the hands of people who, as it turned out, lacked both competence and credibility. After several years of false promises and endless delays, it finally took legal action by the Attorney General of the State of New York, before I regained control over this project.

In the meantime, many new developments have taken place in the tumultuous history of the Middle East, as well as in Christian-Jewish relations. In order to avoid further delays in the publication of this book, I decided to add a minimal number of updates through the insertion of footnotes rather than undertake a more substantial re-write of the manuscript. While I do not consider this an ideal solution, it is the best I could do under the present circumstances.

Many thanks to David C. Dudley and his staff in Denver, Colorado, whose computer skills have made this publication possible.

I. C. R.

I

An Unplanned Career

A funny thing happened to me on my way up the ecclesiastical ladder. I became deeply involved with issues I had not planned to make central concerns in my life, namely Christian-Jewish relations and the state of Israel. I am not saying that I had been indifferent about those matters. Far from it! I think it would be fair to say that I had kept myself better informed on those issues than most people. But I was not personally *involved.* An interested party, yes; an activist, certainly not.

My research and writings over the previous decades had focused on certain theological themes, particularly the question of various religious interpretations of history. Dr. D. Ivan Dykstra, professor of philosophy at Hope College in Holland, Michigan, and one of the best teachers I have studied with, had aroused my interest in that subject. My reading of the Dutch theologian A. A. van Ruler had further whetted my appetite for the topic.

In a very real sense history, as predominantly understood in the Western tradition, could be called a "Hebrew invention." The biblical prophets have taught us to think about history in terms of *telos*—a purposeful destiny. It was their vision of God that made them portray history as a story that is going somewhere. Hence they cast their dream of a new world in the language of the Kingdom of God.

Even though I did not plan my present career as a pro-Israel activist, I do recall one incident rather early in my life that in retrospect can perhaps be considered a sign of things to come. It happened shortly after the liberation of Holland from Nazi rule. I was born in 1925 in the London suburb of Harrow, but when I was four years old the family had moved to the Netherlands, my mother's original homeland.

Since I had been hiding for several years on a farm in the province of

Friesland during the German occupation, I could receive my high school diploma only if I returned to finish my sixth year of gymnasium training, an absolute prerequisite in order for me to enter law school. I felt that I had outgrown high school, but I had little choice.

Our school had a club, named after the Greek muse of the literary arts, Calliope, with a rather illustrious history. Its prime aim was to cultivate forensic skills in students, and I was one of those assigned to give a speech on a topic of general interest. For some reason I chose "Zionist Aspirations in Palestine" as my subject, an issue very much in the news at that time, but hardly the hottest topic of conversation among my high school peers.

That talk, given during Calliope's 20th anniversary celebration in 1946, was my first public speech. It was also my last one on that particular subject for about three decades. So, if that adolescent effort can be considered a seed, it certainly took a long time to germinate.

During the spring of 1948, as the United Nations were arguing and agonizing about Palestine, I was preoccupied with personal matters like getting married and preparing to leave for the United States where most of my relatives lived and my parents had been citizens at one time. I had come out of World War II as a young man who was angry at God and not very interested in the Church. True, some Christians had intrigued me during the years of Nazi oppression, particularly those who risked their own lives in efforts to hide and rescue others, especially Jews. What made people do that, knowing full well that, if caught, they would share that same fate as those they were trying to save?

These people fascinated me, but I felt that God had not performed very well. I regarded my father's death in a concentration camp as the unfairest thing of all—a perhaps somewhat immature but, nevertheless understandable reaction of a teenager who felt that this was one death that should have been a priority concern for divine intervention.

At any rate, by the time I was getting ready to leave Holland at the age of 23, I was in the process of changing my thinking, seriously considering switching from the study of the law I was pursuing at the University of Leiden to philosophical and religious subjects. A Dutch

2

translation of Reinhold Niebuhr's sermons in the book *The Signs of the Times* had influenced me quite a bit.

My father had made the same journey from Holland to the United States at age 24, and we both ended up getting a degree in theology in this country. He, however, eventually returned to Europe, first working in London and later assuming the leadership of a mission in Holland.

Speaking of 1948, in light of subsequent history discussed in this book, it seems of interest to me that the World Council of Churches was founded the same year as the establishment of the state of Israel. I, like most people I knew, welcomed both events with considerable enthusiasm. Little did I realize, however, that one day my own career would become somewhat intertwined with those two historical realities.

Life in America meant quite a change for me. My Dutch Calvinist grandfather, Cornelius Boender, had emigrated to the United States before World War I and, with his wife and 11 children, had settled in Lansing, Illinois. Lawrence Boender, one of my nine uncles, and his wife Cora gave us a home during the first months of our stay in the U.S. He also helped me get a job at the steel and scrap yard in East Chicago where he was a foreman.

Being a "greenhorn" with very limited skills in the English language was not always easy, nor was exchanging the university hall for the junk yard. But I have had a love affair with this country ever since I arrived. While I believe that both good citizenship and Christian faithfulness require that one maintain a certain critical stance towards one's own country, I have never understood the hyper-critics who glibly refer to this nation as fascist. They obviously have never had a true taste of totalitarianism, although some of them have taken guided tours to such countries. As H. L. Mencken once wrote to Theodore Dreiser, who had sung the praises of the Soviet system: "When you were in Russia you saw the show window, but not much else . . . It was as if you had been taken to the best whore-house in St. Louis, and then came out saying that all Americans live like that."

My relatives, who by and large had been quite faithful to the biblical injunction to "be fruitful and multiply", had in their collective wisdom, decided that in this country I was to be called "Connie", a distorted version of my middle name Cornelius, which I had inherited from grandpa Boender. Isaac, they said, could cause problems since people might call me "Ike." This was a few years before Dwight Eisenhower became President of the United States.

I later regretted that I had let this name change happen and eventually returned to my first name, which I had inherited from grandpa Rottenberg. Frankly, there was an element of "force majeur" in the name change to Connie: it was me against so many of them. I was basically faced with a *fait accompli* the moment I came off the boat and my English was hardly adequate to put up a good fight, even if I had been inclined to do so. But, frankly, at that time it seemed that other concerns were of greater importance, like making a living in a totally new environment. Eventually, however, I came to have an ever deeper appreciation for that lovely biblical story about Abraham and his wife Sara who laughed at the idea of bearing a child at their advanced age. Derived from the Hebrew verb for laughing, my name, Isaac, reminds me that history is sometimes touched by divine humor. I am quite happy to go by that name.

Among the wealth of the denominations in this country, we count a Reformed Church and Christian Reformed Church. Both trace their roots to the Netherlands, but the latter was a breakaway from the former. It requires some study to understand the differences between the two, although the founders of the Christian Reformed Church probably thought they'd said it all when they added the adjective. In the late 1940's the feelings between the members of those two churches still ran deep in the midwestern towns that had been settled by the Dutch. The notion of one's son or daughter marrying someone from "the other side" would cause much consternation and could be sufficient reason for having one's name erased from a will.

My grandfather Boender was a secessionist. This meant, among other things, that he had left Holland not exclusively for economic reasons. Although I'm sure those played an important role, his action was also a form of protest against the liberal tendencies in the dominant Reformed Church in the Netherlands, which at that time still had official ties to the State.

In the United States all my relatives were Christian Reformed, but after some exploration my wife and I decided to join the Reformed Church in Lansing, Illinois. We felt that the Reformed Church at large was a bit more ecumenical in outlook, or at least its style of orthodoxy was a touch less rigid than that of the Christian Reformed Church. For instance, I had begun reading extensively in the work of theologian Karl Barth, admiring him both as a theologian and for his resistance to the Nazi ideologists within the German churches. But I soon discovered that my favorable sentiment toward Barth was frowned upon among Christian Reformed preachers and professors. I didn't want to set myself up for trouble once I entered theological seminary, as I had decided to do.

However, I didn't entirely stay out of trouble in the church of my choice either. The Reformed Church in America was then engaged in union talks with one of the small Presbyterian denominations. Eager to be a responsible new member, I went to see Pastor August Tellinghuisen and asked him to show me everything he had to read on the subject. Having done my homework, I concluded that the two small denominations were quite similar in faith and practice, and that union might strengthen their common ministry.

I shall never forget the night of the official vote in our Lansing congregation. The men had come out in force (women did not have the vote in our church at that time). I anticipated a stimulating debate. Instead, we were treated to one speech by Dr. Harry Hager, a well known figure in the denomination and an outspoken foe of union. He predicted many dire consequences from the proposed union. I wondered about this kind of campaigning at the polls, so to speak. How many 'yes' votes might he have turned into 'no' votes? I need not have worried. The final ballot was 1 in favor, 159 opposed.

I sat there dumbfounded. Obviously, I had badly misjudged the spirit of ecumenicity in the fellowship I had joined some short months earlier. Before I could recoup, a deacon who sat next to me whispered in my ear: "I'd like to meet that one guy in a dark alley some night . . ." What if he knew that I, this recent Dutch import, was the one who had spoiled the blessed consensus? On the other hand, what was the meaning of this kind of unanimity? Was it an answer to all the prayers that had been offered asking for divine guidance, or were these people victims of what Aldous Huxley has referred to as "herd poisoning?"

I somehow felt that I had to do something. So I stood up to mutter some emotional words about how during Nazism we had discovered the importance of greater unity among Christians. My remarks were met with silence and soon the meeting broke up.

Later, as I became deeply involved in the ecumenical movement, I learned that conservatives don't have a monopoly on mindless voting patterns. There is plenty of dogmatic unanimity in liberal church circles as well. Furthermore, after we left Lansing in order for me to pursue my theological studies, the members of that local church continued to follow us with their love and support throughout those years of financial insecurity. I have not always found the same charitable spirit toward dissenters among the advocates of ecumenical dialogue and church union.

During the years of theological study in Holland, Michigan, some of my most stimulating intellectual conversations were with Dr. Albertus Pieters, a retired professor who was one of the most interesting patriarchs of the Reformed Church. For years, he had engaged in polemics with the Grand Rapids radio preacher H.R. de Haan, who expounded a fundamentalist-millenialist point of view. Pieters had summed up his perspectives on Israel as a covenant people in the book entitled *The Seed of Abraham*.

Albertus Pieters was a dyed-in-the-wool supersessionist, meaning that he saw no biblical basis whatsoever for the view that the divine covenant with the people of Israel had never been revoked. Or, to say it differently, he firmly believed that the Church is the New Israel that has replaced the rejected Jewish people. All the professors who were teaching at the Seminary when I was there had at one time been students of Pieters and his theological views on this particular question had in essence become the official position of the school.

From time to time my wife and I were invited to the Pieters home for dinner. The meal was always followed by Bible reading which, in turn, was accompanied by Dr. Pieter's commentary. I loved to listen to him. Shortly after dinner he would announce that Mrs. Rottenberg must be eager to return home and put our firstborn child to bed. That was the signal

or his unmarried daughter to drive mother and baby home so that we
could turn to serious business.

Pieters was a great teacher. He held views with firm conviction, but
he loved the give and take of argument. I had begun to read heavily in
European theological writings and thus had the advantage of having discovered some treatises on the subject of Israel and the covenant that had
not yet come to my host's attention. He was in his 80's at that time and
had never been fond of European scholarship in the first place. I recall
particularly a monograph on Romans 9:11 by Karl Ludwig Schmidt that
helped me score a few surprise points.

It was all like a friendly game of polemical gymnastics, but those
were not the issues that would preoccupy me during the following years. I
did become convinced, however, that whatever may be the fallacies
inherent in the fundamentalist/dispensationalist position, supersession
theology could not be the answer either. It simply had too many blind
spots as far as the biblical witness is concerned. For years it has seemed
too bad to me that, as far as many Christians are concerned, there appear to
be only two options available.

I was ordained as a minster of the Reformed Church in America in
June 1955. Shortly thereafter I was invited to join the denomination's
Christian Action Commission. We prepared a "Credo on Race Relations",
which proved to be a helpful guide for reflection and action during the explosive years of the civil rights struggle in this country as well as the
churches. Having participated over the years in the formulation of all sorts
of denominational and ecumenical pronouncements, I eventually came to
recognize that in most cases such statements are produced by a small elite
for a small elite and soon forgotten. I am glad to say that this did not
prove to be the case with the "Credo on Race Relations."

My second denominational assignment, this time as a member of the
Theological Commission, got me embroiled in "The Adam question." A
regional judicatory had refused to license a seminary graduate because,
they claimed, his views on the creation accounts in Genesis were not in
accordance with the Reformed confessions. The matter was referred to the
Theological Commission, which I served as secretary at the time. We issued a report for which I had written the original draft, recommending a

somewhat broader view of biblical interpretation.

The denomination's General Synod in 1960 adopted the Theological Commission's position. Several pastors then proceeded to produce and distribute a counter-document accusing some of us of heresy and other assorted sins. I found their style to be excessively pompous even for preachers and felt that their harsh *ad hominem* arguments were reminiscent of the McCarthy mentality so pervasive in our country during the preceding years. So I decided to write an "open letter", which was printed at my own expense and sent to all ministers in the denomination. It was a somewhat nasty, tongue-in-cheek piece of writing, but I still think that was needed in order to puncture a few bubbles. Theology is serious business, but I have never felt that we should take ourselves dead serious.

I accept the fact that most churches set certain confessional limits for those who wish to be teachers and preachers in that communion. That, it seems to me, is fair enough. After all, nobody is forced to function within any particular denomination. On the other hand, there needs to be some room to test those limits from time to time in order for a church to remain open to reform. Tradition can be enriching but traditionalism is deadening. As the old saying goes, "tradition is the living faith of the dead, but traditionalism is the dead faith of the living."

Shortly after the publication of my "open letter", a professor in one of our seminaries approached me during a national church convention and furtively pushed a crumpled $5 bill into my hand. He asked me to keep the gift anonymous and mumbled something about how nice it would be if professors had a little more freedom to express their honest opinions. I certainly could have used the money, but I was troubled by the air of intimidation that seemed to surround this little exchange. I have never thought of freedom as something that comes our way as a favor. You affirm it, and if someone tries to take it away, you fight for it.

In dealing with matters of faith and morals, a little fear and trembling is not such a bad thing. But it should be the result of an inner sense of responsibility, not of intimidation by others. Heinrich Böll has written that "literature does not need freedom. It is freedom." In a profound sense I believe this to be true of theology as well, (even though or, perhaps, precisely because) it draws its guiding light from revelation.

In 1967 I was asked to serve as "host pastor" for the denomination's General Synod meeting, held that year in Bristol, Tennessee. One of the main functions of the host pastor was to provide a light touch during meal times, which were also used to make various announcements. It so happened that simultaneously with our meeting, the Six Day War was being fought in the Middle East. The rapid and victorious moves of the Israeli Defense Forces provided me with some of the better materials for my monologues. I made no attempt to conceal my bias, but almost everybody loved it nevertheless.

In those days even mainline church leaders were pulling for Israel, a situation that was soon to change. The missionaries to the Arab world who were attending the assembly were less appreciative of my upbeat commentaries.

The following year I joined my denomination's national staff as Secretary for Program Interpretation. My official title was really longer than that, but those were the key words. Edward Hay Associates, a management consulting firm, was then advising the denomination in one of its reorganization efforts. The length of the bureaucratic titles those experts proposed suggested they were being paid by the word.

Speaking of being paid by the word, the first time I had that experience was in 1956, when the *Reader's Digest* used a sentence from a sermon I had preached at an ecumenical Thanksgiving Day service in its "Picturesque Speech" column. The quote had been sent in by someone without my knowledge, and when the $15 check arrived it was a complete surprise. The woman who had submitted it called to let me know that she too had received a $15 check. How I wished that some of my subsequent writings would have been remunerated that well! (I subsequently learned that *Atlantic Magazine* offered Mark Twain two cents a word for his first story, a remuneration that he did not find satisfactory but accepted because of "the awful respectability of the magazine". Considering inflation since 1874, I'm sure Mr. Clemens came out ahead of me, as it should be).

When I was appointed as a church bureaucrat in New York, it meant leaving the suburban Tinton Falls parish I had served for ten years. Those had been good years for our family. In my ministry I tried to combine and hold in creative tension the roles of pastor, scholar, and social activist, seeking to avoid the contempt some pastors called to be "prophetic" sometimes feel for the parishioners they are supposed to serve.

I was proud when the *Daily Register* of Red Bank, New Jersey, gave me a farewell editorial with the heading "A Man of Courage, Dedication.' Not feigning humility, I cite a few sentences: "Not in recent memory has this area been privileged to witness a single individual stir the conscience of the community as did this inspired cleric. He was a front runner in the civil rights movement long before it was fashionable and at a time when many clergymen were silent." I was particularly proud that in the midst of controversy and at times of tension, a relationship of trust and mutual affection had developed between my congregation and me. It still is like a little party whenever we return for a visit to that church.

Most of my colleagues in the church bureaucracy lived in the Ridgewood, New Jersey area, but we decided we preferred the less homogeneous character of the town of Montclair. I joined a car pool that at that time was one of very few private corporations established to transport suburbanites to New York City. Every day our pool of three-seat station wagons drove church executives to a building known as the Interchurch Center, sometimes referred to as "the God Box" because it is the headquarters for many church establishments.

The magazine *Presbyterian Life* had just published an article of mine dealing with the subject of sex education. It received a favorable review from my car pool colleagues during my first ride to New York. Nobody, apparently, had noticed that in the same month in *The Christian Herald* there appeared a protest piece of mine lamenting the party-line mentality that so often prevails in church circles. I somehow suspect that the latter piece would have been a better gauge of how I might behave in a bureaucracy than the article on sex.

My career as a church bureaucrat moved along quite nicely, until the National Council of Churches decided in 1974 to establish an Office on Christian-Jewish Relations. I was asked to represent my denomination on its executive committee and at the first meeting was chosen to be its chairman. I had served on a number of other National Council of Churches committees, since bureaucracies are mostly about committees ınd meetings. But this time, things turned out quite differently. Everyhing apparently changes when "Jewish issues" are involved.

It all looked fine in the policy statement that was part of the grant proposal that had impressed the Lily Endowment sufficiently to support the office during the first three years of its operation. We were, among other things, to "respond to the changing situation and need for new relationships between Christians and Jews, to develop new levels of communication and trust, and to encourage the emergence of new groups for common action." In February 1973 the National Council of Churches Governing Board had voted to create this office "on a priority basis", but the big question was whether the church bureaucrats who controlled budgets considered Christian-Jewish relations enough of a priority to put up some cash. It soon became apparent that the answer was (and still is) "No." Ever since the grant ran out the office has existed in a state of virtual bankruptcy. As I am writing this in 1986 it has been without executive staff for over a year.

It seems to me that the project might have succeeded if there had not been a state of Israel. Especially after 1967, Israel became increasingly central in the life and thought of the Jewish community, while a growing number of Christian leaders came to view the Jewish state as an obstacle to dialogue.

The ecumenical movement or, more specifically, the conciliar movement as represented in the National and World Councils, has had a hard time digesting the reality of Israel as an integral part of Christian-Jewish dialogue. But, more on that later.

For me personally, my involvement in this new ecumenical venture took on increasingly ironic aspects. On one hand, it became the occasion for a thoroughgoing re-education with regard to a number of realities, including the scope of historic Christian anti-Judaism, often leading to vicious anti-Semitism. It also forced me to re-evaluate certain realities, including aspects of my own background and upbringing. On the other hand, some of my experiences relating to the work of the National Council of Churches office were contributing to a growing disenchantment with the church bureaucracy and would eventually lead me on a collision course with the ecumenical establishment. That was a situation I had hardly bargained for when I almost routinely accepted the invitation to join that particular committee. What's one more committee in a world where meetings are a way of life? Well, it all depends.

A few years earlier I had been a member of a committee that was charged with revising the confessional basis of the National Council of Churches . With that kind of assignment, one might expect theological sparks to fly. Quite the contrary. I soon discovered that in some ecumenical circles confessional issues are treated in an almost blasé fashion while passions are reserved for political and ideological agendas. Behind the polite facade of dialogue in the ecumenical movement, just as in the United Nations, one finds intensely politicized and increasingly intolerant processes at work.

Not once during the years that I was chairman of the executive committee of the Office on Christian-Jewish Relations did the various parties within the National Council of Churches that were involved in Middle East issues sit down to explore in open discussions what people believed on those matters and why. Rather, Dr. William Weiler, the executive director and I as chairman found ourselves caught up in a web of intrigue from the very start. The people of the Middle East Office had been at this game for quite a while. As most of them were representatives of Christian missionary interests in Arab countries, their basic view of the "real" Middle East was one that left no room for Israel as an integral part of that region.

Whenever a Governing Board or National Council of Churches Executive Committee was approaching, a small group of "Middle East Desk" and "Justice and Liberation" people would get together to work on a draft statement. It was, of course, important that the proposed pronouncement be "prophetic", which in that particular context usually meant that the critique of some alleged Israeli sin would be severe while Arab countries were spared any kind of condemnation in order not to jeopardize Christian missionary interests there.

By the time Weiler and I were invited to participate in the process, time pressures to meet the scheduled date for the mailing of delegate packets were already being felt. Furthermore, the draft statement usually contained several sentences or even sections of such clearly outrageous quality that the urgent question no longer was what might be the Christian thing to say at this juncture in history, but rather, how a disastrous breakdown in Christian-Jewish relations could be avoided. By the time we had spent our energies expunging the most offensive sentences, the cut-off date had arrived and we were still left with a basically unbalanced document. The strategy in this old political ploy was clear: to forget about dialogue and, by putting others on the defensive from the very start, try to win a battle in the war of petty bureaucratic infighting.

A book in my library written by Markus Barth, New Testament scholar and son of the renowned theologian Karl Barth, contains an inscription dated October 25, 1975. It reads: "To Isaac Rottenberg, in friendship to a fellow-fighter, from the author." What would turn nice scholarly types like us into fighters?

The inscription refers to an incident that took place in Geneva, Switzerland, where a group of ecumenical leaders were meeting. During the summer of 1975 a heated debate had been going on at the United Nations about the question whether Zionism should be declared a form of racism. During the month of November that same year the World Council of Churches was to hold one of its major assemblies in Nairobi, Kenya, and there was some concern that a similar anti-Zionist resolution might be proposed and pushed through at that gathering. We had been asked to meet in Geneva in an attempt to diffuse some of the tensions beforehand and to prepare a document that was designed to stave off any surprise move by delegates in Nairobi.

At this Geneva gathering—where not even one Jew had been invited as an observer—Clovis Maksoud, an editor in Beirut with close ties to the PLO and more recently the official representative of the Arab League at the United Nations, sought to dominate many of the discussions. Since he was not a member of a WCC-related church, it must be assumed that he had received a special invitation in order to reinforce the delegation from Arab churches. He did so by using some of the vilest anti-Zionist rhetoric I had heard since living under Nazi occupation. Barth and I finally decided that it was time to do some blasting of our own. We let Maksoud have it, telling him in no uncertain terms that we would not sit by silently while he poisoned the air with his bigotry.

Such incidents often gave me the feeling that I was playing a part in the theatre of the absurd. Here we were, a Christian ecumenical fellowship, purportedly devoted to dialogue and reconciliation, but behaving like a bunch of third rate politicians. I grew increasingly restless in that environment. Slowly on it became clear to me that I was becoming a member of the loyal opposition, but also that such a role will not be tolerated in most bureaucratic settings, not even when the bureaucracy claims to be devoted to dialogue.

In April 1975, an National Council of Churches sponsored "for staff only" forum on the Middle East was convened at Mt. Augustine Retreat Center on Staten Island, New York. Weiler asked me to send him a memo stating some of my reactions to the proceedings there. The final paragraph in my memo went like this: "I am willing to work for a cooperative Christian approach to the Middle East crisis that has a minimum of propagandistic dimensions to it. For that purpose I am prepared to restrain myself in attitude and speech, and to be admonished by the brothers and sisters if I fail to do so. But, as far as the forum is concerned, right now I am not certain at all whether I am a member of a team or a member of the loyal opposition. We shall see."

Self-preservation is the law of life for most bureaucracies. As a consequence, they tend to become imbued with a fundamentally anti-democratic bias. Critics are to be treated as the enemy. He or she who is not wholeheartedly for us, is against us. Paul Tillich's thesis that the Protestant Principle implies a prophetic stance that leaves room for a self-critical spirit was accepted as theology but rejected as policy. This is a mentality far removed from the spirit of the prayer of Thomas à Kempis: "Grant that I may prudently avoid him that flatters me, and patiently bear with him that contradicts me."

There were times when I began to daydream about the advantages of an academic career. Five years earlier I had been offered the position of dean of my *alma mater*, New Brunswick Theological Seminary. I had declined, being content at the time to stay with the job I had. But I had always thought about teaching as an attractive option.

In 1978, exactly ten years after I had started my bureaucratic career, things came to a head. To tell the truth, I got fired, a subject that will be dealt with in a later chapter. New Brunswick just happened to have vacancy on its faculty and invited me to fill in for a year and also to submit my name as a candidate for appointment. I decided to do so, even though I was developing some doubts about an institution that was steadily lowering the standards for admission, but at the same time has an increasing number of *cum laude* graduates (a situation that is quite common in some of the smaller theological seminaries today).

However, in the end, the committee selected someone from outside our denomination. I had become not only a controversial person by that time, but an individual who, in effect, was "down and out". Such circumstances tend to make any applicant a less desirable candidate and the church like everybody else, needs "winners".

Also in 1978, something else happened that would have a significant impact on my life: the founding of the National Christian Leadership Conference for Israel, of which two years later I would become a full-time employee. The years that followed were not always easy, but, certainly not dull either. The work, which I found stimulating, offered me numerous opportunities to broaden my contacts and perspectives.

Looking back I realized that one sometimes learns to thank the Lord for doors that were left unopened. New Brunswick Seminary, weighed down by what I perceive as its own sterile environment and by what was generally recognized as poor management, went through years of rapid decline and ended up firing half its faculty a few years later. My struggles in National Christian Leadership Conference for Israel were, perhaps, not less severe, but I am quite sure that my working environment was more inspiring. I discovered that a leave from professional church life can be a pause that refreshes.

II

An Unlikely Candidate

Hitler and his henchmen made me very much aware of my two Jewish grandparents in Poland, whom I had never met. In those days, counting one's Jewish grandfathers and grandmothers became a matter of great importance. For millions, it literally became a life or death issue. Having three Jewish grandparents was fatal; having two made one a less desirable human being but not automatically a candidate for a concentration camp and annihilation.

When, after World War II, I arrived in the United States as a cousin from "the old country", my relatives were prepared to receive me as a member of the clan. But they also had to cope with the fact that Isaac Rottenberg is not exactly a Dutch-sounding name like, for instance, VandenBerg. I was different from all the other cousins, because I was part Jewish, and they were accustomed to an environment where uncomplimentary remarks about Jews could be made without any fear of recrimination.

The change of my name from Isaac to Connie was in part an expression of concern, of a desire to give me an equal chance. They did not want me to encounter embarrassment. But at the same time, I suspect, they had to come to terms with at least a touch of embarrassment they themselves felt because of the fact that the family had been infiltrated by this . . . what shall I say? . . . "foreign element".

As recently as the late 1940's, Dutch Americans almost without exception married people "of their own kind", even of their brand of Calvinist denomination, as I have pointed out. My father's background in Poland made him about as different from the norm as an invader from Mars might have been. For the Boender family, the name Rottenberg was enough of a reminder of my "Jewishness". To add Isaac to that invoked a kind of double jeopardy that ought to be avoided.

16

My Jewish background became somewhat of an issue once again when I was being considered for the position of executive director of the National Christian Leadership Conference for Israel. This time, as irony would have it, I was dealing with some of the top leaders in Christian-Jewish dialogue, several of them well-known scholars in the field of Holocaust studies. In other words, these people knew history, particularly the history of Christian anti-Semitism. More than most people, they had come to recognize the evils of treating human beings according to the measure of their Jewishness.

I was not a member of the tribe that has come to be known as "Holocaust scholars", but in a very real sense I was a child of that horrible chapter in history. Elie Wiesel once said that "in a strange way any survivor has more to say than all historians combined on what happened." I am not that kind of survivor, but I lived in the shadows, and I know something about the darkness of those years. When I was 16 years old, S.S. storm troopers invaded our home to arrest my father. They turned everything upside down, not the least the lives of every member of our family.

For years, however, those experiences had not led me to pursue anything even remotely akin to the job of executive director of the National Christian Leadership Conference for Israel. I became a fighter on behalf of Israel in an almost willy-nilly fashion. I had been looking for an academic, not an activist career. In my writings I had always tried very hard to strike a dialectical balance between divergent positions. It felt to me that I was being pressed into a partisan mold because of the politicized ecumenical environment in which I found myself. Of course, I realize that, for better or for worse, we are all in large measure what our experiences have made us. On a less conscious level my journey from a teenage orator on Zionism to executive director of National Christian Leadership Conference for Israel may have involved inner forces more complex than I was aware of.

However that may be, I had in fact become deeply involved in issues pertaining to Israel and I felt that, in a number of respects, I was peculiarly qualified for the job at National Christian Leadership Conference for Israel. Except, of course, for the fact that I was part Jewish. The idea that this automatically might be a reason for disqualification at first seemed very offensive to me. But deep down in my heart I understood that this issue inevitably had to be raised, precisely among people who knew history. The question whether someone like me could function effectively in that job was, sad as it may be, a valid one in light of historical realities.

Historical knowledge can, in curious ways, create its own dilemmas. Take, for instance, the question of conversion or, more specifically, the fact that I was the son of a Jew who had become a convert to Christianity. When discussed in abstract terms, that is simply a matter of free personal choice as to the faith one wishes to embrace. But in the context of Christian-Jewish history, things are much more complicated than that, because, to mention one factor, there has been a long history of forced conversions. For multitudes of Jews the basic choice was either to convert or be killed, to turn or to burn.

There had also been a history of forcible baptisms, little children torn away from their mothers in the name of Jesus and the salvation of their eternal souls. This practice was at times not only condoned but encouraged by clerics (even though it was prohibited by canon law). The more I studied that history, the more I realized the limits of arguments that have logic on their side but lack roots in the realities of life. The hesitation to hire me seemed to me both irrational *and* based on some real concerns. So, I understand what was going on in the debate about how background might affect my credibility in some circles and the organization's effectiveness in others.

Some enemies of the cause would undoubtedly emphasize or even exaggerate my Jewishness, like the pro-Arab apologist Grace Halsell. In her book *Prophecy and Politics: Militant Evangelicals on the Road to Armageddon*, which is loaded with misstatements of all kinds, she refers to me as "a Jew who converted to Dutch Reformed Protestantism"(p. 79). On the other hand, some Jewish leaders might not feel comfortable working in close cooperation with someone with my background.

On several occasions I have received enquiries from Jewish fundraising agencies mentioning that someone had recommended me as an effective speaker and requesting that I send biographical information. I have never felt a need to dwell in detail on my background, but my *curriculum vitae* did include one sentence on the fact that on my father's side I hail from an East European Jewish family. I felt that any attempt to hide that fact would have been dishonest, and, in the end, fruitless. At any rate, there was never a follow-up on the initial correspondence. Even though as the child of a gentile mother, I am not Jewish according to Talmudic law, my very background makes me part of a Jewish-Christian dynamic that has deep and tragic roots in history. There is simply no escaping that fact. However, having said all this, I want to state emphatically that, almost without exception, leaders of major Jewish organizations have treated me with the utmost fairmindedness.

At this point it seems appropriate that I share a few details on my family background, which I have de-emphasized in the past. As I said before, I have never known my grandfather Isaac, nor his world of Hassidic Judaism in Poland. Chronologically, I am two generations re-moved from him. Culturally and perhaps spiritually we seem to be aeons apart. Of course, I realize that the same can be said of Jews who belong to temples, who may be quite strict in their observances, but who are baffled if not embarrassed by the ways of Hassidism. The portrait of my grandfa-ther that hangs in my study is really an enlargement made from a passport photo, the only known picture ever made of him. That he was forced into by the authorities in order to obtain the required identification papers. Grandpa Isaac interpreted the divine prohibition against the making of im-ages to include the invention of photography. He must have looked straight into the lens of the camera, because his soft pensive eyes follow one around the room. I sometimes try to read those eyes and the soul of which they are the reflection. What would this rabbi and I have to say to each other if we could meet today? Would he even be willing to see me?

When my father was roaming across Europe—not yet a Christian but in pursuit of answers about Jesus of Nazareth—he once sent word back to his father through a friend, assuring him that he was well. My grandfather responded with a note quoting the words of Genesis 45:26, where Joseph's brothers report to father Jacob that his son is still alive, but (states the text) "Jacob's heart fainted, for he believed them not." The ending of this story turned out less happy than the biblical narrative, for in my grandfather's case father and son never saw each other again.

My father was born in Dombrowa, Galicia, but spent most of his early years in Krakow. His journey toward Jesus did not start through some sort

19

of Christian missionary campaign. It actually began with a chance encounter in Basel, where he had been sent for three months of Talmudic studies with a renowned rabbinical scholar. It was there that one night in a university hall he overheard a discussion between two students about Jesus and whether he was the one about whom the prophets had spoken.

After months of wanderings through Europe, my father ended up in Holland. There he came into contact with a missionary named Joseph Zalman who worked in Rotterdam, the harbor city from which tens of thousands of Jews sailed for the United States. The mission operated a small cigarette factory where people could find temporary employment while waiting to depart for the new world.

It was there that my father decided to become a convert. It was there that he also became acquainted with my mother. Some years later they met again in the United States where my grandfather Boender had moved his family and where my father eventually immigrated in order to look for greater opportunities to work and study at the same time and, perhaps to pursue my mother. At any rate, they were married in 1920. I was born in 1925, the fifth of six children.

I was baptized and raised in the Dutch Calvinist faith of my mother's family, a somewhat narrow and authoritarian environment. My grandfather Cornelius Boender, whom I did not get to know until I was in my twenties, was a strict disciplinarian. His orthodoxy included the conviction that the English language ought not to be used in church service in the United States. As far as he was concerned, if Dutch was good enough for God, it was good enough for him. The *hollandse* Bible was THE word. All else lacked full authority.

Sometimes I still wonder how the world of Dutch Calvinism and the world of the Krakow ghetto came together in my father's life. It strikes me as a strange combination indeed. Where were the points of contact? True, both traditions show great respect for scholarly pursuits. I'm sure that helped, because my father was passionate about books. Also, the orthodox Reformed way of life tends to be a structured one. Although my father raised many criticisms against some of the rules in the heritage he had left behind, the Calvinism we practiced was hardly free of a legalistic mentality. At any rate, my father remained convinced all his life long that he had never ceased to be Jew.

Therefore, in a sort of awesome sense, it could be called appropriate that, like millions of other Jews, he would end his life in a concentration camp (in his case, Mauthausen), wearing the yellow star of David. I remember walking in Manhattan some years ago with Paul Riebenfeld, an expert on Middle East affairs who was very active in the World Zionist Federation. During our conversation I made the point that my father's conversion had made absolutely no difference as far as the Nazis were concerned. As a matter of fact, since he had authored several books opposing the Nazi philosophy, he had been arrested before most other Jews. "I don't feel at all sorry for him," said Riebenfeld. I think I know what he meant and, if I'm right, I also suspect that my father would have agreed with the basic sentiment behind his remark.

In 1935 my father had made a trip to Germany. Upon his return to Holland he wrote an article raising the question whether, in light of Nazi brutality, Christians have the right to remain silent. "Of course, there is the threat of persecution," he wrote. "So what? There are times when Christians must accept such persecution if they wish to save their souls and preserve their calling as advocates of truth and justice."

Conversion ought not to entitle one to special privileges when the Jewish people as a whole go through the hell of the holocaust. In some cases church leaders made special pleadings for Jews who had become Christians (and also furnished some Jews who had not converted with fake baptism certificates), and a certain number of lives were saved that way. It is all very understandable and every life saved is sacred. But one never can feel entirely comfortable with such selective Christian appeals.

Several years after my father's death I found a letter in one of the file folders that the Nazi's had overlooked. Dated one week before his arrest, it was typed and signed, but had never been sent. In it my father told a friend that we were living through days of mortal danger, but rather than being paralyzed by fear, he planned to speak out till the end. The end may have come sooner than he had expected.

My father was arrested on January 19, 1942. Three months later he was dead. My mother, having been summoned to report to the S.S. headquarters in The Hague, was told that he had been "shot while trying to escape," one of the three or four standard reasons given to family members of the murdered. The officer felt compelled to add that there was no reason for tears since my father was a Jew. My mother stared at him and replied that they never viewed their relationship in racial terms. To that he said simply, "It's the blood in the veins." In those few words is encapsuled a horror story of enormous proportions.

Some time ago a good friend, Rabbi Solomon Bernards, who for years worked with distinction for the Anti-Defamation League of B'Nai B'rith in the area of Jewish-Christian relations, showed me some of the writings of Rabbi Meir of Rothenberg-on-the-Tauber. He told me that this famous 13th century Rabbi, renowned for his scholarship, poetic spirit and his, for that time, remarkable theories about the inalienable rights of individuals, might well be one of my forebears.

Since then I have learned a little more about this fascinating figure. For instance, it is reported that in 1286, exactly 700 years before I am writing this, the great Rabbi Meir was captured in Basel and held for ransom in the fortress of Endisheim in Alsace. In order not to encourage hostage taking, he refused to have the Jewish community pay the ransom money. As a consequence he passed the final seven years of his life in prison. I wouldn't mind at all being a descendent of Rabbi Meir.

I must admit, however, that my education in the traditions of Judaism has been miserably inadequate. I grew up in a home that could boast one of the very few typewriters with Hebrew characters in all of The Hague or even Holland. Yet, I did not learn the Hebrew alphabet until I went to the theological seminary. The Rottenberg children grew up knowing very little about the Jewish festivals, customs and beliefs. I fear that this kind of situation is all to prevalent in families of converts, even though the parent who has made the change is thoroughly convinced that he or she is still a Jew.

But, in my case there was an extra dimension. I grew up in a missionary environment with very aggressive and strongly polemical overtones. My father, as is so often the case with converts, often felt a need to define his newfound faith in contrast to rabbinical teachings. He became an intensely committed and sometimes highly confrontational apologist for

Christianity. I was the eldest son, and friends of the family would, on occasion, voice their fervent hope that I would follow in my father's footsteps.

I remember publicly announced and well-attended debates. The air would be heavy with passion. To me as a child it seemed like high drama; the heated arguments, sometimes even clenched fists. It was like a wild wrestling match, but without physical violence. One night, I recall, an opponent of my father jumped on his chair and made some derogatory remark about "that cursed piece of wood," meaning the cross of Christ. Some of the ladies from refined Dutch families, who were often present at those gatherings, made some shrieking and indignant noises. Many years later I would learn how, in Jewish minds, the cross had become a symbol of Christian anti-Semitism. My father spent most of this time traveling and speaking or in his study writing books, and I never got to know him very well. But, in spite of his spirited style of debating, I remember him as a gentle and courageous man. After his death, the Reformed Church in the Netherlands took over the private organization called "Elim", which he had headed, and provided a pension for my mother who was left with nothing but a 2000 guilder burial policy. (Since my father never had a burial, she gave the money to me as a fund with which to start my law studies.)

After World War II, the Reformed Church in the Netherlands moved away from the emphasis on mission and toward the idea of dialogue. That led to radical change in approach and I sometimes wonder how my father would have reacted to that if he were still alive. Also, what would his response have been to the establishment of the state of Israel? How would my father have felt about some of my writings, or my activities as executive director of National Christian Leadership Conference for Israel? These are questions about which one can only speculate.

It seems to me that converts face such complex adjustments. Perhaps this is particularly true for Jews. In Judaism, faith and life come, as it were, in a package: there is the individual, but there is also that strong sense of peoplehood and of a destiny that is inextricably tied up with THE LAND.

When my father came to the United States in search of an education,

23

he spent some time at Moody Bible Institute in Chicago. But the flirtation with fundamentalist/millenialist theology was short lived. Eventually he studied at the staunchly Calvinist Christian Reformed seminary in Grand Rapids, Michigan and graduated from McCormick Theological Seminary in Chicago, a Presbyterian institution. I don't know whether my father didn't feel at home at Moody or whether members of my mother's family prevailed upon him to pursue his studies at an institution more in line with their brand of Protestantism.

It would hardly have been surprising if my father had embraced some form of fundamentalist evangelicalism. Quite a few Jewish converts had done that before him and a number of them since. Some have become prominent evangelists. On the one hand, this has always puzzled me. All the emphasis on "saving souls", as if there is a body-soul dichotomy, strikes me as fundamentally un-Hebraic. The unworldly tendency in so much evangelical theology has always seemed to me in conflict with the earthiness of biblical thinking.

On the other hand, I realize that converts are frequently people in search of "high intensity religion", the kind of religion found more in evangelical than in so-called "mainline" Christian circles. In evangelicalism, faith is often lived with passion, and I can understand why such passion has a certain appeal to restless and questioning Jewish souls.

At any rate, I find it intriguing to speculate on how my own life and career might have developed if I had been raised in an evangelical-millenialist environment. I still could have ended up as a pro-Israel activist, because many believers in that particular tradition are today among the staunchest supporters of Israel. However, it is not very likely that I would be heading an ecumenical network like National Christian Leadership Conference for Israel. My basically "mainline" upbringing (albeit with strong evangelical sympathies), and my experience in the ecumenical movement made me a viable candidate for that job, even though I came burdened with what might be called a certain "baggage".

I was eager to get the position at National Christian Leadership Conference for Israel, not only because I was unemployed and was badly in need of a job, but because I saw it as an opportunity to deal with some unfinished business as far as the mainline church establishment was concerned. I knew that world and its internal anti-Israel politics like few other people did. I had been part of that world, knew how it operated and felt that I had both the theological and organizational background to confront it with some effectiveness.

The position was advertised in several periodicals. There were few applicants. Among those considered, I was the only one who knew the truth about the organization's financial condition. The irony of the situation was that the money spent on advertising the job had virtually depleted the tiny balance in National Christian Leadership Conference for Israel's bank account. In the end, it turned out that I was the only person crazy enough to take the job.

III

National Christian Leadership Conference

for Israel:

A New Chapter in an Old Story

The decision to found the National Christian Leadership Conference for Israel (NCLCI) was based on some excellent ideas, but also on a few inaccurate assumptions. Certainly the core notion that Christian support for Israel ought to transcend narrow sectarian interests was an idea whose time was long overdue. On the other hand, the expectation that one could find broadbased financial support in Christian circles for a network like National Christian Leadership Conference for Israel was somewhat naive, as past history might have taught us. In short, the people who were the prime movers in establishing the National Christian Leadership Conference for Israel demonstrated both vision and a slightly pollyannish view of life.

The immediate occasion for National Christian Leadership Conference for Israel's beginning was the 30th anniversary of Israel's independence in 1978. That also happened to be one of those years when the U.S. Congress was debating the sale of sophisticated weaponry to Arab countries. Some 400 Christian leaders, representing a broad spectrum of churches, gathered at the Hyatt Regency Hotel in Washington, D.C.

There are very few subjects on which the people attending that conference could have reached a consensus. They had, however, one concern in common: the security and well-being of the state of Israel. They agreed that Israel's enemies should not be furnished the means for her potential destruction.

I have often referred to Israel as a great ecumenical catalyst. Love and concern for that country have a way of bringing together the most extraordinary combinations of people. People who would otherwise have little occasion to meet, let alone cooperate with one another. Still, this is not just an ecumenicity of political expediency. It goes much deeper than that. In spite of profound theological and social-political differences, these Christians share certain fundamental perspectives on God's dealings in history and particularly on the nature of the divine covenant with the Jewish people. To say the least, most of them are convinced that this covenant has not been revoked or transferred to the Church. Christians enter into a relationship with the God of Abraham, Isaac and Jacob only by becoming incorporated into the divine and eternal covenant with Israel.

True, bringing people together for dialogue is not the same as establishing an effective network of support and, on many occasions, Israel has also become a stumbling block to better Christian-Jewish relations. However, I have become increasingly convinced that an encounter with Judaism and the reality of Israel is of immense significance to the life of the churches, including their search for greater unity among Christians.

The word "ecumenical", like the word "catholic", even though commonly used in rather narrow ecclesiastical context, has connotations too rich to be confined to any particular group or organization. Those words seek to reach beyond churchly realities. They aspire to open up vistas of a unity that encompasses humanity and the world in which we live.

In that sense, Israel must be seen as the great ecumenical catalyst. In ancient times the Jewish nation and its ethos were formed around a fundamental confession of unity: "Hear, O Israel: the Lord our God is one Lord." This is not just a matter of addition and/or subtraction. Rather, it is and expressions of the unitary nature and purpose of the Divine Creator and Lord of history. It was through the history of Israel that a certain kind of vision concerning unity has entered our world. Any ecumenical movement that ignores this fact will eventually become anemic and lose its vitality.

But we must return to the Washington Hyatt in 1978. Those attending felt good about what was happening there. Here they were, Christians of many stripes, united as friends of the Jewish state: members of church hierarchies, evangelists, labor leaders, academicians, people from the art

27

world, prominent politicians from both the Republican and Democratic parties. It is not surprising that the question arose whether there ought not to be a framework wherein such contacts could be maintained and further cultivated on an ongoing basis. A resolution to that effect was proposed and enthusiastically endorsed.

Thus National Christian Leadership Conference for Israel was born. In a way something new was being started here, but in another sense it was the beginning of a new chapter in an old story. There were antecedents; forerunners who had laid foundations on which others could build. The immediate predecessor to National Christian Leadership Conference for Israel had been Franklin Littell's Christians Concerned for Israel (CCI), formed after the Six Day War. At that moment of agony and trauma for the Jewish community, some of the leaders who had devoted years to improving relations with the churches were looking for signs of support from their dialogue partners. Instead, in most instances, they were met with an ominous silence.

The situation was not that Israel was totally without friends in the Christian community. But so much of the dialogue is conducted through church establishments and, therefore, with people who in the very nature of the case are caught up in all sort of internal political dynamics, no matter how much they might like to see themselves as officers in the Lord's army at the "prophetic" frontiers. The question had to be raised as to how the voices of the grassroots friends of Israel in the churches can be made more effective and their support more visible. Littell, a professor at Temple University, and his wife almost singlehandedly provided the network through which those Christian efforts might be reinforced. Many of their contacts were with people from academia, but church and community leaders were represented as well.

Christians Concerned for Israel became incorporated into National Christian Leadership Conference for Israel. But CCI itself was, in a sense, a revival of a previous endeavor, namely the American Christian Palestine Committee founded in 1946 and disbanded in 1961. And before that, the Christian Council on Palestine had been very active during World War II as the groundwork was being laid for the establishment of the an independent homeland for the Jewish people in Palestine. Earlier yet, during the 1930's, the Pro-Palestine Federation of America, whose membership consisted mainly of Christian clergy and teachers, had vigorously advocated the Zionist cause. Some of the people involved in those various organizations were John Haynes Holmes, Paul Tillich, Daniel Poling, William F. Albright, as well as many other prominent and not so prominent Christians, both clergy and laity.

But, in fact, the story goes yet further back. We can point to the 16th century and the teachings of the Restorationists, pious Protestants who were persuaded by their reading of the scriptures that the God of Abraham, Isaac and Jacob would eventually restore his people and that this would involve a return to the Holy Land. Restoration and Return, when capitalized, became terms of profound theological meaning, understood as touching on the divine destiny of history. For those people these were issues of world historical significance. God's covenant with Israel was believed to have implications for all creation and all history.

The Restorational Movement has its own list of martyrs to the cause. As early as 1589, Francis Kett, a fellow of Corpus Christi College in Cambridge, was burned alive as a heretic because he taught the eventual return of the Jewish people to their ancient homeland. Some Christian supporters of Israel today may face less than friendly treatment in a sometimes hostile ecclesiastical environment, but surely nothing as radical as what happened to poor brother Kett.

The same thread of Restorationist thinking can be traced through 17th century Puritanism as well as through the 18th and 19th centuries. I shall not include the details of that story here. The well-known words of President John Adams sum up some of the basic sentiments, including the less than noble undertones that were usually part of the picture:

"I really wish the Jews again in Judea, an independent Nation, for, as I believe, the most enlightened men of it have participated in the amelioration of the philosophy of the age; once restored to an independent government, and no longer persecuted, they would soon wear away some of the asperities and peculiarities of their character. I wish your nation may be admitted all the privileges of citizens in every part of the world."

At times Christian Restorationists caused consternation among Jews who were not at all happy with this emphasis and, for their own reasons, considered those views to be heretical. A case in point was the 1891 petition, composed by the evangelist William Blackstone and signed by more than 400 prominent Americans. It urged President Benjamin Harrison to join them in promoting the return of the Jewish people to Eretz Yisrael. This was six years before the first Zionist Congress in Basel, convened by Theodor Herzl. A rabbi named Emil Hirsch felt deeply offended by this Christian evangelist's activities and took to the road himself as a sort of one-man truth squad, assuring everybody who would listen that Jews had no such aspirations whatsoever and only wished to be good citizens in whatever country they resided.

History is so full of ironic as well as tragic twists. The good rabbi, although perhaps not consciously, may have reacted against those who at times have supported the idea of a Jewish homeland from racist motives and as a convenient way of ridding their country of Jews. In 19th century Europe, for instance, we find certain nationalist movements supporting the Return for all the wrong reasons.

One further observation on the Blackstone affair. Peter Grose, in his book *Israel in the Mind of America*, says that it "contained one lesson that would be learned and relearned over the coming half-century of Zionist agitation: the futility of grand public statements unaccompanied by pointed and discreet political pressures" (p. 37). It seems to me that "Christian Zionists" still have a long way to go in learning and relearning that lesson.

The danger I see in the "mainline" churches is that they are strong on dialogue but weak on solidarity. Among evangelicals, on the other hand, I see a good deal of strength in the area of inspiration, but often a failure to recognize the importance of organization and the kind of mobilization that turns goodwill into action. The end result in both cases tends to be friendly talk but little active support.

I certainly do not mean to disparage dialogue, or to suggest that it has failed to produce any concrete results. I consider myself a veteran dialoguer, and I am proud of it. Without that movement, to give one example, many church education materials would still contain the same myths and misinformation about Jews and Judaism that they did some years ago. Dialogue has definitely made a difference.

But dialogue can become somewhat seductive and it easily becomes a substitute for action. When dialogue becomes an end in itself, we produce talk without end (it goes on and on, but doesn't go anywhere). During the crisis of 1967, during the Yom Kippur war in 1973 and at other critical moments in Israel's history, the question of solidarity became an increasingly urgent one. If dialogue means that people enter into each other's historical experiences, how then can one party be left so isolated during moments of deep suffering? One is reminded of the old rabbinic question: "How can you love me [or even care for me] if you do not know what hurts me?"

A classic illustration of what I am talking about occurred during the Sixth National Workshop on Christian-Jewish Relations, held in Milwaukee during October 1981. I think there were about 1400 of us attending that conference, a multitude of eager dialoguers buzzing about the hotel, listening to speeches, meeting in small groups and all in all feeling excited about it all. In the meantime, the U.S. Senate was in the final stages of a debate on the sale of AWACS to Saudi Arabia.

I had the eerie feeling that in our Milwaukee hotel we were living in a world all by ourselves, totally detached from the world of Washington D.C. and AWACS. Finally, on Wednesday—the day of the Senate vote—Father Robert F. Drinan broke the spell during a speech in which he reminded the solemn assembly that the Senate vote that afternoon could have more far-reaching consequences for Jewish-Christian relations than anything we had done that week. Because of the intervention by a few activists, a drive was started immediately to raise funds and send telegrams to the members of the Senate urging them to vote down the AWACS proposal. In order to avoid conflict, it was emphasized that this action was not part of the Workshop's official agenda and that participation was entirely voluntary.

For me personally, the issue of solidarity and, therefore, the need for a network like National Christian Leadership Conference for Israel became an increasingly urgent matter. I am not talking about knee-jerk support for anything Israel does. Solidarity does not preclude criticism. It does, however, lend credibility to whatever critiques one may feel compelled to utter.

As to the question of inspiration versus organization, it must be said that some of the most exciting gatherings in support of Israel in recent years have been organized by evangelicals. Many of them have a real gift to put on a good show. I see nothing wrong with that, except when the "proclamations" issued become exuberant to the point of embarrassment and people go home feeling good but not inspired to do good works where it really counts. I am not implying that prayer does not count or that praising the Lord does not count. But there are moments when a letter to the President or members of Congress can make a crucial difference and therefore, may be THE Christian thing to do.

In the meantime, a little caution in language may help enhance Christian credibility. For instance, I have seen an evangelical statement assuring the Jewish people that if—God forbid—another Holocaust were to occur, Bible-believing Christians would be marching with Jews to the crematoria. I do not say that certain individuals might not act that way, but I do believe that those who behave heroically and commit acts of supreme sacrifice are not necessarily the same people who have signed statements. The truth is that none of of us can be quite sure how we might behave in moments of extreme crisis. It behooves us all to exercise a measure of humility in our public pronouncements, while prayerfully hoping that in the moment of decision we shall not compromise our conscience and betray our principles.

A remarkable Dutch woman, Etty Hillesum, not yet 30 years old, wrote in her diary as she was preparing to depart on the journey that would lead her to Auschwitz and death: "I don't fool myself about the reality of my situation and I even let go of the pretension that I will be a help to others. I will always be motivated by the desire to help God as much as possible, and if I succeed in doing that, well, then I'll be there for others as well. But one shouldn't entertain heroic illusions about such things." Indeed, and least of all those of us who have not had to travel that kind of *via dolorosa*.

As to support for Israel right now in the rather safe surroundings of the USA, I have come to the conclusion that the trouble with Christian friends of Israel is not that there are so few, but that they are so ineffective. Again, I do not claim that nothing has been achieved, but, rather, that in a country where the public at large tends to be sympathetic to the Israeli cause, Christians rarely play a role as a distinctive force on critical issues.

A major source of our ineffectiveness lies, I believe, in our fragmentation. I am realistic enough to recognize that the answer to that problem is not to be found in centralization. It could not be done, and even if it were achievable it would, in my judgement, not be desirable. There are many mavericks in pro-Israel Christian circles and there is immense diversity, not only in theology, but also in programs and general approach. That's fine! But some consultation, plus at least a minimum of coordination and cooperation, would surely benefit the common cause. It could be achieved without compromising anyone's integrity or independence.

National Christian Leadership Conference for Israel was founded on the principle of inclusiveness. From the very beginning it has sought to be a forum where people who share this particular concern can interact with each other and reinforce each other's efforts. To cultivate such a network, one that is considerably more inclusive than existing ecumenical councils, takes tact and much patience. I don't claim that I have always displayed those virtues, but I have enjoyed the experience of trying to pioneer at these outer edges of the ecumenical frontier.

It didn't take me long, however, to discover that "networking" of the National Christian Leadership Conference for Israel variety is a hard item to sell to the faithful. People may agree that it is a good idea, but in order to raise money one needs more than that. Dr. Marion de Velder, my one-time boss in the church bureaucracy, used to say that some projects do have "suction," while others simply do not. Or it is said that a cause must have "sexiness" in order for people to reach for their checkbooks and send generous contributions. Hunger, earthquakes and other assorted calamities tend to bring forth a flood of donations as I well know from my denominational leadership days. The whole notion of "networking", I think, lacks romance and will always be hard to finance.

Furthermore, for some of our conservative Christian friends the aims of National Christian Leadership Conference for Israel seemed to lack even a modicum of missionary motivation. It all sounded a bit too political. Language is so important when dealing with various forms of spirituality. Anyone who receives fundraising appeals from evangelical sources knows what I am talking about. Since National Christian Leadership Conference for Israel seeks to address itself to a very broad spectrum of the Christian community, our mailings were cast in a "tongue" that to some Christian believers must have sounded rather flat, yes, even "secular".

On the other hand, for many of our more liberal friends we often seemed a bit too partisan. They much preferred an "evenhandedness", forever dealing in "moral equivalencies" in an attempt to assure everybody that they stand above all parties. There is something to be said for keeping one's lines of communication open and, to be sure, in no dispute will one find all truth or righteousness on one side of the issue. But the never ending balancing act that somehow seeks to press everything into a neat system of symmetry strikes me as resting on either intellectual laziness or a lack of moral nerve. For instance, I see a qualitative difference between the Irgun's actions during the British Mandate against predominantly military targets and attacks on schoolchildren, athletes and civilian air travelers in the name of Palestinian rights. Hence, as is common practice in some church circles, to call Israeli leaders who at one time served in the resistance movement terrorists, in the same sense that Abul Nidal is a terrorist, strikes me as moral subterfuge.

At any rate, money has been a perennial problem for National Christian Leadership Conference for Israel. This may not necessarily be devastating for the dreamers of dreams, but it surely is debilitating. I have never given up on the vision of what could be, the belief in the potential of a network like National Christian Leadership Conference for Israel. But constant worry about finances, the ceaseless struggle for survival, the endless curtailment of even the most basic programs of action, have a way of draining creative energy and eroding the spirit of idealism.

To say the least, I began my stewardship for National Christian Leadership Conference for Israel affairs with a handicap. On February 1, 1981, I was handed the organization's checkbook with a balance of $178.82, plus a file with overdue bills in excess of $12,000. Mr. Stephen McArthur, National Christian Leadership Conference for Israel's first executive director (who previously had worked for the American Israel Public Affairs Committee (AIPAC) in Washington D.C.), and some of the initial organizers of National Christian Leadership Conference for Israel had greatly underestimated the difficulty of raising funds for this type of venture. They may not have been aware that AIPAC, too, in the early years of its life had had to face a struggle for survival.

After working for National Christian Leadership Conference for Israel for a little more than a year, Mr. McArthur suddenly announced that within three days he would leave the job in order to become the manager of a promising young singer who very soon was to become a newly rising star on the Nashville scene. The young lady, it turned out, was the sweetener in a scam operation that deprived several McArthur family members of hard earned resources which they had invested in this "opportunity of a lifetime".

Dr. Franklin Littell, National Christian Leadership Conference for Israel's president at the time, proposed a rescue mission in order to deal with the emergency that had been created by McArthur's sudden departure. Mrs. Littell would manage the operations of the organization as his assistant for a salary that was guaranteed by the American-Israel Friendship League. Furthermore, none of the funds raised during this interim period were to be used for the paying of bills inherited from Mr. McArthur, whom Littell suspected of mismanagement. Those bills were to be left for future disposition, which in the end meant that they were left for me to worry about.

I had been on the job only for a few months when I received an invitation from Mr. Lawrence Goodman, a Chicago businessman with national real estate interests, to be his guest at an AIPAC banquet in Washington, D.C. Mr. Goodman had recently become a staunch believer in the power of public relations and the potentials it offered to strengthen support for Israel among a wide public. In order to try out his ideas on the matter, he had founded the Institute for Mideast Research and hired the services of an advertising firm.

The hot issue of the pro-Israel community at that time was the sale of AWACS to the Saudis. Over dinner I discussed with Mr. Goodman the idea of convening a "Congress" of Christian supporters of Israel in Washington, D.C., mentioning in an all too transparent fashion that, unfortunately, National Christian Leadership Conference for Israel's debt situation would make it difficult to pull off such a plan.

Larry Goodman was an upbeat sort of guy, and he felt that finances ought not to stand in the way, a sentiment I eagerly interpreted as an offer of support. My reading of the situation was considerably reinforced when two weeks later Mr. Goodman, accompanied by a P.R. consultant, flew to Minneapolis where we were holding a National Christian Leadership Conference for Israel executive committee meeting. We decided to move ahead on the "Congress" and, until 2:00 a.m., discussed ideas and drew up specific plans. When, before I went to sleep, the P.R. man asked me how much I thought it would take to put the show on the road, I replied modestly that $20,000 should go a long way. He thought that sounded rather reasonable. I had sweet dreams that night.

The Congress was held during October 1981, just as the U.S. Congress was approaching the decisive vote on the AWACS issue. In short, our timing turned out to be superb. It also turned out that we had totally misread the situation as far as funding was concerned. The end result: National Christian Leadership Conference for Israel incurred and additional debt of over $10,000. I made a deal with the hotel about monthly payments, and my wife had to hold a job in order to handle our personal finances.

In the meantime, I had met a remarkable gentleman by the name of Gilman Hill. Gil, a deeply devoted evangelical businessman from Denver, was engaged in oil and gas exploration. He is a fervent Christian Zionist, who put his investments where his faith was when he ventured some of his capital in oil explorations in the Mt. Carmel region in Israel.

Gilman Hill's fundamentalist-millenialist faith was to him not a matter of abstractions. When you believe in the infallibility of the Scriptures, you act on it. Take for instance the book of Deuteronomy, Chapter 33, Verse 24:

> "And of Asher He (the Lord) said,
> Blessed above sons be Asher; Let him be the favorite of
> his brothers, and let him dip his foot in oil."

On ancient maps, I'm told, the territory of the tribe of Asher was shaped like a boot and the tip of the toes almost touches the foot of Mt.

Carmel. For Gil and his associates, the words of the Scripture, supplemented by geological testing and other research, justified a risky gamble that oil might be found in that region of Israel.

In my 'mainline' ecumenical involvements I was not likely to meet people like Gil Hill. Most people in that movement make hardly any effort at all to even understand the spirituality and biblical interpretations that are so much a part of dispensationalist Christian's outlook and life. I firmly believe that the ecumenical frontiers need widening, although I realize that the difficulties posed on both sides are many. And frankly, it has to be admitted that my warm feelings toward Gilman Hill are also influenced by the fact that he was the first person to come to my organization's rescue with a major donation.

Hill's support for National Christian Leadership Conference for Israel did not last very long. Perhaps it was because the oil business had come upon hard times. My hunch is that, as distinct from his other favored projects, we just did not fit into the charismatic-evangelical ethos which, in those circles, tends to set apart the brother from the neighbor. We did not speak the same language and we basically live in different worlds of spirituality. I could not turn National Christian Leadership Conference for Israel into an evangelical entity; that would have been against my nature, but more than that, it would have militated against the organization's original purpose. But I shall always be grateful to Gil, not only for his financial gifts, but also for his personal graciousness.

Where to turn to next? I received much advice as to whom to contact as potential contributors to National Christian Leadership Conference for Israel, but in many cases, I did not stand a prayer. In some cases, prayer is precisely what I came away with. For instance, a friend urged me to visit Mrs. Leslie Hromas at the American Christian Trust (ACT), located immediately adjacent to the Israeli Embassy in Washington, D.C. Since I was told that everyone who stays at that lovely home devotes some hours per day to prayer and scripture study, I thought that the proximity to the Embassy was, perhaps, for the purpose of greater spiritual impact. (The magazine *Spotlight* gave a different explanation, offering the sensational charges that the evangelicals who constituted the membership of ACT were engaged in spying on behalf of Israel.)

Mrs. Hromas was very pleasant. She informed me that the center was being financed by a group of pro-Israel friends in Southern California. Before my departure she assured me that some aid for the work of National Christian Leadership Conference for Israel should not be considered an impossibility. In the meantime, I and my organization would be added to the ACT prayer list. I did attend a few ACT functions in Washington in the year that followed, but financial support was never mentioned again.

Fundraising does make one aware of the idiosyncracies of some of the rich and usually not-so-famous. In the fall of 1985, the Israeli press reported that a Mr. Ara Tchividjian had arrived in the country with six of his grown children in order to found a movement of Christian penance. One report stated that the founding meeting took place at the La Romme hotel in Jerusalem with some 50 guests flown to Israel, including heads of Jewish organizations, professors, clergy, theologians and an "anonymous local rabbi", among several other Israelis.

A year earlier (May 1984), I had attended a founding meeting of the Ecumenical Center for Christian Repentance, sponsored by the same Mr. Tchividjian. As a matter of fact, I was asked to submit a list of names of persons who might be invited and flown to Key Biscayne, Florida, for that occasion. I made numerous telephone calls to potential participants and the National Christian Leadership Conference for Israel network was well represented. Those of us attending were under the impression that we were participating in the establishment of an ecumenical educational center where Christian leaders could become sensitized to the truth of historic Christian anti-Judaism. It sounded like a great idea.

For three days we were guests of Mr. Tchividjian at the local Sheraton Hotel and listened to lectures delivered by this fascinating gentleman. All through he proceedings several TV cameras reeled away, recording every detail of this historic event. However, in the months and years that followed, the participants in that gathering did not hear again about the Center for Christian Repentance. It crossed a few repentant minds that, perhaps, we had been paid to play the role of props on Mr. Tchividjian's stage. Hopefully, the efforts in Jerusalem turned out to be more fruitful.

While I wished that more pro-Israel Christians would have supported the work of National Christian Leadership Conference for Israel, I do not deny that some Christian individuals and groups have made considerable contributions to development in Israel through the Jewish National Fund and other agencies. I have been particularly impressed with the fact that some of those groups, instead of establishing a separate Christian agency to handle distribution of the funds, have been willing to entrust that function to local Jewish authorities and to do so without strings attached. It seems to me that, in Christian benevolent activities that is a somewhat novel development, practiced also nowadays by some church agencies that are engaged in development projects abroad.

I have often been asked how much money National Christian Leadership Conference for Israel received from Israeli sources or Jewish organizations. The answer is: not one penny. As a matter of fact, National Christian Leadership Conference for Israel's budget was raised entirely from individual donors, although office space was made available through the America-Israeli Friendship League. Are some of the contributors Jewish? Yes, indeed. The original goal at the time of National Christian Leadership Conference for Israel's founding had been that 90-95 percent of its funding should come from Christian sources. I must admit, with some sadness, that strict adherence to that principle could have meant the early demise of the organization.

The sentiment expressed by my friend Frank Eiklor of Shalom Ministries in one of his newsletters is much like my own. "During a couple of past financial crises, I asked a small number of Jewish friends to help. Frankly, I regretted it . . . Anti-Semitism is a Gentile problem and should be fought by Christian giving," he wrote. A Christian pro-Israel network, too, should be supported by Christian giving, and I feel a deep gratitude to the hundreds of Christians who have sent donations. On the other hand, while I wished that contributions from Jewish friends had not been necessary for survival, I feel profoundly indebted to some of the wonderful and loyal Jewish friends of National Christian Leadership Conference for Israel, not only for the money they have given, but for the kindness they have shown us and their encouragement in many difficult moments.

During some of my down moods, when unpaid bills were piling up, I gained a measure of comfort from the words of I. L. Kenen, founder of AIPAC, who reported in his book *Israel's Defense Line: Her Friends and Foes in Washington*, that payment of his salary was sometimes delayed because funds were not available. AIPAC's fortunes changed very much after the Six Day War, and even more so after the Senate's vote in favor of selling AWACS to the Saudis. I don't know what it will take to evoke stronger support for Israel among Christians.

The truth is that National Christian Leadership Conference for Israel's problems were not new; its perennial state of near-bankruptcy too is part of an old story. As a matter of fact, as I trace the history of Christian organizations in support of Israel, I doubt that there ever has been a day when ecumenical Christian pro-Israel activities received support that by any measure could be called adequate. In some cases it can even be said that Christian organizations, at least to a degree, served as fronts for agencies controlled by Zionist leadership, who made many of the day-to-day decisions. In my years with National Christian Leadership Conference for Israel all the decisions were made by the dedicated core group of Christians of the executive committee. I have never met a Jewish leader who has even expressed the slightest desire that it should be otherwise.

Since confession is considered good for the soul, I ought to mention in all frankness that the situation at National Christian Leadership Conference for Israel was not helped by the fact that I am not a very good fundraiser. It is just not my forte, and I do not like to do it. I have always felt empathy with people like the late Senator Hubert Humphrey who, I have been told, complained frequently about how demeaning fundraising activities can be.

The games we play in order to raise money are just too embarrassingly transparent. True, some of the honorees at our fundraising dinners are eminently worthy of receiving a special tribute. But I have also attended dinners where labor leaders with questionable reputations were honored in the name of America-Israel friendship mainly because the local unions were prepared to fill the ballroom tables at $1,500 a piece, a price they were quite willing to pay in return for a gesture of respectability.

One can only hope that those honorees to whom the process is very familiar because they have gone through it so frequently, will be able to maintain a sense of humor about it all. Otherwise, they may end up in rather sad shape, like the man in the story told by Charles Silberman in his book *A Certain People*. This person insisted on supervising the most minute details of the dinner at which he was to be the guest of honor, even to the speech praising him for his achievements, which he wrote himself. When the chairman read the text of the tribute, the honoree burst into tears.

I grew up in an environment where the emphasis was very strongly on the "helping professions". So I did not meet many people who had set their minds to making money. During my adult years, too, I tended to associate with persons who perceived themselves as being "people oriented", which usually meant that they held jobs that paid modest salaries but were supposed to be high on the scale of personal satisfaction.

We were never told that wealth was bad, just that it was a risk to one's spiritual health. The imagery of Psalm 73, portraying the arrogant greed of the wealthy power elite, sound and sleek in body, self-satisfied in spirit, adulated by crowds who lacked the courage to put character above pomp and circumstance, all that was very real to me. They are the people who have made "it" and who for that reason alone are treated with deference. As it says in Proverbs 14:20: "The poor is disliked even by his neighbor, but the rich has many friends."

Through the years I have discovered that there is another side to the story. I have met millionaires whom I have come to admire because of the kind of people they were and because of the way they lived with wealth. Money can become a terrible captivity, but in a vastly greater number of cases, lack of money leads to a dismal loss of independence.

I found that out once more during the Spring of 1986, when I was forced to focus my mind on money as I had rarely done before. It all had to do with the mortgage on my home and the drop in interest rates at the time. Refinancing seemed the right thing to do, but I found myself in a sort of Catch 22 situation. I regularly used a capital credit line, backed by the greatly inflated equity in my home, as a source of bridge loans to keep

National Christian Leadership Conference for Israel and my family afloat during deficit periods. Before the bank would give me a new loan, those debts had to be paid off. After matters had been settled, I could return to the old practice of interim financing.

In an attempt to resolve the dilemma, I did something that I found embarrassing: I wrote a letter to a person who had given National Christian Leadership Conference for Israel major support in the past and asked for a 90 day loan. My embarrassment turned into a sense of humiliation when I did not receive a reply. It was then that I decided to focus my mind a little more on financial matters. For six months I suspended writing on this book and read ferociously in investment literature. I became introduced to the world of stocks and bonds, of metals and mutual funds, of future contracts and options.

Richard Band's book *Contrary Investing* with its numerous illustrations of the herd mentality in money markets found an instant resonance in my mind. I had come to know that same kind of mentality so well during my days in the church bureaucracy. But I had never given much thought to the fact that money is to be made by betting against the conventional wisdom.

I decided to test the truth of this thesis in the rather treacherous field of commodity trading and discovered that it works. First, necessity had forced me to run the National Christian Leadership Conference for Israel in a somewhat entrepreneurial fashion. Now I found myself applying the same spirit of entrepreneurship to areas I had never even dreamed of entering. That strikes me as one of the more ironic twists of my life.

On the other hand, for people involved with Israel the non-conventional approach may well be a most appropriate one. Within the churches, afterall, activist friends of Israel are likely to function as a fringe element for some time to come. Furthermore, Israel itself is a land where the spirit of "make do" and experimentation with the less conventional often, out of necessity, had become a way of life.

IV

Dialogue: Dream and Reality

The World Council of Churches (WCC), as we noted earlier, came into being during an Assembly held in Amsterdam, August 22-September 4, 1948, just a few months after the establishment of the state of Israel. For a decade prior to the Amsterdam gathering, the organization had existed in embryo form, listing itself as "the World Council of Churches in process of formation." The long interim period was caused by the fact that World War II had forced a postponement of the official founding of the Council.

The heart of the WCC agenda has always been "unity", and the basic approach whereby it hopes to achieve this goal is "dialogue". Active attempts to bring about greater unity between the churches, which for centuries displayed not only great diversity, but often considerable mutual hostility as well, had been going on for at least half a century. As usual, the initiatives for this visionary movement were taken outside the "official" church establishment: in the Bible societies, the YMCA/YWCA organizations, the World Student Christian Federation, etc.

Major Ecumenical Missionary Conferences, held in Edinburgh (1910), Jerusalem (1928), and Tambaram, India (1938) had established the basic framework of co-operation and the network of interdenominational contacts, which eventually would lead to the founding of the WCC. These were all predominantly Protestant enterprises. The Roman Catholic Church was not much involved in unity efforts during the pre-Vatican II era.

The Christian world mission movement, which had undergone tremendous expansion during the 19th century, gave a powerful impetus to the search for greater unity. Western church divisions, often more determined by history and culture than by theology, were being exported to other continents and were increasingly becoming cause for confusion (certainly among the "natives" to whom love was being preached), frustration and embarrassment. Members of ancient tribes who began to look and act like Scottish Presbyterians or American Baptists often came across more like comic figures than like people who might have and impact on their own culture.

World War II and the sufferings it caused contributed in a somewhat ironic fashion to the breakdown of Christian divisions. For instance, missionaries from countries occupied by the Nazis were left stranded in various parts of the world and, in many instances, received support from church agencies in the free world. Prison camps also played a role as catalytic agents toward greater Christian unity, as Catholic and Protestant leaders, thrown into forced association, often discovered that they were united not only through their common resistance to Nazism, but also by spiritual bonds, which had been left unexplored before.

In addition the Nazi war against the Jews introduced a wholly new dimension into the ecumenical agenda, namely Christian-Jewish relations. The churches could not ignore the fact that during this period of great suffering and pain among the general populace of occupied and war torn lands, a horror of incredible proportions had occurred in the Holocaust; the systematic murder of six million Jewish men, women, and children.

For instance, less than one year after the liberation of Holland from Nazi rule, leaders of the Netherlands Reformed Church, convinced they would "have to come to a renewed confession against the false gods and temptations of this century, both those around us and within us," appointed a special committee charged to explore the feasibility of a new confessional statement. The document resulting from this church's reflection on its experience during the Nazi era was entitled *Foundations and Perspectives of Confession*. It contained two features not commonly found in Christian credal statements: an article on "history" and another one on "Israel." As already pointed out, once people begin to focus on the faith of Israel, they inevitably begin to reflect more seriously on the meaning of history, because history, as predominantly understood in Western thought, basically is a "Hebrew invention."

Through the centuries, the most common Christian response to Jewish suffering has been that it was the logical result of the Jews' rejection and crucifixion of Jesus. The argument in essence was a straight and simple one: the Jews have rejected Jesus; God in return has rejected them, has cast them off as his covenant people and has chosen the Church in their stead. The Dutch Reformed confessional statement sounded a very different note, however, claiming that the divine covenant with the Jewish people had never been revoked. It affirmed that the Jews "remain the people of the promise" and that those who are offended at this "take offence at God's sovereign action, to which they themselves owe their salvation." In short, as the famous theologian Karl Barth used to say, people who have such a hard time accepting the eternal covenant with Israel, in effect saw off the branch on which they themselves are sitting.

Forty years later, I regret to report, that same Reformed Church in the Netherlands refused to renew the contract of its "theological advisor" in Israel. The *Jerusalem Post* (August 8, 1986) quoted Dutch ecclesiastical sources as stating that this person had identified too closely with Jewish concerns and had failed to comply with instructions that he meet with PLO representatives. Eventually he was offered an extension of his contract if he was prepared to accept severe limitations on what he would be allowed to say publicly. This incident is symptomatic of what has been happening in the Protestant ecumenical world during the past four decades.

Dialogue is the holy ground on which the ecumenical movement stands or falls. For instance, once the dialogue approach is exchanged for an ideological approach, the ecumenical movement has lost its soul. After all, dialogue is not just one among many techniques; it is a way of ecumenical life. It calls for nothing less than a new way of relating to one another. Dialogue implies that one has not only an open mind, but also a heart that is responsive to overtures of understanding from people with whom one has, perhaps, profound theological or social-political differences. True dialogue embodies in a very special way the art of listening as an expression of loving other human beings. As Bishop Krister Stendahl has so often pointed out, one of its first fruits is that one refuses to bear false witness against other believers, portraying one's own position in the most positive light and the other person's faith fellowship according to its most questionable features.

From the vantage point of the 1980's it is sometimes difficult to recall the sad estrangement, even enmity, that existed between Baptists and Methodists, Presbyterians, and Episcopalians and—above all—Protestants and Roman Catholics only a few decades ago. The dialogue with Jews was in sadder shape yet, having hardly advanced beyond the situation in the second century when the church father Justin Martyr wrote his famous *Dialogue with Trypho the Jew.* In this book, which the historian Adolph von Harnack has called "the victor's monologue," the Jewish "partner" is accused of "obstinacy of heart" as well as "feebleness of mind." In sum, Jews who could not be argued into becoming Christians were not only dumb; they clearly had a character defect as well. Thus began the process whereby Christians increasingly defined themselves in anti-Judaic terms. Dialogue became polemics, and polemics derailed into diatribe and, further along the road, pogroms.

The ecumenical movement sought to change all that, and it must be said that the dream of moving from confrontation to new forms of relationships has at least partially been fulfilled. Much re-thinking has been going on in certain Christian circles with respect to Jews, Judaism and Israel. Helga Croner has compiled two volumes of ecumenical documents entitled *Stepping Stones to Further Jewish-Christian Relations*, which demonstrate the considerable progress that has been made in redefining Christian positions. The critical observations on certain ecumenical policies and practices that I will be presenting are in no way meant as a denial that the Christian-Jewish dialogue has often made a difference for the better.

As one studies various ecclesiastical and ecumenical pronouncements on the Church and the Jewish People, several themes stand out. A central point in many of those documents has been the rejection of so-called "supersession" or "displacement theology", the teaching on which millions of Christians have been nurtured over many centuries: that the Jews stand eternally condemned and that the Church is the "New Israel" that has replaced the old and discarded covenant people.

We have already referred to the new confessional statement of the Netherlands Reformed Church. In 1967, the WCC's Commission on Faith and Order issued an important study document on the relationship between the Church and the Jewish people. This statement, usually referred to as the Bristol Declaration, affirms the following: "We believe that God formed the people of Israel. There are certainly many factors of common history, ethnic background and religion, which can explain its coming into existence, but to Old Testament faith as a whole, it was God's own will and decision that made this one distinct people with its special place in history."

The document goes on to say that God "chose this particular people to be the bearer of a particular promise and to act as his covenant partner and special instrument." It finally expresses the conviction "that the Jewish people still have a significance of their own for the Church." These sentences have the flavor of the kind of compromise that is so often characteristic of ecclesiastical (and particularly ecumenical) documents. Some would have wished a stronger affirmation, like the one in the Dutch Reformed statement declaring that the Jewish people "remain the people of the promise" because "the gracious gifts and calling of God are irrevocable." However, for some representatives, those from the Orthodox churches in particular, such a clear-cut anti-supersessionist position was unacceptable.

A number of later ecclesiastical pronouncements, on the other hand, were much more explicit in their affirmation of God's continued covenant with Israel. One illustration is the famous document adopted in 1980 by the Synod of the Rhineland in Germany, stating simply: "We believe in the continuing election of the Jewish people as the people of God . . ." Another example is "A Declaration of Faith" in the Book of Confessions of the Former Presbyterian Church, U. S., which puts it in very plain language: "We can never lay exclusive claim to being God's people, as though we had replaced those to whom the covenant, the law and the promises belong. We affirm that God does not take back his promises. We Christians have rejected Jews throughout our history with shameful prejudice and cruelty".

This particular declaration of faith does not only condemn anti-Semitism, as numerous ecclesiastical and ecumenical bodies have done, (including most major assemblies of the World Council of Churches) but it also confesses Christian complicity in the persecution of Jews throughout the Church's history. As it was put by a Lutheran World Federation body some years ago: "We confess our peculiar guilt and we lament with shame the responsibility our church and her people bear for this sin (of anti-

Semitism),'' adding "we can only ask God's pardon and that of the Jewish people.'' More recently (in 1987) a United Church of Christ statement that studiously avoided any reference to the people of Israel, asked "for God's forgiveness through our Lord Jesus Christ,'' because of the church's history of anti-Jewish theology and actions.

There can then be no doubt that through dialogue, which was conducted on a world scale through such bodies as the World Council of Churches, many Christians have been induced to rethink traditional theological positions on Jews and Judaism and to face with greater honesty than ever before the historical role of the churches in the teaching of contempt. However, once it is accepted that the covenant with Israel has not been revoked, new questions arise, such as, what does the covenant encompass? Or, to put it quite specifically, what about the land dimensions of biblical covenant promises?

We read in Genesis 17:7: "I will establish my covenant between me and you and your descendants after you throughout their generations for an everlasting covenant . . ." If we accept that promise as still valid in our day, what then about the next verse: "And I will give to you, and to your descendants after you, the land of your sojournings, all the land of Canaan, for an everlasting possession . . . ?" Has that promise been invalidated? Many evangelicals answer "Of course not!'', without any equivocation whatsoever. Some even see scriptural grounds for speaking about "biblical boundaries,'' claiming that "all the land of Canaan'' definitely included today's West Bank plus quite a bit more.

In "mainline'' ecumenical circles, even those where anti-Semitism is repeatedly and vehemently denounced, that issue is usually considered a bit more problematical. Critics of any kind of covenant/land position scornfully speak of "theological tribalism'' and "real estate theology.'' Such primitive particularism, they insist, has been transcended by a more universalist message that comes to us through the gospel of Jesus Christ. Nevertheless, some documents that have been the product of ecumenical dialogue do indeed affirm that the divine promise of the land is part of the covenant message still valid today.

In 1970 the General Synod of the Reformed Church in the Netherlands once again assumed a pioneer role by issuing a statement entitled

"Israel: People, Land and State". This expresses the hope that their efforts at theological reflection on those issues would "start a broad discussion, which up till now has sorely been lacking in our church, in the sister churches abroad and in the World Council of Churches." They not only declared the land to be "a vital aspect of the election of Israel" and proclaimed their joy in the "reunion of people and land," but also stated that "in the present situation a state gives greater opportunity to the Jews to fulfill their vocation than any alternative can offer." In short, the state of Israel, too, receives a positive place within the realm of theological reflection.

Subsequent ecclesiastical documents have made the same point, sometimes referring to the state of Israel as "a sign of the mercy and faithfulness of God to the Jewish people." However, the hope of the Dutch church leaders that the WCC would place those issues on its dialogue agenda has hardly been fulfilled. Quite the contrary, Israel has increasingly become a topic of controversy. As the ecumenical processes became more and more politicized, this issue was moved from the realm of dialogue into the sphere of ideological dogma and diatribe. A brief survey of what has happened at the six major World Council assemblies since the organization's founding in 1948 gives an interesting picture of how things have evolved and to what extent the dialogue has degenerated into politics of self-righteousness.

In 1948, the Council declared that "to the Jews our God has bound us in a special solidarity linking our destinies together in His design." Anti-Semitism was condemned as a sin against God and man. With regard to the Middle East situation, the Council appealed to the nations to deal with the problem not as one of expediency, but as a moral and spiritual question that touches a nerve center of the world's religious life. That latter statement was sufficiently vague as not to offend anyone.

The next assembly was held in Evanston, Illinois in 1956. This time when theologies of hope were stirring in the ecclesiastical air, the theme was "Jesus Christ, the Hope of the World." A group of prominent theologians concluded that this would be an appropriate occasion to say something about Israel as a sign of God's faithfulness in history and, therefore, in some sense, a source of hope. Their proposal was voted down after the Assembly had received a telegram from the Christian statesman Charles

Malik in Lebanon, urging the delegates to say and do nothing that might give offense to Arab Christians. In more recent years, Charles Malik has found plenty to criticize in the ideological preoccupations of the WCC. No doubt, at that time, his desire was to de-politicize the Council's voice on Middle East issues. In fact, he helped de-theologize the Council's approach to the question of Israel.

The next Assembly, held in New Delhi in 1961, dealt with the theme "Jesus Christ, the Light of the World." Questions pertaining to the relationship of the Christian faith to other (particularly Eastern) religions were predominant at this conference. The issues of anti-Semitism and Israel did not come into sharp focus in India. As a matter of fact, the section under "I" in the index of the assembly's reports ends with "investment portfolios".

By the time the World Council met in Uppsala, Sweden in 1968, the theological climate was undergoing rapid and radical changes. The theology of hope was being replaced by "a theology of revolution". The so-called Third World agenda, dealing with issues of poverty and oppression, became increasingly central to the ecumenical movement's concerns. That in itself, it seems to me, should be no cause for complaint. Poverty and oppression, too, are issues with profound theological implications. But, unfortunately, the dialogical approach was more and more replaced by an ideological rhetoric with a distinctly anti-imperialist slant. More unfortunately yet, it became fashionable to refer to Israel as an outpost of Western imperialism in the Middle East. As church historian Martin Marty put it in *Context* (March 1, 1971), "being anti-Israel has become part of the anti-Establishment gospel, the trademark of those who purport to identify with masses, the down trodden and the Third World."

During the 1960's various radical theologies were much in vogue. For some Christians the basic questions had to do with the need for a radical reinterpretation of traditional beliefs. They posed the challenges: What can a person still believe in this modern age, and how does one speak about God in a secular era? For others, the fundamental issue was not how to adapt to modernity, but rather how to counter the forces of conformity. They asked, what is a Christian lifestyle? Instead of emphasizing radical theological criticism, this movement advocated radical biblical obedience. Its basic stance was more counter-culture than contra-orthodoxy.

Among radical Christians of the second type, the United States was sometimes referred to as "the great whore of Babylon" mentioned in the book of Revelation. There was a tendency to use apocalyptic terminology when describing what were perceived to be the crises of our age, particularly, the sins of the West. The radical evangelical paper *Sojourners*; first called the *Post-American*, was started during the days of anti-Vietnam war protests. History was frequently analyzed in somewhat Manichaean terms as the struggle between the forces of Light and Darkness. The imagery is always one of sharp demarcations.

At the same time, the New Left was falling more and more in love with the language of excess, an intellectual climate in which some Christian radicals seemed to feel right at home. Radical Christian journals, like *Témoignage Chrétienne* in France, felt free to once again engage in explicitly anti-Judaic writings. In this country people like Father Daniel Berrigan certainly did not go that far, but in his astonishing October 1973 speech to the Association of Arab University Graduates, in which he referred to himself as "a Jew in resistance to Israel," he proceeded to attack the Jewish state in such vitriolic language, that one wondered whether any boundaries of restraint were left.

All those cultural-ideological ingredients were already brewing as the World Council of Churches met in Uppsala. But something else was part of the picture as well. The Six Day War had been fought in the Middle East only one year earlier. That same year, the WCC's own Faith and Order Commission had issued the so-called "Bristol Declaration" on the Church's relationship to the Jewish people. Politically that document was now considered an ecumenical hot potato, even though its authors had very carefully avoided all explicitly political issues.

So what did the Uppsala Assembly do? It simply ignored the whole question, including the work of its Faith and Order Commission. Once again, the ability or inability to engage in dialogue was determined more by current events than by the Christian faith and the vision that had inspired the founding of the Council. Thus one further step was taken in the process of de-theologizing the question of Israel, as well as in the decline of ecumenical dialogue.

By 1975, when the Council held its fifth Assembly in Nairobi, the politicization of its agenda had grown apace. During the early years of the ecumenical movement the slogan most often cited had been "Let the Church be the Church!" The Church was seen as a unique fellowship of faith, full of human frailties and follies, but nevertheless empowered by the presence of the divine spirit and living under a divine mandate. In short, it was claimed that the Church is more than one of the many voluntary associations in the world, at least for those who have committed themselves to Jesus Christ as Lord. Hence it was felt that the Church must present its own kind of witness to the world.

As the years went by, however, a new slogan emerged: "Let the world set the agenda!" The central idea here was that the Church, rather than being isolated from worldly concerns, should be sensitive to the sufferings and aspirations of humanity. In other words, a claim of uniqueness may never be turned into a form of escapism and social irresponsibility.

As valid as the basic intention may have been, in practice the slogan came to mean that the churches issued an endless stream of statements on every conceivable social issue and that somehow the churches, instead of sounding a voice of their own, seemed to be able to express themselves only in a language that was both bland and bombastic. Someone has appropriately characterized this style of communication as United Nations English.

In 1975, it will be recalled, the U.N. spent months in a rhetorical orgy on the question about whether Zionism is a form of racism, ending up with the predictable, albeit absurd, conclusion that indeed it is. That organization too, one recalls with sadness, at one time was inspired by dreams about dialogue and reconciliation. I have already told the story about the pre-Nairobi meeting which was held in Geneva in order to avoid a U.N.-type resolution at the upcoming WCC assembly and the role played on that occasion by Clovis Maksoud, now representative of the Arab League at the U.N. This meeting had been convened by WCC General Secretary, Dr. Philip Potter, with delegates nominated by Christian communities in various countries. Consequently, the composition of the group was such that an honest-to-God encounter and debate could take place.

In 1983, as the sixth WCC Assembly, scheduled to meet in Vancouver, Canada, approached, the anti-Israel forces within the WCC decided to once again hold a meeting in Geneva. This time it was not under the official sponsorship of the Council, to make sure that no dissenting voices could be present. This self-appointed group of partisans, financed by the Middle East Council of Churches, came to Vancouver carrying a draft statement that no longer even gave the appearance of being fair. In short, they came, not for dialogue, but to pull off a political coup. The climate they found was sympathetic (or, at least, indifferent) enough for them to succeed.

I will not dignify the document by presenting details of its content. *The Christian Century*, hardly a rabid pro-Israel periodical, observed in an editorial (Aug. 17-24, 1983) that the Vancouver resolutions could just as well have been formulated at the U.N. and indicated "a total lack of concern for Christian-Jewish relations." That about says it.

It is a sorry, but not unusual story. A movement started by dreamers and visionaries, is step-by-step undermined by people who know how to manipulate the bureaucratic machinery. There are still many wonderful, decent and idealistic people around. But they are not into playing that sort of game, and the top leadership is either unable or unwilling to put a stop to the nonsense. It happens in politics, in labor unions, and also in churches.

At a press conference during the Vancouver meeting WCC General Secretary Philip Potter was asked about the obvious biases and imbalances in the document on the Middle East. According to press reports his response went as follows: "The Jews have other voices speaking on their behalf." In other words, through our imbalance we balance the scale for the poor Palestinians and the PLO. Having no other voice, they, therefore, deserve the compassionate concern of the WCC. If that means partisanship instead of rapprochement, well, so be it. But why then, one wonders, did the Council reject every proposal to say something about the plight of people in Afghanistan, who were being murdered *en masse* by Russian troops? The truth, of course, is that power plays, not compassion, determine the agenda. The officially recognized Russian churches, having declined the invitation to participate in the founding assembly of the WCC in

1948 because they feared that the Council would become a platform for critics of totalitarianism, later decided that the potential rewards might justify the risk of joining. And so they became members. However, every time a position was recommended that would displease the Soviet rulers, the Russian Orthodox churches forced its removal from the agenda by threatening to withdraw from the Council.

Most pathetic of all was the inability at Vancouver to respond with fervor and conviction to the plaintive cry of the Russian priest Vladimir Rusak who, living under the cross of Communism, wrote in an open letter to the Council: "It is difficult to reach you, so very difficult, much more difficult than to reach God, yet I cannot remain silent." Selective indignation, the endless quest for "moral equivalencies" and political deals, eventually blur the vision and quench the inner fires of the soul.[1]

References to Israel in WCC documents were cast increasingly in the form of questions rather than affirmations. On that issue, ambiguity became the mark of ecumenical witness, while on other, particularly political, topics the "prophetic" witness became ever more apodictic and cocksure. For instance, in 1974 tens of thousands of dollars were spent to convene an International Consultation on "Biblical Interpretation and the Middle East." Did they talk about the divine covenant promises in the Bible, touch perhaps on the question of covenant and land? No, such issues were now too hot to handle and the delegates decided early in the proceedings that they ought to focus on the question of justice in the

---

[1] After six more years of struggle and suffering, Vladimir Rusak was finally allowed to leave the Soviet Union and taste a life of freedom in the West. In the meantime, some of the top leaders of the World Council of Churches, including its General Secretary, Mr. Emilio Castro, have begun to ask some critical questions about the organization's so-called "quiet diplomacy" in the face of religious persecution in socialist societies.

For instance, in 1988, Rumanian Orthodox Metropolitan Antonie of Transylvania, succeeded in stopping a move to condemn the Rumanian government for human rights violations by threatening to leave the meeting. "I think we didn't speak strongly enough, that is clear," Castro is reported to have said to the media, "... that is the price we thought we needed to pay in order to help the human rights situation inside Rumania." Of course, "noisy diplomacy" remained the rule in statements protesting the sins of non-socialist countries.

Middle East.

Jews and Israel are still mentioned in the minutes of the meeting, but in the form of questions. "Does the New Testament nullify the theological meaning of the Jewish people and its continuing existence?" "Can we evaluate and decide questions of the promise of the land, the election of Israel, etc. on the basis of the New Testament, and from a Christian perspective?" "In what sense can Christians identify with the right of the Jewish people to Statehood?" It should not be hard to guess what kind of answers some of the participants in such a consultation would give to those questions.

Every once in awhile people within the Council, like the members of its Consultation on the Church and the Jewish People, would address the questions and seek to provide some answers. One would think that those efforts were welcomed as an open invitation to engage in dialogue. But in fact such ecumenical endeavors were handled with a good deal of hesitation, even embarrassment. Whenever such a situation arose, the issues were put on the bureaucratic escalator from committees to subcommittees, then to sub-sub-committees where behind-the-scenes maneuvers could apply the proper revisions and corrections.

Take, for instance, the "Guidelines for Christian-Jewish Dialogue" on which the WCC's Consultation on the Church and the Jewish People, and the Jewish People worked for a number of years. It all started in 1977 when the Consultation group met in Jerusalem. I thought the choice of meeting place was excellent; it afforded me my first opportunity to visit Israel. But some people within the Council were infuriated. They saw it as damaging to Arab interests, and never forgave Dr. Franz von Hammerstein, the Consultation's executive director, for this "trespass". In fact, he did not survive very long as a WCC employee after that Jerusalem meeting.

Still, a draft document was finally produced and approved on several top levels of the Council's bureaucracy, including in January 1982 by the Division of Dialogue with People of Living Faiths and Ideologies, the overarching agency of which the Consultation was a sub-division. The draft contained some helpful and hopeful statements.

Then, at the last minute, came the denouement. The democratic process came to a sudden halt. A small inner group of the bureaucratic elite announced that they would further "revise and reorder" the text before the document became official. As a result, a separate section on "the Land" was taken out and, after being eviscerated, subsumed under the section entitled "Towards a Christian Understanding of Jews and Judaism." Furthermore, the phrase "the indissoluble bond between the land of Israel and the Jewish people" was deleted, while the phrase "the need for Palestinians for self-determination and expression of their national identity" became "the quest for statehood by Palestinians." Silence on the bond between Israel and the Jewish people but a strong endorsement of statehood for the Palestinians. Surely, some of the Jewish partners must have wondered whether this was the best they could get after years of dialogue with church representatives.

There has, of course, never been unanimous enthusiasm in the Jewish community for dialogue with Christians. There are those who, as a principle of faith, oppose any form of theological dialogue. To them, as to some conservative Christians, the very idea of dialogue seems to imply a relativizing of the faith and betrayal of the truth. As recently as 1986 the Rabbinical Council of America reaffirmed its position that theological discussions, as distinguished from conversations on social and human welfare issues, ought to be avoided.

Others remain skeptical about Christian motives and are particularly concerned that the dialogue process might be manipulated for missionary purposes. The fear of proselytizing is extremely strong in the Jewish community, but we shall deal with that in a separate chapter.

Then there are people who feel that, in general, the dialogue is overloaded with friendliness and tends to lack honest confrontation. Eliezer Berkovits, in a 1966 article in the periodical *Judaism*, put it quite sharply when he raised the question about who the people are who are so eager to engage in dialogue. Scornfully, he provided his own answer: "They are either Jews without memories or Jews for whom Judaism is exclusively a matter of public relations, or confused or spineless Jews unable to appreciate the meaning of confrontation in full freedom."

No doubt, public relations play a role in the interfaith enterprise, as do political calculations. And, I would think, quite understandably so. There is no need to romanticize all that goes on in the name of Christian-Jewish relations. On the other hand, sometimes the politics and P.R. may be a bit overdone. There have been times when Jewish leaders seemed excessively eager to show gratitude to church officials for little favors. For instance, after the slaughter of innocent worshippers in the Istanbul synagogue in 1986, several church bureaucrats spoke out in protest, and Jewish organizations cited their words in mailings across the land. But some of those same leaders had been silent at times when it was much less safe to speak out, when nothing less than Jewish survival was at stake. In some cases, as during the 1967 and 1973 wars, a few of those same leaders had called for cut-off of U.S. arms shipments to Israel when it was in a life and death struggle with enemies who were heavily armed by the Soviet Union.

Still, it seems unfair to me to accuse staff members of Jewish organizations who are professionally involved in relations with the Christian community of avoiding confrontation at all cost. I know from personal experience that this simply is not so. We all live with dilemmas and ambiguities, except perhaps some inhabitants of academia, professors who dwell within the certainties of their own theories. So, yes, Jewish bureaucrats, too, play games, and sometimes it is done under the large umbrella of dialogue and defense of Jewish interests. But that is not the whole story.

Of course, the whole story of Christian-Jewish relations is quite complex. One of the major mistakes we tend to make is to overestimate the role of national establishments. They are part of the picture, even an important part, but in the final analysis perhaps only a small part. It is certainly not the only game in town. In numerous local communities all sorts of activities go on that never hit the headlines. Men and women of goodwill, Jews and Christians, join together in a common search for better understanding as well as for ways to serve the community in which they live.

So, in spite of the noises that sometime emanate from solemn ecclesiastical assemblies, and at times seem to jeopardize progress that has been made, the dream is kept alive by people who may never be in the limelight but who quietly seek to obey the biblical injunction: do justice, love kindness and walk humbly with your God.

V

The Prelate and the Presbyterian Bureaucrat

"Valerian Trifa, an Archbishop with a Fascist Past, dies at 72." Thus read the heading of a rather lengthy obituary in the January 29, 1987, issue of the *New York Times*. The article pointed out that at one time, this man had been an honored prelate. In 1955, he had given the opening prayer before the United States Senate. Furthermore, the obituary observed, "he was also appointed to the Governing Board of the National Council of Churches, although he was later removed." That last sentence stands in need of a little elaboration as well as a touch of correction. Rather than remove the archbishop, the National Council of Churches reached a compromise arrangement whereby Trifa, without resigning, promised not to show up at meetings any more.

In this chapter, our focus turns to the National Council of Churches and particularly to the so-called "Trifa Affair." The way this affair was handled tells volumes about how ecclesiastical processes function when key figures in the church establishment embrace a dogmatic approach rather than a dialogue approach.

There is obviously more at stake here than the National Council of Churches' position on Middle East issues. The treatment of Israel at National Council of Churches meetings and in National Council of Churches resolutions is basically one aspect of a broader ideological agenda . It is an agenda that is not unique to church bodies at all. Both the Christian Right and the Christian Left are constantly in danger of becoming mere fellow-travelers of certain political positions that are part of partisan agendas. Commitment to those positions can, and in many cases does, lead to a loss of critical thinking. As a result, church constituencies are fed propaganda in the name of prophecy, precisely the kind of thing Christian friends of Israel are often accused of being engaged in (and, no doubt, sometimes are engaged in). Whenever this happens, dialogue is sacrificed and so is a sense of fairness.

As to Trifa's promise not to show up at National Council of Churches meetings anymore, it should be pointed out that he had not attended National Council of Churches sessions for a number of years and, although quite active in the ecumenical movement, I did not know about the man's existence until a group of young people belonging to the Jewish Defense League decided to stage a demonstration at the October 1976 National Council of Churches Governing Board meeting held at the Roosevelt Hotel in New York City. They had come to protest Archbishop Valerian Trifa's membership in the Governing board, because they claimed that, as a member of the Nazi Iron Guard in Rumania during World War II, he had instigated violent attacks against Jews, leading to the horrible murder of several hundred of them in the so-called "Kosher butchering" in the municipal slaughterhouse of Bucharest.

The young Jews of the J.D.L., it turned out, had decided to act after the latest issue of *Esquire* magazine, featuring an article on the Rumanian Orthodox prelate, appeared on the newsstands. A central character in the story was a New York dentist, Charles Kremer, who had lost many relatives during the Nazi reign of terror in Rumania and had devoted years of effort as well as a considerable portion of his financial resources, to expose the real Viorel Trifa, who later had adopted the name of Saint Valerian. Incidentally, Saint Valerian's special day is January 21, the same day the Trifa inspired pogrom had started in 1941.

As I became embroiled in the "Trifa Affair", I came to know Charlie Kremer rather well. He was not the easiest man to deal with, but he was possessed with the sort of ornery determination as well as a good deal of courage that is needed to pursue a wolf in archbishop's clothing like Trifa. In the process, it turned out, he would have to take on a large segment of the ecclesiastical establishment as well.

By 1976, interventions at ecumenical gatherings had become rather common events. In 1968, my first year as a church bureaucrat, I had witnessed in that same ballroom at the Roosevelt Hotel a temporary takeover of the dais by James Forman and a group of young cohorts, who served as his bodyguards as well as intimidators of the assembled church delegates. Forman, a Black radical whose star shone brightly albeit briefly as he traveled from one ecclesiastical assembly to the next, demanding millions of dollars of reparation money to make up for injustices inflicted upon Black people. I recall returning to my office on the subway train in a mild state of shock. I felt as if I had just witnessed a major hold-up attempt. But soon, as the occupation of church offices became a rather common practice, this sort of confrontational interaction seemed like a regular part of bureaucratic life.

By and large denominational establishments treated the invaders of their offices and the riflers of their filing cabinets with a certain deference, but above all with great understanding. At one point a group of Reformed Church seminary students from New Brunswick, New Jersey, decided to get into the act too, as a sign of their solidarity with the oppressed people of the world. As we were showing them (before our 4:30 p.m. departure for the suburbs) which offices had the most comfortable couches to sleep on and the softest rugs, their leader burst out in a mixture of anger and frustration that we did not have to be so damn nice about it all because it made him feel uncomfortable.

Forman did not get his millions of ransom money, but most "mainline" denominations did vote through substantial sums of money for new programs designed to help Black people as well as to demonstrate the sincerity of their repentance. It was somewhat like the indulgences in medieval times but on a higher inflation scale. Of course, there were also groups of people who very badly wanted to be heard by the ecumenical bureaucracy without making any demands for money, but who never learned the confrontational game very well. The Coptic Christians were a good illustration of such a group.

My first contact with Coptic Christians occurred in October of 1977 when a delegation came to visit me in my office at the Interchurch Center. For years they had sought to plead the cause of their brothers and sisters in Egypt who were constantly subjected to harsh and discriminatory measures. But they never succeeded in getting past the middle-level church executives who occupy the various denominational Middle East offices. Their repeated efforts always had met with the same result: they were sent on their way with a sympathetic headshake plus handshake, but never had the issues been dealt with by the National Council of Churches leadership. Not once did the National Council of Churches speak a churchly word on their behalf, not to speak of a "prophetic" pronouncement on the issue.

Why, they wanted to know, was the cause of the Palestinians such a central concern to the National Council of Churches and why was their voice not being heard? I had to explain to them that there were various reasons for their plight. First of all, they had never found out how the system works and how to find out when and where meetings were being held. But more important than that, in the political scheme of things, to allow them to voice their grievances publicly would pose an embarrassment to the church establishment. Oppression of the Coptic Christians simply did not fit into the priorities of the Council's social agenda.

Gabriel Habib, General Secretary of the Middle East Council of Churches, said as much in a speech he delivered in the Interchurch Center of August 15, 1977. In that talk, which was later distributed among an inner circle in printed form, he gave the following advice: "When dealing with those other areas of tension [i.e. other than the Palestinian-Israel issue], one should carefully take into account the effects on the future of the Christian communities in the Middle East. For example, we have to be extremely careful in dealing with, or even mentioning the right of Copts in Egypt, because of the negative effects this might have on the life of the Christian community in that country. Emphasizing the problems of the religious minorities in the Middle East today is a double-edged sword." In sum, it is safe to attack Israel, but risky to even mention oppression of fellow Christians in Arab countries. Therefore, silence becomes the better part of political-ecclesiastical wisdom.

At any rate, a few weeks later, once again in the ballroom of the Roosevelt Hotel, Coptic Christians staged one of the quietest and most polite interventions that an National Council of Churches Governing Board meeting had experienced for some years. At the end of a plenary session they approached a somewhat astonished National Council of Churches president to present their concerns and distributed some literature as the delegates were leaving the hall. Denominational staff members with Middle East portfolios hastened to assure the powers that be that they had not provided those people with information about the place and schedule of the meeting.

A year earlier, when the Jewish Defense League had appeared on the scene, things had been a bit noisier and a good deal nastier. Dr. William

P. Thompson, a lawyer and the Stated Clerk of the United Presbyterian Church, served the National Council of Churches as president at the time. He was a rigid and humorless bureaucrat whose expertise on parliamentary procedure (a potent weapon he would not hesitate to use for his own purposes) was recognized by all. To me he always seemed a man who, in Shakespeare's words, "hath no music in his soul." The fact that he had once served on the U.S. legal team during the Nuremberg trials had not made him sensitive to Jewish concerns and certainly had not made him sympathetic toward Israel. He had a hard time keeping his anti-Israel sentiments below the surface of the well-controlled parliamentarian persona.

These character traits of the then National Council of Churches president no doubt played an important role in how the intervention by the Jewish Defense League and the Trifa affair in general were handled. One thing is sure, those young Jews were received quite differently from Jim Forman and his cohorts in 1968. The air was heavy with hostility. Personally, I must confess, I have little use for storm trooper types of whatever ideological brand, but it seemed clear to me that the fact that those Jewish youths were considered Outsiders with a capital "O" added a few degrees to the intensity of the anger directed at the disturbers of the Governing Board peace.

Dr. Thompson virtually lost his parliamentary cool. He threatened to shut off the microphones before he would allow any of the protesters to speak to the delegates. By contrast, Forman had been given unlimited access to the mikes without a word of complaint. At one point Dr. Thompson vacated the chair temporarily in order to vent his resentment at the protesters. There even was talk of calling the police, something that had been inconceivable during previous interventions.

A chronology of the events that followed, based on the official releases at the time, gives an indication of the moral paralysis that can take hold of a "prophetic" establishment when one of their prelates is involved, particularly when dealing with Jewish concerns. True, people were taken somewhat by surprise, because most of those active in the ecumenical movement did not realize that Trifa was a member of the Governing Board. He certainly had not played an influential role. Very few of us had ever heard of the accusations that were being levelled against him, although it eventually came out that some National Council of Churches insiders had had forewarnings. Now that the facts were being exposed, however, and since militant Jewish youths had confronted the Council on the issue, defensiveness took over with a vengeance. "His Eminence the Archbishop" was being attacked. (The title, it later turned out, he had bestowed upon himself after a take-over of the Rumanian Orthodox Church, which was achieved by applying Nazi goon squad tactics to those who opposed him.)

The following items in my chronology tell the basic story:

October 8—The Governing Board's Credentials Committee, to whom the matter of Trifa's membership had been referred, reported: "We cannot ask any communion to defend its internal policies or practices of delegate selections." In other words, if the Orthodox Church in America wishes to have an alleged war criminal represent them on the Board, there is no constitutional way for the National Council of Churches to refuse accreditation to such an individual, or even to morally challenge the sister church.

October 14—National Council of Churches President William P. Thompson let it be known that he was prepared to meet with "responsible Jewish leaders" in order to explain to them that, both from the point of view of civil law (a person is innocent until proven guilty) and church law (the National Council of Churches constitution) a "wait and see" attitude was the only correct stand to take until Archbishop Trifa had had his day in Federal Court. He referred to the "great anguish" inflicted upon the Orthodox Church because of the "hearsay" charges. In the meantime, Trifa's lawyers were busily at work to make sure that their reverend client would avoid a day in court at all cost.

October 15—At my request the Committee on Christian unity of the Reformed Church in America adopted a statement expressing deep concern about the manner in which the Council had addressed the issue of Trifa's membership, calling the position of the National Council of Churches Credentials Committee "spiritually and morally untenable" and making the point that "we, who do not hesitate to address others with the moral claims of the gospel, should not remain silent when our fellow member churches are involved." How, after all, could a Council of Churches, which in so many cases had presented itself as the voice of conscience on national issues, now take refuge in the claim that there is no accountability whatsoever in the churches' relationship with each other? A few days later, Dr. Marion de Velder, General Secretary of the Reformed Church in America, received a letter from Dr. Thompson reminding him of his right to propose a constitutional amendment.

October 18—A *N. Y. Times* article quoted official National Council of Churches spokesman Warren Day regarding the allegations made against Trifa: "We did a lot of checking and it doesn't hold up under any kind of investigation."

October 20—The *N. Y. Times* published the following letter, which I had submitted a few days earlier: "Dr. William P. Thompson, president of the National Council of Churches, has expressed the hope that Jewish leaders would agree that the council's action in the Archbishop Trifa Affair was the only responsible one that could be taken. It is my hope that both Christians and Jews will reject that position.

> "The right of every accused person to a fair trial is a moral issue. The shadow hanging over the whole National Council of Churches as a result of the allegations that one of its governing-board members is an unrepentant Nazi war criminal is also a profoundly moral issue. It is, in my judgement, not a responsible act on the part of the National Council of Churches to sit back and say that we must await the judgement of a Federal court, possibly years from now. On numerous occasions, the National Council of Churches has gathered and evaluated evidence dealing with violations of human rights and torture. Why is that suddenly such an impossible thing to do when a member of our own ecclesiastical community is involved?"

October 21—A number of National Council of Churches staff members requested that a special session of the executive committee be called to consider the matter of Archbishop Valerian Trifa's membership on the Governing Board, pointing out that the allegations against him were so serious that "the moral responsibility of the Council is being challenged." They on their part challenged the position so passionately advocated by Dr. Thompson, that the argument of constitutional restraint was the final answer.

October 26—The Rev. Father Varile Hategan, speaking on behalf of the Department of External Affairs of the Orthodox Church in America, wrote a letter to National Council of Churches General Secretary Claire Randall, reporting that the Department had "unanimously and emphatically decided not to withdraw Archbishop Valerians' representation on the Governing Board of the National Council of Churches." He also chided the Board for not adequately insuring the safety and security of its members. One got the impression that poor Trifa had been traumatized by the protesting Jewish youths.

October 27—The Holy Synod of the Orthodox Church in America announced that they had appointed an "episcopal commission to review allegations against Archbishop Valerian Trifa," adding that they were wholly opposed to anti-Semitism as, they were sure, His Grace the Archbishop was also.

October 31—The executive committee of the National Council of Churches met in special session in Chicago. They expressed gratitude for the fact that the Holy Synod had initiated an ecclesiastical investigation and suggested that they might consider asking the Archbishop "to refrain from executing his duties" as a Governing Board member until church and civil proceedings are concluded.

November 12—The National Council of Churches issued a news release "to provide accurate and up-to-date information about the situation surrounding the charges and the Council's response to them." The appointment of a commission by the Holy Synod of the Orthodox Church in America is noted as something of special significance. What better medicine for bureaucratic dilemmas than the appointment of a committee, no matter whether the committee functions or not?

On February 4, 1977, the Orthodox Church in America announced that Trifa would not function as a member of the Governing Board of the National Council of Churches during church and civil proceedings now under way, claiming that the "atmosphere surrounding the case and the person of the Archbishop" would make it impossible for him to function effectively.

On October 7, 1982, six years minus one day after the demonstration at the Roosevelt Hotel, Archbishop Valerian Trifa was ordered deported from the United States. In order to save him from execution in his homeland Rumania, Portugal granted him asylum.

In the preceding account I have focused heavily on the role of Dr. Thompson. And rightly so. After all, he was the organization's president and greatly influenced the procedures that were followed. But my main concern is not really with Bill Thompson the man. As a matter of fact, since he was defeated as a candidate for the Stated Clerk position in the newly formed Presbyterian Church (U.S.A.), he has become an almost forgotten figure in the Protestant establishment. Beyond the man, however, I am intensely interested in the mind-set he represented, as well as in the question concerning the cultural-spiritual climate in which people with such a mentality gain influence and power.

How does a dialogue movement take on the characteristics of a dogmatic establishment? Some will say that organizations, like human beings, eventually begin to suffer from "tired blood." They see history as moving in rise and decline cycles. I'm sure there is some truth to that theory. Yet, one seeks to understand some of the processes and internal dynamics by which such disintegration takes place.

It is my belief that the betrayal of dialogue in the ecumenical movement can, at least in large measure, be attributed to certain liberal bureaucrats with a locked-in agenda. This, I realize, is a contradiction in terms. The very root-meaning of the word "liberal" tells us that it has something to do with freedom, openness and the ability to engage in continual re-evaluation of positions in light of new evidence and historical developments. A locked-in agenda means that there has been a sell-out of liberal spirit. We end up with a liberalism that has lost its soul, an unliberal liberalism.

In some circles, "liberal" has come to mean that one takes a solid position on "the Left," which is no longer a way of thinking or a historical dynamic, but a dogma. "The Left", when detached from an ongoing internal debate, becomes a rigid system. In his book *The Emergent Church*, the Catholic scholar Johann Baptist Metz distinguishes between "rigorism" and "radicalism," claiming that the former derives from fear while the latter finds its source in the "freedom of the Church's call" (p. 8). Metz, who uses these ideas in his attacks on bourgeois religion in a post-capitalist age, has thus become greatly admired in "progressive" theological circles. But the truth is that the Protestant bureaucracy, while seeing themselves as representatives of biblical radicalism, is through and through bourgeois in mentality. The radical rhetoric these people espouse has little to do with their life styles or the way they run their ecclesiastical operations. The result is "rigorism" under the guise of "radicalism," a sort of fundamentalism on the Left.

Dialogue needs a sense of dialectic. Without it, we end up in the sterile world of monologues, a phenomenon apparently well suited for TV news programs. Anyone who has ever listened to "exchanges" between, let us say, the Rev. John H. Buchanan, chairman of People for the American Way, and the Rev. Jerry Falwell, leader of the Christian Right, knows what I am talking about.

Whatever qualms one might have about the so-called dialectical theology that was popular some decades ago, it must be said that it turned out to be a fruitful soil for the nurturing of a dynamic ecumenical movement, inspiring some of the visionary leaders who turned dreams into reality. How ill at ease, one suspects, would a Reinhold Niebuhr be in the non-dialectical environment of church life today, dominated as it is by church leaders who proclaim that they will "let the world set the agenda." Unfortunately, they chose to imitate some of the worst features of what in some circles passes as the "liberal agenda."

A rather dramatic and profoundly ironic illustration from outside the church world, of what I have in mind took place during January, 1986, when PEN held its International Congress in New York City. Here one saw gathered the literary elite of the world. One would think that, of all people, writers want to promote a climate where an open exchange of views can prevail and where tolerance for diverse opinions is matched by contempt for all forms of intellectual intimidation. In theory, I'm sure, that is what the vast majority of these people would affirm. In practice, however, they apparently had a hard time pulling it off.

Cynthia Ozick used the Op Ed page of the *New York Times* (January

22, 1986) to air her complaints about what had transpired at the Congress. The event, she wrote, had been turned into "a narrow tower of political babble," transformed into "a booming ritual monolith where you felt you had to watch your step" i.e. be sure to say the right thing or face the scorn of the crowd; i.e. take a solid position on "the Left." She concluded her essay with a haunting question: "Is that really what free writers want . . . one more intellectual uniform?"

But, perhaps Cynthia Ozick is not considered a bona fide spokesperson for the progressive wing of the literati of the world. So we turn to Norman Mailer, the man who had raised most of the money for the Congress and who has few rivals for the title of Mr. Liberal among American authors. In an interview, also reported in the *New York Times* (January 27, 1986), he expressed dismay at some of the things that had been going on and blamed it all on what he called a "catatonic leftism", adding scornfully that "most of the leftists around today wouldn't even know how to spell that word 'dialectic'." I think they know how to spell it, but they have somehow lost the spirit of a true liberalism, one that knows the difference between passionate discourse and propaganda.

Joseph Epstein has coined the phrase "the virtucrats". They are to be found on the Left as well as on the Right, both secular and religious. They go for certainty, "prophetic" certainty to be sure, the kind that has God on its side or something that serves as a substitute for the Deity. A dialectical approach to issues or the slightest sense of ambiguity are seen as a sign of wavering that cannot be tolerated among true believers.

The current peacemaking campaign in some mainline Protestant churches offers a prime example of how ecclesiastical virtucrats influence denominational policies. It is a drive that manifests highly propagandistic overtones dressed up in pious terminology. The 1987 Assembly of the Presbyterian Church U.S.A. was a case in point. To see those people seriously consider the question whether their denomination's position in the United States today is similar to that of the Confessing Church in Hitler's Germany shows that absurdity knows few bounds when the Church and Society curia go on a crusade. Finances fortunately set some limits. The cost of mailing the proposed document, "Presbyterians and Peacemaking: Are We Now Called to Resistance?", to the church's members proved to be so high that the Assembly voted in favor of delay and a period of further study.

Peacemaking is probably as close to a perfect cause for a propaganda campaign as one can get. The horrors of war are terribly real. Who would want to give even the slightest impression that he or she is a warmonger? Although I have noticed that in denominational peace literature those who do not follow the establishment line are actually referred to as "idolators," people who worship false gods, like national defense, or who have the audacity to raise questions about national security.

Some church editors, who are not always among the most independent people to start with, because so many of their magazines are highly subsidized by denominational funds, soon tend to fall in line. The Christian Reformed journal *The Banner*, published an editorial entitled "Pursuit of Political Peace" (November 10, 1986), assuring readers that he is not "a radical pacifist," the editor concludes his essay be recommending "exchanges between Russian Christians and American Christians, artists from here and artists from there, Soviet people and North American people."

So far so good, although I find it a bit amusing that trips to the Soviet Union (usually highly subsidized with denominational funds) are always piously referred to as "peacemaking missions" and I remember many enthusiastic reports by pilgrims to Russia during the Stalin era. In this connection it may be worth quoting the remarkable confession in 1950 by Anna Louise Strong, daughter of a Christian pastor and passionate apologist for socialism. Wrote she: The people I really cared for, on whose side I felt myself to be fighting, they winced so if a single human weakness in the U.S.S.R. were noticed. So I let my audiences pressure me into giving what I knew was a partial picture. I told no lies, but I didn't tell all the truth" (*New York Times*, February 27, 1984).

People-to-people contacts undoubtedly have their value, but it is unfortunate, to say the least, when they produce partial pictures about the situation in totalitarian societies. Or when people, who usually display a good deal of common sense, suddenly romanticize the results that such exchanges can be expected to yield. For instance, the editor of *The Banner* concludes the aforementioned editorial with the declaration that "we will not kill people whom we love, and they won't kill people they love." Now really? Isn't it a touch naive to suggest that the issue of modern warfare and the conduct of a superpower conflict will be determined by church delegations whose members have engaged in brief encounters during what can fairly be described as guided tours?[2]

The editor of my own denomination's official magazine, *The Church Herald*, also wrote an editorial a few years ago, entitled "The Morality of Deterrence" (November 18, 1983). In discussing the option of opposing "any further nuclear deployment", he made the observation that "taking that position, one would have to risk a degree of political subjugation, but being righteous would have to take precedence of being politically free." In other words, let's accept a little slavery in exchange for security or, as some would say, survival. But in this case, as compared with those who hold a non-establishment position, the search for security is not called a sinful idolatry; it is counted as righteousness! I am reminded of a remark Sidney Hook is reported to have made to the effect that people who make

---

[2]Under the leadership of Mikhail Gorbachev, changes have taken place in the Soviet Union since I finished the manuscript for this book that no one in the West had imagined, least of all the Christian apologists for the old system, who presented the churches with their "partial pictures." These changes have come about, because Gorbachev was finally forced to face the fact that the centrally controlled and utterly oppressive system simply did not work, and had the courage to acknowledge this. The full picture of the true conditions in Russia is now being revealed through the passionate revolts of people who had never ceased to thirst for freedom, both in the Soviet Union and its satellite states.

As noted before, ecclesiastical prelates and bureaucrats are now publicly admitting that at times they let themselves be used as propagandists, something that should have been clear to anyone who ever listened to the carefully selected delegates from the Eastern bloc to ecumenical meetings. Less than one year before the downfall of the Rumanian tyrant, Nicolae Ceausescu, church officials there referred to him as "a hero among the heroes of our country . . . a man whose mind and soul have realized the interests of the people," while they were busily levelling sanctions against the truly heroic dissident priests in their midst.

I suspect that recent developments in the world community will tend to lessen the ideological tone of ecumenical dialogues. My hope is that this will strengthen the role of those church leaders who have never been comfortable with the excessive politicization of both the World and National Council of Churches. In short, I believe that things look more hopeful for world peace, as well as for honest ecumenical dialogue.

survival the supreme value are declaring that there is nothing they will not betray.

Still some, I'm sure, will never lose the passion for freedom. To them the cry of Patrick Henry will still make sense in the nuclear age: "Is life so dear, or peace so sweet, as to be purchased at the price of chains and slavery? . . . I know not what course others may take, but as for me, give me liberty or give me death!" My own antidote to editorials that tell readers to see righteousness in the choice for slavery is to listen to Odetta, the great Black singer:

> "Oh freedom, oh freedom,
> Oh freedom over me. And before I'll be a slave
> I'll be buried in my grave; go home to my Lord and be free."

While the good old fashioned ways of dealing with idolaters are no longer viable, the liberal establishment is not at a loss when it comes to ridding itself of troublesome dissenters. Moorhead Kennedy, one time foreign service officer and hostage in Iran, found that out. He discovered that the spirit of the Ayatollah is alive and well in liberal Protestantism. He tells the story in his book *The Ayatollah in the Cathedral.*

After his return to the United States, Mr. Kennedy was approached by two prominent peacemakers in the liberal church world, Bishop Paul Moore of the Episcopal Church and Rev. Bill Coffin of Riverside Church. With supporters like that, who would expect to become the subject of a heresy hunt? But, Christian doctrine is one thing; political orthodoxy is something quite different. On the latter score Mr. Kennedy apparently failed the test.

The trouble started shortly after he had established a Peace Institute at the Cathedral of St. John the Divine in New York. While being openly critical of certain aspects of U.S. Middle East policies and sympathetic toward a number of positions favored by "the Left," Mr. Kennedy expressed some reservations about the Nuclear Freeze Movement, or at least suggested that a diversity of opinions be heard. Peacemakers of the pure kind simply are not supposed to entertain notions like that. And so another idolater had to be dealt with by the liberal establishment. Soon the Peace Institute died in the spirit of conflict.

72

Another preposterous illustration of the lack of tolerance among some liberal church leaders is to be found in the fact that as many as four attempts have been made in recent years to silence an independent Presbyterian journal. *The Presbyterian Layman*, with a readership far larger than any of the official Presbyterian magazines, has been a voice of dissent within that denomination for many years. Social activist bureaucrats, solid adherents to liberation theology, have repeatedly brought charges of un-Presbyterian activities before the General Assembly of the church and have demanded that, because of "journalistic excesses" and lack of compliance with denominational pronouncements, the paper no longer be allowed to claim an association with the denomination. Closing down papers that voice dissent is, of course, a favored tactic among totalitarian states. But to see it attempted in a historic Christian community with a great tradition of freedom is baffling indeed.

Most of such pathetic campaigns start with pious-sounding phrases like "the partisan church", which is supposed to be a corollary of the God who has a "preferential option for the poor". But soon the partisan church, rather than being a compassionate fellowship, turns out to be a party-line church, where intolerance is practiced in the name of liberation theology and denominational mailings are used to pursue ideological goals. Local parishes are presented with " a partial picture", as happened, for instance, when the 1985 "Peace with Justice Week" packets, sent out by national denominational staffs, listed a whole variety of trouble spots in the world about which Christians ought to be concerned, but omitted any mention of Afghanistan.

Some countries are always treated with a best-case scenario. Others, the United States in particular, are portrayed in a worst-case scenario. I see nothing "prophetic" in such procedures; on the contrary, it strikes me as representing a triumph of prejudice.

After this rather lengthy detour we return to the central theme of this book: Christian attitudes toward Israel. I believe that the preceding reflections are relevant to our topic. A Christian Left that has lost its liberal spirit poses, it seems to me, a peculiar threat to Christian-Jewish relations. The lines of communication all too easily become overloaded, leading to breakdowns in even the most basic understandings. First, there is the issue of historic Christian anti-Judaism which inevitably must be faced if dialogue is going to have any integrity at all. But now the situation tends to become burdened with additional baggage, namely the anti-Semitic impulses which historically so often have been part and parcel of the radical Left, both religious and secular. All this becomes then tied up with a Third World agenda whose valid and urgent concerns increasingly become obscured rather than advanced by mindless sloganeering and anti-imperialist rhetoric that portrays Israel as an invader in an otherwise freedom-loving region.

It is not surprising that under such circumstances the PLO and a Nazi prelate have a much better chance of getting the benefit of the doubt than the state of Israel. It is also no wonder that the Office on Christian-Jewish Relations of the National Council of Churches really has gone nowhere since it was established. I reported earlier that the executive position of that office had been vacant for several years. As I am writing this, it had just been announced that the position has been filled. The appointee, a Presbyterian pastor, is receiving strong financial support from his own denomination. Hopefully this means that new Presbyterian leadership has produced a more positive attitude toward Christian-Jewish relations.

VI

Creative Transition

A "sloppy firing", according to an article by Robert Johnson in the *Wall Street Journal* (March 20, 1987) has a scenario that runs somewhat like this: "You know, Phil, there are times in a man's career when . . . I mean, it's always important to consider your options, and I think it's more and more important in your career now. You know, Phil, there are a lot of reasons for it, and I guess I'm not saying this very well . . . Listen Phil, if you want to continue this, let's go have a drink. But I'll tell you now, you've been loyal to us for 15 years, that's really loyalty, and I know this is tough. But strange as it may seem, Phil, let's just remember that this is the first day of the rest of your life. Really, that's all I have to say, except that although this is an ending, it's not like an ending-ending, you know. You'll get paychecks for a while, at least. Look, this is Friday. On Monday, I'll see personnel and find out just how long you get 'em."

This story sounds very similar to my own firing in 1978 by the Rev. Arie Brouwer, then General Secretary of the Reformed Church in America and my immediate superior, now General Secretary of the National Council of Churches of Christ. First came the chitchat. How had the dinner gone the night before with Professor and Mrs. Hendrikus Berkhof? The Dutch theologian, an old acquaintance of my wife and me, was the special guest of the Reformed Church in America during its 350th anniversary celebration, which had just been held during a General Synod meeting on the Columbia University campus in New York. I responded with a few cheerful chitchats of my own, mentioning such momentous details as that Dr. Hendrikus Berkhof had tasted his first "rusty nail" ever.

Then followed the hemming and hawing stage, the uh . . . I've been wondering how to say this and the ah . . . you've made a tremendous contribution to this organization and I personally very much appreciate the role you have played, but . . . uh. . . .ah. . .you really must look for other employment. "But please remember Isaac," Arie Brouwer repeated several times, "I want this to be a creative transition. . ." Finally, I was assured that some sort of financial arrangement could be worked out.

Even in my state of near-panic I thought this phrase "creative transition" sounded so precious, even more so than "just remember this is the first day of the rest of you life." Having lived in a society where the term "Besonderes Heilsverfahren" (special healing procedure) was a euphemism for the liquidation of "incurables" by overdoses of drugs secreted in their food, I consider "creative transition" a rather mild form of Orwellian double talk. Nevertheless, it seems to me a significant indication of how the corruption of language tends to permeate all bureaucratic structures, those of the churches not excluded. We Christians don't act like "them"; we don't fire each other; we simply provide people with creative transitions.

To say that I was stunned at hearing Brouwer's announcement about my imminent departure would be somewhat of an understatement. Perhaps the word "shatter" comes closer to it. For ten years I had worked with this man. We had a close, although not always smooth, relationship. Year after year he had rewarded me with a high performance rating. My last performance review had occurred only a few weeks earlier, and there had not even been a hint about a precipitous decline in the quality of my work to the point of zero. This guy had played games with my life, and that's exactly what I told him.

In a letter I received a few weeks later, Hendrikus Berkhof wrote: "We had several talks about your work and I can testify that from what you said it was clear that you had not the faintest awareness of what was hanging over your head." In retrospect I realize that the innocence I projected was based on a good deal of naiveté. The truth was that I was not as politically savvy as I had believed myself to be, not an uncommon state of mind among people who are about to receive the professional axe.

Lee Iacocca, who was unceremoniously shown the door by Henry Ford a few weeks after I lost my job, notes in his autobiography that not once during their fateful final encounter did Ford use the word "fired". Now, Arie Brouwer is not a Henry Ford and Isaac Rottenberg is not a Lee Iacocca. Furthermore, compared with the auto industry the ecclesiastical bureaucracy is a mini-business. But what matters, I think, is the style and the mentality, which are quite similar among the God-players in business and the church.

Brouwer mumbled something about recent tensions that had necessitated radical measures. But he also assured me that the transition could be done more creatively (i.e. there would be more cash available) if I agreed to depart quietly. Instead, I decided to make a few noises, involving a certain cost that I have never regretted.

The day before firing Iacocca, Ford had called nine key board members to set the stage and protect his flanks. In our tiny church establishment Arie needed to call only four persons: namely the members of the so-called liaison committee, chaired by Mr. Carl VerBeek, a Grand Rapids attorney who served in the triple capacity of being Brouwer's legal counsel as well as prosecutor and judge in my case.

In the Church we often like to believe that we have no need of "legal niceties" such as prevail in the secular world. After all, among us business is conducted by the rule of love. It is one of the self-delusions by which many Christian leaders live publicly. On the inside, however, there is a much greater sense of realism. An associate, who had become a good friend—and who eventually succeeded me—looked me straight in the eye and in a calm, cool and collected voice advised me that Arie Brouwer had the power to ruin my future career within the denomination and would not hesitate one moment to do so if I gave him a hard time. It's a tough world, including the world of the One Holy Catholic and Apostolic Church; those who manage the "house of the Lord", no matter what name the ecclesiastical establishment may go by, know how to play hard ball when they believe that their vital interests are at stake.

There are aspects of Iacocca's story that I could readily identify with: the anger one feels about the hurt that is inflicted upon one's whole family; the disappointment experienced when board members behave as if they are helpless creatures who don't know how to handle messy situations and who just wish to have the whole business over with as quickly and quietly as possible. There are so many agendas at work in such situations. The chairman of my denomination's executive committee, a retired regional executive who had become president of our

General Synod as well as an honorary doctor as the rewards for good behavior, reacted to me as if I were undermining everything he had ever stood for.

One member of the board, a district school principal from Interlaken, New York, articulated that mentality most clearly when he wrote me that he believed in being a team player; if someone did not fit that mold, well then, for the good of a smoothly running organization that person should be gotten rid of. The spelling mistakes in that school principal's letter served as a strong reminder to me that team players, even mediocre ones, do indeed sometimes have a way, not only of surviving, but of rising to the top.

Below the surface of piety that came my way during the weeks that followed my dismissal, I sensed a good deal of moral paralysis. "I hear what you are saying," wrote one church leader, "I feel your pain. May God bring good out of apparent evil." This man occupied a top position among non-staff denominational leadership at that time. Didn't he know that in order to bring good out of apparent evil God usually needs the services of disciples who show a little backbone?

Then there are the people who have charmed you while you were on the way up but carefully avoid you when you are down, because the association may not be safe to one's professional health. Or others who for some reason have nurtured a slight grievance against you and who now, for the first time, feel free to send signals that convey the unmistakable message that you had it coming. I am not suggesting that those grievances were necessarily groundless. People "on the way up" can very easily grow insensitive to the feelings of others and do things that rightfully cause resentment.

When I first joined the new team at denominational headquarters we were determined to build a bureaucracy that, above all, would be different. We would not become an establishment in the usual sense. Somehow we were going to reverse the law of bureaucratic gravity that normally causes high ideals to become dragged down into the muddles of organizational mediocrity. We were going to institute a person-centered style of administration. The then very popular techniques of sensitivity training were going to help us pull it off.

It all began in 1968 when the Reformed Church's national establishment went through a major organizational shake-up, usually referred to in church circles as a "restructure for mission". The first task of Arie Brouwer, hired as the Executive Secretary for Program, was to put a new team together. Some of my friends warned me against joining the new administration, reminding me that as a seminary student Brouwer had gained considerable notoriety as a member of a triumvirate who, in the name of strict orthodoxy, harassed those professors suspected of deviations from pure doctrine. However, after a brief hesitation I not only joined, but also proceeded to persuade my friends who saw themselves as part of the progressive wing in the church, that we were now dealing with a new and more mature person, who was endowed with considerable leadership abilities. I still think I was partly right. The part on which I was wrong would have significant consequences for my personal life.

It had just become fashionable to send new church executives to expensive seminars where they would be introduced to the glories of Management by Objectives as well as to the miracles of the Human Potential Movement. Funds were not an obstacle at that time. My first experience of this kind was a three week training course in the San Francisco area, starting with a full week of sensitivity training sessions.

For many of us these were mind-blowing experiences. In some cases they became like counter-conversions: an emotional unloading of what we had been taught were essentials of a Christian lifestyle, especially the negatives of no dancing, no drinking, etc. It was all liberation, a raw celebration of life that had a neo-pagan touch about it, accompanied by a confrontational style of relating to others that sometimes had highly sexual overtones. It was like a "gospel of the gut", inner stirrings that received an almost revelatory significance.

I shall never forget my first session in the sensitivity group. In a context that I no longer recall exactly, I used the term "big shot". Dr. David Hunter (at that time Deputy General Secretary of the National Council of Churches, a man of imposing physical stature and one of the few people in the room who was not a novice at this kind of experience) attacked me in no uncertain terms for using that kind of language. Not knowing David from Adam, I immediately made my second mistake by stating that he impressed me as a person who might be a big shot (in the best sense of the word, of course!) and asking him what his job was. He replied in rather colorful non-ecclesiastical language that he would be damned if he was going to tell me what he did for a living. Later David and I became pretty good friends.

We were full of excitement as we started to build our open, self-critical and person-oriented organization. We were high on hugging and tight embraces, enamored with psychic probings ("I really want to know where you're coming from!") and intoxicated with a new sense of freedom. The sexual connotations were by and large acted out more in the form of suggestive language than in promiscuous behavior, although staff parties of the ecumenical "jet set" could be rather wild affairs (especially, as some of my readers will recall, at the John Marshall Hotel in Richmond, Virginia) as the spirit of Zorba moved mightily among the saints of mainline officialdom.

My job description stipulated that "the incumbent must possess sound theological knowledge" and that "the position must act to some extent as the staff's conscience." I thought that I had landed in the best of all possible worlds: I was being paid to fulfill a gadfly function.

Although I eventually became quite skeptical about sensitivity training techniques, I have never regretted my participation in conflict labs, encounter groups and other group dynamics experiences. The potentials for manipulation in the name of liberation are immense. But we also learned to work with groups of reserved Dutch Calvinists in ways that introduced elements of celebration into our rather somber assemblies. Furthermore, much of what was at first a faddish innovation eventually became part of conventional life. Looking back, I realize that I should have taken some of the stuff about open confrontation within the bureaucratic context less seriously. The boss who sends you to those sessions is the same person who will make sure that you do not apply the principles in dealing with him or her.

In the meantime, it can be reported with certainty that life at 475 Riverside Drive in New York, where many church bureaucracies have found a home in the Interchurch Center, has not been radically changed by the Human Potential Movement. It takes more than a few techniques to humanize any bureaucracy. Personally, I have become convinced that bureaucracies basically operate according to certain Kafkaesque principles that are quite similar whether one lives in a capitalist, socialist or any other kind of society. Our notion of building a new kind of bureaucracy had been the product of our inexperience and naiveté.

When, with the help of Rockefeller money, the Interchurch Center was built during the Eisenhower era, the basic idea behind the "475" set-up was the creation of an environment where a truly dynamic ecumenism could develop. Proximity was thought to promote, not only efficiency and more effective cooperation, but above all a creative encounter between the various Christian traditions. This, in turn, would lead to mutual enrichment and the strengthening of the ecumenical idea of unity without uniformity.

It did not happen that way. Instead, the striking thing about life at "475" is really the sameness of it all. A process of homogenization has led to a party-line mentality, which had made creative interaction an ever harder goal to achieve. In the world of innumerable meetings (the locale changes from floor to floor, but the attendees are usually the same), in the world of memos and endless reams of xeroxed materials, language eventually is turned into jargon; distinctiveness of perspective is replaced by group-think.

As I have indicated earlier, my troubles with ecumenical bureaucratic procedures intensified when I moved into the areas of Christian-Jewish dialogues and Middle East concerns. I discovered how fierce the infighting can be in an establishment that ostensibly was devoted to dialogue. At the risk of sounding repetitious, I will recount events that took place during the Spring of 1978, which provide, at least in part, a backdrop for my dismissal.

When one operates in a highly politicized environment, the people who control the process can exercise great power. They run the bureaucratic machinery; they set the agenda and structure the meetings; they manage the mailings that go out to delegates and decide which guest speakers will address the assembly. Thus, in many subtle and not-so-subtle ways, they can influence the tone and, to a considerable degree, determine the outcome of large gatherings. On such points church conventions and political party conventions function according to the same rules.

We in the Office on Christian-Jewish Relations realized that in essence we were fighting a losing battle. Damage limitation became our major task, not a very creative role in a dialogue movement. Any bureaucrat who wishes to survive knows that the only legitimate way to raise issues is to go through "regular channels". We had tried that many times, only to discover that those channels were controlled by people who were unsympathetic to our concerns and in many cases hostile to our efforts.

Some of the events taking place during the May, 1978 Governing Board meeting of the National Council of Churches convinced me that the time had come to do something irregular. So I wrote a nasty letter to the *New York Times,* blasting the NCC for the dismal state of affairs into which it had fallen.

But let me explain. First, prior to the meeting that was held in Minneapolis, Frank Maria, representing the Antiochean Orthodox Church with its close ties to Damascus and always eager to fan the anti-Israel feelings within certain Council circles, had presented a document to the Middle East Committee of the National Council of Churches purporting to deal with human rights in Israel. As usual, the piece was grotesque in its distortions, and nobody expected it to be adopted by the Council in the form it was offered. That, however, is not so important for people who have a propagandist purpose in mind. The simple fact that their twisted ideas can be introduced into the process gets them the attention they want. Therefore, even when defeated or when the document is radically revised, the effort is considered worthwhile.

Responding to Maria's document, I wrote a memo to the members of the Middle East Committee with a copy to Dr. Claire Randall, then the National Council of Churches's General Secretary. This stated in part: "I personally would not fight it if the National Council of Churches wanted to initiate a wide-ranging debate on human rights in the Middle East. There are lots of issues to talk about and there is enough blame to go around. I'm not sure that such a debate would contribute to a ministry of reconciliation right now, but there are certainly valid issues to be raised. I will, however, fight like hell if ideologues within the National Council of Churches use that organization for their own propagandistic purposes, or if, in truly hypocritical fashion, church bureaucrats talk loudly about human rights in Israel to cover their silence on human rights in Arab countries in order to protect their missionary interests there."

In the end Maria was outmaneuvered, and his document never came up for discussion. Still, he was not left entirely empty-handed. In those days U.S. Nazis felt a strong compulsion to march through Skokie, Illinois, the home of many Holocaust survivors. Sister Ann Patrick Ware, a Roman Catholic nun who worked for the National Council of Churches' Faith and Order Commission, had written a 13 sentence resolution expressing concern about the increasingly aggressive activities of neo-Nazi groups. This had been duly processed and made part of the agenda sent out to the delegates. It was the shortest piece in the packet.

That same mailing contained a very long and complicated policy document on Affirmative Action, a more than mildly controversial issue among National Council of Churches constituents, one would think. But the Governing Board was able to digest it and adopt it within a matter of minutes. By contrast, the brief resolution on neo-Nazis was debated for several hours until the lunch break forced some sort of action, which was to send it back to a committee for a rewrite. What was the problem? What kind of severe hang-ups might have produced such hesitation to speak a few simple words protesting hate-mongering Nazis marching through Skokie?

The real problem, one suspects, lay beyond the specific issues verbalized. For instance, some people argued that if the Council was going to talk about the Nazis and the Jews in Skokie, there ought to be equal time for an attack on the Ku Klux Klan. Never mind the fact that over the years the Council had passed many resolutions condemning anti-Black racist groups without anyone demanding that they should include a section on anti-Semitism. In a cynical gesture bordering on obscenity, the new version of the resolution was later read to the Council by none other than Frank Maria.

There was still more to come! "Suddenly" (Dr. Claire Randall later told Jewish leaders that she was taken by surprise, but some of us had been tipped off in New York a few days earlier that such an action was afoot) a new resolution appeared on the scene, accusing Israel of using cluster bombs in Lebanon. A "native American" claimed, while roaming around

Southern Lebanon, to have picked up the fragments, later presented as evidence. Since this resolution contained a pious reference to the "sanctity of human life", it was suggested that mention should also be made of the murder of civilians by PLO terrorists along the Haifa road that had precipitated the Lebanon incursion. Fair enough, said the Council's own reference committee, only to have its recommendation for such an inclusion voted down by the Governing Board at large. Apparently, only certain people fell within the purview of the Council's concern for the sanctity of human life. Israeli Jews were not among them. My letter of protest about this kind of National Council of Churches shenanigans appeared in the May 24, 1978 issue of the *New York Times*. A few weeks later my career as a church bureaucrat came to a sudden halt.

Now, in all fairness it should be said that Arie Brouwer's fury had little to do with my stance on Israel. It had, however, everything to do with his standing among the inner circle of the ecumenical establishment. He had made some basic career decisions of his own. Those included a climb up the ecumenical ladder.

Much was made of the fact that I had not only signed my name, but had added my title, Director of Communications, Reformed Church in America. This, it was claimed, made it sound as if I spoke for the church at large. That criticism contained a valid point, but by identifying my position I enhanced my chance of the letter being published. Furthermore, I had done the same thing in a letter published by the *N.Y. Times* during the Trifa affair and not a word had been said about it. Of course, there was a difference! That letter had attacked Dr. William Thompson, Brouwer's rival (whom he eventually defeated) in the race to become General Secretary of the National Council of Churches. This time it was his stature that, he felt, was at stake.

There were other non-Israeli related dynamics at work as well, and it would be a distortion of the total picture if I were to leave them unmentioned. The year 1978, when the denomination was celebrating the 350th anniversary of its continuous ministry in this country, was an important milestone in the history of the Reformed Church in America. In June, General Synod met in the city that at one time had gone by the name of Nieuw Amsterdam. The main celebration took place in the historic Marble Collegiate Dutch Reformed Church which traces its roots back to 1628, when New York was a colonial outpost of Holland.

But festivities were not the only agenda of the General Synod meeting. Business items on the agenda included the somewhat sticky issue of the "Spoolstra Affair", involving a complaint of unjust treatment by a Rev. Franklin Spoolstra against a regional Synod in the Chicago area. The 30 minutes that Brouwer had scheduled for the Synod's executive committee to deal with the matter stretched out into many hours of debate, including two late night sessions. Brouwer began to worry about his image as an effective manager.

What was the issue? Spoolstra had received a call to become pastor of a church and had accepted. Although the local judicatory had given its approval, they subsequently had second thoughts about it and refused to install him in that church because certain objections had been raised against him.

One detail, not mentioned earlier was revealed at the Synod meeting: that Mr. Spoolstra had never been told about the nature or content of the objections raised. Rather, he was advised that it was in his best interest if those things were kept silent. But was it due process?

Brouwer pushed for an affirmative vote on his original recommendation that the regional Synod's position be sustained. He was supported by Carl VerBeek, one of two lawyers serving on the executive committee. The latter's argument went, that in the church we don't have the same strict constitutional protection prevailing in the secular judicial system. Some people, including myself, were not so sure about that. The study of law had been my first love and, looking back, I realize that I joined the anti-Brouwer position with an alacrity that lacked basic bureaucratic prudence. We lost . . . for a little while.

Instead of sleeping, David Alford, the other lawyer, (from the small village of Middletown, New York) spent part of the night writing a minority report that stirred up the whole issue again the next morning. "A common criminal is entitled to be informed of the charges against him and an opportunity to refute them," Alford wrote. "Is a minister of the Word entitled to know what objection is offered to his installation? Is it a sufficient answer to the charges made here of secret condemnation that it is in his best interest not to know? Is it sufficient to say we act with Christian love and intentions with which a certain highway is notoriously paved? If such procedure is approved, what minister is protected from irresponsible and illegitimate objections to his installation in any church at any time? Such procedure undermines the foundations of Christianity and citizenship."

During the earliest days of the Dutch presence in America, Peter Stuyvesant, the first Director General of New Netherland, represented the spirit of an arbitrary authoritarianism. He was a man imbued with a deep suspicion of the non-conformist who, he feared, might foment rebellion. He was also of the opinion that Jews should not be allowed to settle in New Amsterdam. But there is another side to the Dutch heritage, one that made Holland a free haven for non-conformists and a land of rebels against autocratic rule, be it by the church or by the state. Both these streams of tradition were, it seemed to me, still evident at the 350th anniversary General Synod of the Reformed Church in America.

I believe that among the many speeches that were made during that anniversary celebration, few words deserve to be remembered more than David Alford's eloquent minority report. The end result of the whole affair was that Mr. Spoolstra's complaint was dismissed on a technicality while the regional Synod was reprimanded and admonished to follow better procedures in the future.

But I had been a poor team player. Brouwer felt that my behavior had come close to a betrayal. I am sure that in his frustration he really believed that I had committed the unforgivable sin. To return once more to Iacocca, in his account he says that he was fired on an impulse but that in the end it had been inevitable. One only sees those things from a certain distance in time, but I am sure that the same was true in my case. And, as a matter of fact, Brouwer knew that I was exploring other career possibilities. But anger looks for an outlet. The exercise of power is a common reaction of people who happen to be in a position of power.

This story has an ironic twist. During the preceding months, Arie Brouwer had chaired a special National Council of Churches committee, which issued a report challenging the U.S. Government on the rights of citizens before grand juries. The whole document was filled with a passion for due process. That is precisely the reason why so many "prophetic" ecclesiastical utterances come across as pious hypocrisy. They are often the products of religious establishments that strike out at the sins of the world, while blissfully lacking any sense of self-criticism.

The last meeting of top Reformed Church staff that I attended in Brouwer's office had a one-item agenda: floor covering. During one dark night a xerox machine in the print room had, for some mysterious reason, caught fire and caused considerable damage in our offices. A major repair and redecoration job was called for. The decision between carpets or tile had already been made in favor of the former. The question now was whether top executives (in whose offices usually originate noble pronouncements about "God's preferential option for the poor") should be allowed to select more expensive carpeting. I chose the cheaper brand, a decision with which it turned out I only had to live with for a very short time.

The heady days for the Reformed Church establishment in the late 1960's had been turned into the hangover days of the late 1970's. We were not what we had imagined ourselves to be. There was less hugging and kissing and more interpersonal conflict. Visions about great programs to advance the Kingdom of God were increasingly dimmed by petty preoccupations.

Some will say that I am trying to demonologize the church bureaucracy. The word "demythologize" would come closer to the truth. For a decade I unashamedly referred to myself as a church bureaucrat. I have few regrets about those ten years. There are people in the church hierarchy for whom I have great respect. Bureaucrats of all kinds will be with us till kingdom come. I always felt that as long as that is the case, some of them ought to be people like me.

A human being, wrote Blaise Pascall, is "a Nothing in comparison with the Infinite, an All in comparison with the Nothing. . ." He also said that a human being "is but a reed, the most feeble thing in nature; but he is a thinking reed." (*Pensées*, 72 & 347). We are a complex mixture of the angelic and the demonic, of wisdom and folly. Bureaucratic environments rarely bring out the best in our humanity, nor in our sense of humor. Hence the need to demythologize.

The Rev. Arie Brouwer, who rarely had gone wrong in planning his career, became General Secretary of the National Council of Churches. There was a slight miscalculation when he thought that his efforts to promote closer ties with the Soviet Union would earn him the Russian Orthodox vote in his campaign for General Secretary of the World Council of Churches. The Russians, for certain reasons of their own, decided to cast their vote for the South American theologian Emilio Castro, thus giving him the victory. However, the National Council of Churches came to the rescue. By any standard of "making it" in the world of ecumenical, becoming that organization's General Secretary must be counted as a success.

And the Rottenbergs? Two weeks after my dismissal we moved into a new home for which we had signed a contract a few months earlier. Exactly two weeks before firing me, Brouwer had put his signature to the documents approving our mortgage from church funds at a reduced rate, a perk to which executives were entitled. So much for long range planning and management by objective! As a form of partial compensation I held on to the low rate loan for three extra years.

Well-meaning persons tried on several occasions to arrange for a hand-shaking session which to them meant reconciliation. I refused, seeing it as basically a political gesture "for the good of the party", as they say, designed not to bring about a fair resolution but to assure my silence. Two months later a colleague wrote me with an apparent mixture of surprise and dismay: "You still come across to me as angry." "You're so right," I wrote back, "I am mad as hell."

Why, one wonders, are Christians often so uncomfortable with any kind of anger? "Be angry, but do no sin," advise the Holy Scriptures. I know that the danger of self-deception ought never to be underestimated. But neither, it seems to me, should the problems that are associated with a kind of spurious piousity that stifles honest anger and tends to turn it into guilt. From my perspective, that is not love but sheer sentimentality and potentially a danger to one's health.

In conclusion, let me say that I do believe in creative transitions and consider it important that persons in various church positions believe in it too. Because across the board, in conservative as well as liberal churches, firings of pastors and other church personnel are becoming increasingly common. (And the same might be true in the world of American synagogues). However that may be, creative transitions are not handed out by benevolent religious superiors or boards. The worst clergy today can do is to entrust themselves completely to Mother Church, who presumably will always take care of us. The modern world demands greater maturity than that. It also requires, I believe, that those who feel the "calling" develop broader interests and skills that count for something if by chance they once again find themselves "on their own." I discovered that, thank God, there is life after "475", a center of ecclesiastical bureaucracy that is steadily losing some of its influence. During the past few years, for instance, several major denominations, like the Presbyterian Church and the United Church of Christ, have shown an interest in moving their national offices from the Interchurch Center in New York to the Middle West, indicating a successful revolt by grass roots forces.

There is no doubt in my mind that the ecumenical movement will keep right on moving without the heavy concentration of church executives in the "Vatican-along-the-Hudson". Some endeavors to engage in dialogue, with the Jewish community for instance, may well be enhanced by such moves toward decentralization. Creative transitions indeed![3]

---

[3]When, in 1984, Arie Brouwer was nominated as General Secretary of the National Council of Churches, some members of the search committee told reporters that they had been particularly impressed with the brand of piety with which the candidate approached various issues. Realizing full well that I would be accused of sour grapes, and admitting openly that I was not the most objective commentator on the subject, I went public with a little essay, entitled "The Selling of an NCC General Secretary—A Dissenting Opinion." In that piece I ventured the view that, in the end, Brouwer's appetite for power, rather than his piety, would determine his relationship to colleagues and other church leaders. When Mr. Brouwer was forced to resign in 1989, that particular prediction had turned out to be right on the mark. However, Arie Brouwer was not forced to join the poor, whom bureaucrats love to portray as God's favored children. His lawyer negotiated a severance payment that, according to my rough calculations, would require $1,000 contributions from a few hundred local congregations to cover. Church justice moves in mysterious ways!

VII

Vatican Affirmations and Vacillations

"The big, the inevitable, question to the Church is that of the permanent election of the Jewish people and its meaning for Christians." Thus spoke Cardinal Roger Etchegary of Marseille, France (now residing in Rome), during an "intervention" at the 1983 Synod of Roman Catholic Bishops. "So long as Judaism remains exterior to our history of salvation," he added, "we shall be at the mercy of anti-Semitic reflections." Then followed this expression of penitence: "May we learn how to ask pardon of the Lord and our brothers who have so often been nurtured on 'the teaching of contempt' (Jules Isaac) and plunged into horror and holocaust."

If the permanent election of the Jewish people is indeed the big and inevitable question to the Church, it has to be admitted that the addressee has succeeded in avoiding that question for many centuries. One even wonders how many members of the hierarchy present during Cardinal Roger Etchegary's speech would wholeheartedly endorse the sentiments he voiced, not to mention the millions of priests and local church members around the world.

Still, the Cardinal spoke from an historical context in which his affirmations make sense and that context is the Second Vatican Council and subsequent official pronouncements from Rome. We are talking about an extremely short historical period. Before that there was a very different history, covering many centuries which, according to the U.S. Catholic Bishop's declaration in 1975, were "replete with alienation, misunderstanding and hostility between Jews and Christians."

To state things a bit more explicitly, those were the centuries of ecclesiastical anti-Judaism in theology and anti-Jewish legislation in practice. It was the era of the "Jew badge", instituted and enforced by the Church.

Those were also the days, not only of anti-Jewish fulminations, but also of forced conversions and forced baptisms, surely among the worst violations against the human spirit. And, to mention more recent history, motivated by strong anti-Communist impulses, powerful figures within the Vatican put their hopes in Hitler's forces and, after World War II, even became involved in helping Nazis escape from Europe and hence from justice.

Vatican II, the basic context of Cardinal Roger Etchegary's remarks, meant a decisive turning point in the history of Catholic-Jewish relations. Perhaps we should say in a more direct way it was an encounter between Pope John XXIII and the French historian Isaac, the man who coined the now famous phrase "teaching of contempt", that began to bring about change in Catholic attitudes toward Jews and Judaism.

From all accounts the Jewish historian did have quite an impact on the recently elected Pope, who already was preparing to open up the windows of the church to the world in order to let the breezes of new insights and inspirations refresh the stodgy atmosphere in the Catholic establishment. Some people, among them Pope John's confidant Loris Capovilla, have intimated that the thought of making the Jewish question and anti-Semitism central concerns at the forthcoming Council had not occurred to the Holy Father until his meeting with Isaac on June 13, 1960, just one week after he had created the Secretariat for Promoting Christian Unity.

In my own life as a young, recently ordained pastor, Pope John XXIII became an important figure. I was deeply impressed by his diary, *Journal of a Soul*, which tells us so much about the spiritual formation of this humble giant among the saints. "The whole world is my family," he wrote in 1959. Drawing on "a strength of daring simplicity," he declared himself "ready for the Lord's surprise moves." Not only did he put the "Jewish question" (as a *Christian* problem!) on the Council's agenda, but together with Cardinal Bea, he made sure that it stayed there, despite the efforts of some within the hierarchy to get it removed or, at least, to have its impact weakened.

One of the most moving prayers of Pope John XXIII was not published in the book *Journal of a Soul* but one he is reported to have written on June 4, 1963, a few days before his death. "We realize now that for many, many centuries our eyes were so blind that we were no longer able to see the glory of your chosen people, nor to distinguish on their faces the signs of the special status of our brothers. We have come to see that the sign of Cain is on our foreheads. Century after century our brother Abel lived in blood and tears on account of our trespasses because we had forgotten your love. Forgive us the curse which we have so unjustly inflicted upon their flesh. We have crucified you for a second time, because we did not know what we were doing. Lord, help us turn from the evil way we have gone in history and church history. Let our conversion consist of a concrete renewal. May the peace of God, which guards our lives and thoughts, fill our hearts in Christ Jesus our Lord."

Two and a half years later, the Vatican Council promulgated *Nostra Aetate*, a declaration on the Relationship of the Church to the Non-Christian Religions. Containing a special section on the church's relationship with the Jewish people, the Declaration speaks about "the spiritual bond linking the people of the New Covenant with Abraham's stock." It reminds the faithful that it was through the people of Israel that the Church received divine revelation. It advocated "fraternal dialogues" and affirmed that Christ's death "cannot be blamed upon all the Jews then living, without distinction, nor upon the Jews of today". Finally, it deplored "displays of anti-Semitism directed against the Jews at any time and from any source."

The use of the (in this context) rather weak verb "deplore" seemed more than a little surprising to many readers of the document. One explanation given for this word choice was that "condemn" in a Council document should be reserved for matters of formal heresy, and Pope John explicitly had expressed that this Council not engage in such condemnations. Nevertheless, an exception on this particular point would have seemed most appropriate. Anti-Semitism often did develop within the churches as a form of heresy; in this case the Council would not just have condemned the aberration of some individual, but a most grievous error of the Christian world at large.

The statement declaring that not all Jews living in the time of Jesus and since that day should be blamed for his death was also considerably weaker than an earlier proposed version, which had expressed the hope that Christians "may never again present the Jewish people as one rejected, cursed, or guilty of deicide." Quite understandably, such revisions in proposed drafts caused great disappointment in many circles. But it was also generally recognized that this was the best that could be achieved in the theological/political climate of that moment.

Dr. Eugene J. Fisher, Executive Secretary of the Secretariat for Catholic-Jewish Relations, National Conference of Catholic Bishops (U.S.A.), frequently has pointed out that he finds the real breakthrough in *Nostra Aetate*, not in the rejection of collective guilt, important as that is, but in the paraphrase of Romans 11, "the Jews still remain most dear to God because of their fathers, for He does not repent of the gifts he makes nor of the calls He issues." With those words Rome sought to transcend a long tradition of supersession theology. A people that remains most dear to God cannot at the same time be a cursed people, replaced in the divine covenant by the Church. Vatican II constituted a definite shift in 1900 years of Catholic-Jewish relations, or rather, the lack thereof. It meant the beginning of what some Catholic scholars have called an "irreversible movement" that, step by step, would produce radical change of perspective within Catholicism.

Fisher has claimed that *Nostra Aetate* is, for all practical purposes, the beginning of Catholic Tradition (as distinguished from tradition with a small "t", summed up in the phrase "teaching of contempt") on the relationship between the Church as "People of God" and "God's People, Israel." Never before had the Church really dealt with those issues as a matter of *doctrinal* concern. Previous Councils, like the Fourth Lateran Council (1215), had plenty to say about Jews, but the mean-spirited and discriminatory canons issued at that time were not of a doctrinal nature. I realize, of course, that that fact gave little comfort to the victims of those laws nor did it in any way alleviate the sufferings of all who were subjected to them. Nevertheless, in view of the way things work in Christian theological tradition, I think that Fisher's observations about the theological significance of the developments started at Vatican II have a good deal of validity.

In my opinion, a graphic portrayal of post-Vatican II developments would, while showing up and down movements, exhibit a gradually ascending line. In analyzing developments within the World Council of Churches from Amsterdam (1948) to Vancouver (1983) we, unfortunately, were forced to draw the opposite conclusion. It was downhill process.

Although, as we shall see, things turn less positive within the Catholic community as well, once the "Israel factor" becomes part of the equation. In that respect the Protestant and the Catholic dialogue movement share a common weakness or, in today's parlance, show similar serious hang-ups.

But first let us trace the line of progress in Catholic-Jewish relations. On December 1, 1975, the Holy See issued "Guidelines and Suggestions for Implementing the Conciliar Declaration, Nostra Aetate par. 4." In comparing the various Catholic documents I have been helped by materials that arrive regularly from the office of Dr. Eugene Fisher, and particularly from a paper he wrote, entitled "The Evolution of a Tradition: From Nostra Aetate to the 'Notes'."

By the time the Guidelines were issued, Rome had overcome its reluctance to use the word "condemned". Now all forms of anti-Semitism and discrimination are, indeed, condemned "as opposed to the very spirit of Christianity." Also, there is a specific reference to contemporary Judaism, something that had been lacking in *Nostra Aetate*, although it was there by implication. The need for an explicit emphasis on this point is so important, however, because many people (including a famous historian like Arnold Toynbee) viewed Judaism in essence as a fossilized relic of something that had died soon after the death of Jesus and the rise of Christianity. When in recent years the fossil proved to be very much alive—in short, when history refused to comply with the theory—and the state of Israel as well as the Hebrew language were revived, some proponents of the Judaism-is-dead theory had a hard time concealing their resentment.

Over against the historical fiction of the fossil, the Guidelines put the unmistakable teaching of the Catholic Church, that Judaism has continued to evolve as a vital reality: "The history of Judaism did not end with the destruction of Jerusalem but, rather, went on to develop a religious tradition." Throughout the 1975 document the Jewish people, who in 1965 were still mainly defined in terms of biblical categories, are portrayed as a living, neighborly reality; as a people of faith, whom Christians, also a people of faith, must learn to understand through open dialogue: two communities of faith, drawing in part on a common prophetic tradition, that will be a blessing to humanity by cooperating in the areas of justice and peace.

After one more decade of internal discussions as well as dialogues with people of other faith-perspectives, the Vatican, in 1985, came out with "Notes on the correct way to present the Jews and Judaism in preaching and catechesis in the Roman Catholic Church." The use of the term "Notes" would seem to suggest that the document is perceived as one further step in a process of development, not as final dogma, much less as summa theologica. The "Notes" are meant to give some assistance to those who are charged with teaching responsibilities in the church. Above all, they seek to serve as an authoritative educational tool in an effort to portray Jews and Judaism in a fairer and, hence, more positive way than has often been done in the past.

Before discussing the content of this 1985 document, a few parenthetical observations may be in order. When we read the best in recent ecumenical literature on Jews and Judaism, we may be inclined to conclude that we have come a long way, especially when the present situation is compared with a very bad past. One visiting theological seminaries, however, soon discovers that in may instances that literature is not being studied or assigned for reading. In short, numerous pastors continue to be trained without any clear understanding of the long tradition of teaching of contempt, both in Catholic and Protestant churches.

If pastors are ignorant of the past, one can imagine what happens at the level of the local parish, especially in church schools where millions of children receive their knowledge about the Bible and the story of Jesus from mostly untrained teachers. The gap between the best of what is being published "up there" among the relatively small group of people who are preoccupied with these matters, and what goes on in local churches and Sunday schools is immense. At that level many myths and misinterpretations, repudiated by reputable scholars still are being disseminated as gospel truths.

That having said, I personally have little doubt that, on the whole, the Catholic community has tried harder to correct the situation, and done a better job in revising educational materials, than either "mainline" Protestants or evangelicals. People like Dr. Eugene Fisher and Sister Rose Thering, professor of education at Seton Hall University, have done pioneer research in this field that has led to numerous changes, often brought about with the eagerly sought assistance of Jewish scholars. True, not all Catholic teachers use the materials available to them. Perhaps, some do not use them too well, but the overall movement is in the right direction.

It seems to me that it is in that context, that the "Notes" must be viewed, As the introduction points out, Pope John Paul II himself set the tone when, in 1982, he told delegates of episcopal conferences and other experts, meeting in Rome to study relations between the Church and Judaism: "We should aim, in this field, that Catholic teaching at its different levels, in catechesis to children and young people, presents Jews and Judaism, not only in an honest and objective manner, free from prejudices and without any offenses, but also with the full awareness of the heritage common [to Jews and Christians]."

Once more the "Notes" seek to move a few steps beyond what was affirmed in the preceding Vatican pronouncements. New areas are opened up for exploration, such as positive elements in the contribution of the Pharisees, who traditionally have been treated with almost total negativity in Christian teachings. Other emphases are reinforced and, in some cases, reformulated in light of what has been learned during the preceding years. For instance, the danger of anti-Semitism is pointed out with renewed urgency as an evil that is "always ready to reappear under different guises."

Citing John Paul II who, in an address to the Jewish community of Mainz, West Germany in 1980 referred to "the people of God of the Old Covenant, which has never been revoked," the "Notes" too present a strongly anti-supersessionist message. But, beyond that, there is a very positive assessment of Jewish history which, as the 1975 document stressed, did not end with the destruction of the Temple in 70 A.D. This history, we are now told, "continued, especially in a numerous Diaspora which allowed Israel to carry to the whole world a witness, often heroic in its fidelity to the one God and 'to exalt him in the presence of all the living' (Tobit 13:4), while preserving the memory of the land of their forefathers at the heart of their hope."

More on the reference to "the land" in a moment. In this section I have sought to give a broad picture of positive developments in Vatican thinking concerning Jews and Judaism. The "Notes" deal with a number of issues, like various approaches to biblical interpretation or liturgical practices in the church and the synagogue. While they have provoked considerable debate, I have chosen not to dwell on them here.

In the Catholic community the voice of final authority obviously resides in the Holy See. But the role of the various national conferences of Catholic bishops should not be underestimated. Some of the statements they have issued represent dramatic breakthroughs in Christian-Jewish dialogue and, in turn, influenced subsequent Vatican documents.

Then there are the words and actions of the Holy Father as he travels around the globe, particularly important in the case of someone like Pope John Paul II, who operates on the world scene with such a well attuned sense of symbolic drama. I have already cited some of his words when addressing Jewish leaders in Mainz, West Germany, in 1980. One year earlier, during a very dramatic visit to his native Poland, the Pope had visited Auschwitz and there spoke movingly about the millions of murdered Jews.

In such missions of goodwill, unintentional blunders do occur. During his Auschwitz visit, for example, the Pope singled out Edith Stein for special mention. She was a convert who later came to be known as Teresa Benedicta of the Cross. The Holy Father, I am sure, did not foresee what sensitive Jewish ears would hear in this one sentence, which at the very least raised the question whether a Christian martyr of Jewish descent is more important than those who died faithful to their Jewish tradition. Such incidents demonstrate that even the most well-meaning among us Christians have a long and hard journey to travel toward a mind-set truly attuned to the feelings and historical experiences of our Jewish brothers and sisters. Nevertheless, through this visit the Pope sent a significant signal to the Catholic faithful, even though later disputes about the opening of a Carmelite convent on the site of Auschwitz temporarily introduced renewed elements of ambiguity into the message the Catholic Church wishes to convey. That matter was finally settled in early 1987 with the decision to move the convent some distance away.[4]

---

[4]As things turned out, the 1987 negotiated settlement wasn't that final after all. During the summer of 1989, the dispute flared up once again. The Carmelite nuns were supposed to have relocated their convent to a new site, which was also

Even more dramatic was the Pope's visit to the Great Synagogue in Rome during the Spring of 1986. His very positive message on that occasion was all the more welcome because several Lenten homilies, delivered by him only a few weeks earlier, had raised serious questions among Jews as well as concerned Christians, including some prominent Catholics, whether supersession theology really was a thing of the past. In the Great Synagogue the Pope once again affirmed that "the Jews are beloved of God, who has called them with an irrevocable calling." The homilies, I suspect, reflected a long-standing past that is dying only slowly, while the message in the Great Synagogue represents the wave of the future. At least, I fervently hope that this will prove to be the case.

Speaking of hope, we have already noted that the 1985 Vatican document spoke of the Jews who, throughout their history, have preserved "the memory of the land of their forefathers at the heart to their hope." But what about our faith and our hope as Christians? Or, to repeat the question raised when discussing the Protestant ecumenical world: If the covenant

---

to serve as a center for Jewish-Christian dialogue. The designated date was February, 1989, but that deadline was not met. A small group of Jews from New York then staged a protest at the convent, which led to some rather ugly incidents. Cardinal Glemp, Poland's Roman Catholic Primate, and the Archbishop of Cracow both reacted in anger, accusing the protesters of fomenting anti-Polish sentiments, especially because of their alleged power over the media, and threatening to abandon the plan to establish a center for dialogue. Not only Jews, but also many others, including John Cardinal O'Connor of New York, expressed shock at those statements. In February 1990, ground was finally broken for the new convent.

In November, 1989, the U.S. Catholic bishops unanimously adopted a policy statement on the Middle East, a development followed with considerable apprehension by the Jewish community. In the end, because of a careful balancing of Israeli and Palestinian rights, the document did not become a matter of controversy. But other issues, such as a meeting between Pope John Paul II and Yasir Arafat, or the matter of formal recognition of the State of Israel by the Vatican, or statements made by church officials regarding certain unique claims of the Catholic faith, have kept, and will no doubt continue to keep, Catholic-Jewish relations in a certain state of ferment. That, it seems to me, is a healthier condition for dialogue than the bland consensus that comes with the avoidance of conflict.

promises are still valid today, if, as the Holy Father has said, these have never been revoked, does that include the "promised land" and does the answer to that question affect our faith and our hope?

Where does the Catholic Church stand on that question, which also encompasses the issue of the status of Jerusalem? In the midst of much ambiguity and ecclesiastical/political gamesmanship, it could with certainty be said that the Catholic Church has moved beyond the position of Pope Pius X, who in 1904 held a meeting with Theodor Herzl, shortly before the latter's death. The founder of the modern Zionist movement was looking for the "goodwill" he did not get much of during his visit to the Vatican. A statement made by the Pope on that occasion ranks among those unfortunate famous remarks to which the world is treated with sad regularity by religious and secular leaders alike. "We cannot approve of the Zionist movement," declared the Holy Father. "We cannot prevent the Hebrews from going to Jerusalem, but we could never sanction it. The Hebrews have not recognized our Lord; therefore, we cannot recognize the Hebrew people . . ."

Two weeks later a mild spirit of charity had apparently taken over as the Vatican Secretary of State, Cardinal Merry del Val, wrote in a letter to Herzl: "If the Jews believe they might greatly ease their lot by being admitted to the land of their ancestors, then we would regard that as a humanitarian question. We shall never forget that without Judaism, we would have been nothing." The first sentence in this quote seems to imply some goodwill toward, or at least a toleration of, a non-political type of Zionism (the Jews are allowed to live in the land as a favor, a humanitarian gesture). The second sentence seems to appreciate Judaism mainly as a *preparatio evangelii*, an instrument to bring forth Christ and the Christian Church.

At any rate, in 1917, Pope Benedict XV, protesting the Balfour Declaration, still manifested a spirit of Catholic imperialism when he wrote: "Our apostolic charge makes it a duty to demand that the rights of the Catholic Church in Palestine, when they are so manifestly superior to the rights of others involved, should be respected and safeguarded prior to all others; not only the claims of Jews and infidels, but those of members of non-Catholic confessions, no matter what their race and country."

As Father John F. Morley has so clearly shown in his book *Vatican Diplomacy and the Jews during the Holocaust 1939 - 1943,* the Vatican suffered from a longstanding phobia about a Jewish majority in Palestine, convinced that this would be very much opposed to Catholic interests. Still in 1943, while debating the feasibility of sending rescued Slovakian children to Palestine, Monsignor Domenico Tardini, a principal assistant to the Vatican Secretary of State wrote: "The Holy See has never approved the project of making Palestine a Jewish home . . . And the question of the Holy Places? Palestine is by this time more sacred for Catholics than . . . for Jews."

The words spoken in the Rome synagogue in 1986 were indeed a world removed from the remarks by these papal predecessors. Still, the question of Israel is far from resolved. It continues to haunt Catholic-Jewish dialogue. In *Nostra Aetate* the whole subject was treated with silence. That was not an oversight during the early stages of dialogue. In fact, it represented a clear defeat for those who had attempted to raise the issue. A first draft document proposed at Vatican II was rejected precisely because it hinted at the possibility of extending diplomatic recognition to Israel. This defeat led to a withdrawal into safer territory and *Nostra Aetate* ended up focusing mainly on what, in a fondly condescending fashion, is often referred to as "the Israel of old." Later Vatican pronouncements sought to correct this by making positive statements about Jewish history since the destruction of the Temple in 70 A.D.

But the question of Israel could not be silenced that easily. In 1966, one year after the promulgation of *Nostra Aetate*, Father Cornilius Rijk, a Dutch biblical scholar, was assigned the task of follow-up and implementation. Once again, he and associates sympathetic to his views went to work on a draft document designed to attribute a certain theological significance to the rebirth of the state of Israel. However, in 1969 this preliminary draft was leaked and published in *The Catholic Review* of Baltimore. This raised the level of internal Vatican politics to a feverish pitch, showing that church politics and bureaucratic infighting are by no means a Protestant monopoly, least of all when the issue of Israel is at stake.

Father Thomas F. Stransky, a founding staff member of the Vatican

Secretariat for Promoting Christian unity, wrote in *America* (February 8, 1986) that "politics should not be allowed to place theology in chains," while knowing full well the dynamics of church discussions when the Middle East is involved. So, according to Father Stransky, "no matter how purely theological and pastoral the conciliar intentions might be, any positive development in Catholic-Jewish relations would have political implications in the Middle East, saturated with Christian, Moslem and Jewish conflict. Beleaguered minority Catholic communities would express that anxiety through their bishops. And Arab diplomats to the Holy See would bluntly state their disquiet" (p. 92). A little later he mentions his surprise "that, while, over the past two decades, the results of the dialogue have been changing the theological and pastoral horizons, the political pressure, subtle or not so subtle, has stubbornly refused to subside" (p. 93).

The meek, whom the gospel calls blessed, better step aside. Ecclesiastical infighting can become quite fierce, devouring in many instances the more gentle and scholarly spirits who have little stomach for that sort of game. It was, therefore, not surprising when Father Cornelius Rijk, Director the Vatican's Catholic-Jewish Secretariat, withdrew in 1973, two years before the Guidelines were issued. Msgr. George G. Higgins, at that time Secretary of Research for the U.S. Catholic Bishops Conference, gave us a glimpse into how rough the politics can get, when he went public with a protest piece against the machinations of Father Joseph Ryan, S.J. (N.C. Features, 12/11/72). He charged that Father Ryan, who was stationed in Beirut but a frequent speaker for pro-Arab groups in the U.S., tried to play the Vatican off against the U.S. hierarchy. Higgins specifically accused him of seeking to undermine the work done by Father Edward H. Flannery, then Executive Secretary of the U.S. Bishop's Committee on Catholic-Jewish Relations, by writing surreptitiously to Flannery's superiors, discrediting his work.

Father Flannery, in his 1982 Barnett R. Brickner Memorial Lecture, has stated that "in a sense the Jewish-Christian dialogue has stumbled over the State of Israel and to a point has been thereby weakened." On a number of occasions, I have heard him refer to Christian silence in 1967, when Jews feared that their survival as an independent nation was in jeopardy, as a decisive moment in Christian-Jewish dialogue. It did not mean its death, but it did introduce the dynamic of Israel in a way that would lead to repeated friction.

Nevertheless, some progress has been made. The 1975 Vatican document of "Guidelines" once again remained silent on the question of Israel. But conferences of bishops in several countries began to speak out, some of them even before 1975. For instance, the French bishops, in their Declaration of 1973, stated: "It is at present, more than ever, difficult to pronounce a serene theological judgment on the movement of return of the Jewish people on its land. In this context, we cannot forget as Christians the gift once made by God to the the People of Israel of a land where it was called to reunite."

In 1975, the U.S. Catholic bishops declared that "an overwhelming majority of Jews see themselves bound in one way or another to the land of Israel. Most Jews see this tie to the land as essential to their Jewishness." They went on to make the point that "whatever difficulties Christians may experience in sharing this vision, they should strive to understand this link between land and people which Jews have expressed in their writings and worship throughout two millennia as a longing for the homeland, holy Zion." They added that this in no way implied agreement with specific policies or political positions.

In this statement the U.S. Catholic bishops seemed to be practicing what the "Guidelines" preached, namely to take into consideration "by what essential traits the Jews define themselves in the light of their own religious tradition." Finally, in a 1983 message, the Brazilian bishops spoke of "the right of the Jews to a calm political existence in their country of origin, the State of Israel."

Encouraged no doubt by such collective efforts on the part of conferences of bishops, some members of the hierarchy have also taken individual initiatives. In the case of Archbishop Peter L. Geraty, then Archbishop of Newark, New Jersey, this took the form of a pastoral letter which has received wide distribution. Picking up on what had already been stated in the "Guidelines" and the Declaration of the U.S. Bishops, it affirmed the following: "Dialogue demands respect for the other in his or her self-understanding. For most Jews an essential component of this self-understanding is a point of focus on the Land of Israel and the city of Jerusalem. Leaving political issues in their myriad details to be solved in the context of the Near East and its peoples, we Christians rejoice with the Jewish people that a representative portion has come to the land promised to the patriarchs, and hope that they will find there a continuing abode of peace for the creative response of Judaism to the call of God." Now even Jerusalem comes into view as an essential and authentic component of Jewish self-understanding.

But what about the Bishop of Rome, Pope John Paul II? He too began to make explicit references to the State of Israel. For instance, in his 1984 Easter message he stated: "For the Jewish people who live in the State of Israel and who preserve in that land such precious testimonies to their history and faith, we must ask for the desired security and due tranquility that is the prerogative of every nation and condition of life and of progress for every society."

All this brings us to the "Notes", the Vatican document of 1985. The silence on Israel is finally broken. The "Notes" refer to the "often heroic" witness of the Jewish people to the whole world, to their "fidelity to the one God . . . while preserving the memory of the land of their forefathers at the heart of their hope." Then follow these sentences: "Christians are invited to understand this religious attachment which finds its roots in Biblical tradition, without however making their own any particular religious interpretation of this relationship . . . The existence of the State of Israel and its political options should be envisaged not in a perspective which is in itself religious, but in their reference to the common principles of international law . . . The permanence of Israel (while so many ancient peoples have disappeared without trace) is a historic fact and a sign to be interpreted within God's design."

What exactly does all this mean? Does the statement fail to affirm the right of Israel to exist, as some Jewish leaders read it? Does it empty modern Israel of any possible religious significance for Christians? In short, is the document essentially supersessionist in outlook, regarding the promises of the "old covenant" as having been abrogated? Or, as Dr. Eugene Fisher explained it, does the pronouncement, when read against the backdrop of papal statements about Israel, support that country's right to exist, but sound a warning against a fundamentalist-biblicist approach to Middle East problems? Is the Vatican reacting against evangelicals who talk, not only about a theological basis for affirming the rebirth of Israel as a sign of God's faithfulness to the prophetic witness, but also about "biblical boundaries" and the like?

The reference to the principles of international law seems to contain an implicit recognition of the right of Israel to exist. After all, international law is not a bad foundation on which to base a country's legitimacy. But is that all Christian believers have to say on the matter? The document tells us that Jewish attachment to the land "finds its roots in Biblical tradition." Of course, that could mean "old covenant" tradition, no longer valid or authoritative for Christians. But there is more. The permanence of Israel, including, one assumes, the most remarkable (miraculous, some of us would say) rebirth of this ancient nation, is not only a fact of history, but as such also "a sign to be interpreted within God's design." Is that another way of talking about the divine covenant promises, which are coming true today?

So many questions come to mind. The problem with this particular section of the "Notes" is that it lacks clarity. And clarity on this issue is precisely what is so desperately needed. In the midst of so much confusion, how are Catholic teachers going to use these "Notes" in a constructive way? The great danger is that they will take the text and fill the gaps with entrenched biases with respect to the biblical message concerning Jews and their destiny.

If the covenant with the Jewish people has not been revoked, why does it seem so difficult to apply that in a clear way to the promises of the land, without thereby giving the church's imprimatur on specific Israeli policies? The answer might be summed up in one word: politics. I refer to both internal Vatican political infighting and the peculiar dimension that is added by the fact that the Vatican also functions as a state, which means involvement in all sorts of diplomatic entanglements.

Protestants, too, have minority groups in Arab countries. They, too, have often felt constraints on what they can say and do, because they fear for the safety of their people and the survival of their missions. For the Vatican, with its diplomatic *nuncios* across the world, the situation becomes even more complex. For instance, it introduces the question of formal recognition of certain countries but not of others. When it comes to the formal recognition of Israel, Catholic leaders are obviously very much divided.

For a whole variety of reasons, the Vatican is not prepared to extend formal recognition to Israel at this time, and the "Holy Land" tradition, especially the issue of the status of Jerusalem, is charged with historical passions. For these reasons any formulations about Israel and its role in history have to be approached with extra carefulness. Quite frankly, they are bound to be characterized by premeditated ambiguity.

Nevertheless, over the years there have been many official contacts between the Vatican and Israel. Israeli officials, prime ministers, presidents and foreign ministers have been received quite formally at the Vatican. These were treated as visits of state. So, *de facto* recognition is definitely there. Perhaps it could even be said that *de iure* recognition exists, but not *formal* recognition, not a representation from the Vatican in Jerusalem at the ambassadorial level.

What difference does it make? For millions of people, including no doubt many Christians, very little. It is seen as something that is mainly symbolic. But to declare something to be symbolic does not make it insignificant. Jews have a very strong historical sense. They have lived through many centuries of rejection and persecution. Vague statements, or even friendly gestures, do not necessarily persuade them that a new day has dawned. They look for daring and affirmative action. Hence the importance they attach to formal recognition of the State of Israel by the Vatican. Jews have appreciated some of the dramatic symbolic acts the present Pope has engaged in. But this particular symbolic act would speak louder than any of the official pronouncements and what it would say is this: we Christians of the Catholic persuasion have once and for all abandoned the view that Jews are a pariah people, condemned to eternal wandering as punishment for the alleged killing of Christ.

True, the Vatican does not have an ambassador in Jordan either, and true, there are still unresolved border disputes. But that is also the case with a number of other countries with which the Vatican has, nevertheless, established formal diplomatic relations. So why, Jews want to know, are we treated by a different standard? Logical sounding but nevertheless lame arguments will not do; a long history of Christian hostility has left too much of a heritage of suspicion.

The Vatican, like the National and World Councils of Churches, is eager to keep the line of communication open to both the Arab and the Jewish worlds. That is understandable, even laudable, as it could cast the churches into a reconciling role in the Middle East. By and large, however, they have not functioned that way at all. Their search for even-handedness has tended to tie them up in awkward theories about "moral equivalencies", leading to more questions than trust. Such questions were raised, for instance when, in 1982, Yasir Arafat was received by the Pope, a gesture that may have produced some political benefits for both parties involved, but that to most Jews was incomprehensible since it seemed to give credibility to the murderers of Jewish men, women and children.

Diplomatic intricacies and the requirements of *Realpolitik* are, no doubt, part of the picture here. They sometimes raise troublesome questions about the meaning of Christian integrity in the midst of all this international gamesmanship. The Pope's reception of Kurt Waldheim in 1987, praising the man's alleged achievements while ignoring the serious questions that were being raised about his character and his actions during the Nazi period, did little to enhance the Vatican's credibility. On the other hand, it is very easy to become overly self-righteous in condemning the accommodations that others make while demanding understanding for one's own dilemmas. None of us functions in an atmosphere of purity that transcends politics.

Having said this, however, I continue to be haunted by the question why ecclesiastical even-handedness in the Middle East so often seems to have the result of placing Israel in a position of disadvantage. I have seen that happen time and time again in the Protestant ecumenical movement. It also is true in Rome. There is an element of political practicality involved, even of political expediency. But I fear that it goes deeper than that. To put it quite bluntly, I can honestly come to no other conclusion than that the sin of theological triumphalism continues to influence Christian attitudes towards Jews, Judaism and the State of Israel.

This sin has been confessed over the past decades by a number of ecclesiastical and ecumenical bodies. It has been admitted that such triumphalism has meant untold suffering for the Jewish people over many centuries. It is a sin from which many Christians have sought to repent.

But this sin, like all other sins, is never totally overcome. To claim, for instance, that one if free of all pride, would be one of the most boastful statements a person could make. There is a constant need for self-critical honesty, to confess ever anew that continued change is called for. It will not be a painless process. Healing usually is not.

The topics of the State of Israel and Jerusalem are among the most touchy and troublesome in Christian-Jewish relations. We tend to handle them with utmost care, because we do not want to shatter the precious treasures that dialogue has yielded thus far. However, what can be worked out rather neatly during programs of the National Workshop on Christian-Jewish Relations, avoiding confrontations that might cause a measure of discomfort, usually becomes a more knotty problem when real or imagined Christian "interests" in Jerusalem are at stake.

In a letter dated December 1, 1986, the National Christian Leadership Conference for Israel addressed an "open letter" to the sponsors of the National Workshop on Christian-Jewish Relations, by all counts the major regular gathering point for people who are concerned about such issues. The letter expressed some disquiet about how the topics of Israel and Zionism were being handled in the dialogue movement. Everybody knows that the "Israel dynamic" is stirring constantly just below the surface, occasionally bursting into the open with explosive force. Nevertheless, these issues are rarely confronted with the sense of urgency that one would expect such an obstacle to candid dialogue to receive. "We are aware," the letter stated, "that in most National Workshop programs something has appeared on Israel and Zionism and that in a few instances those issues have been dealt with in a rather tangential fashion. In most cases those topics were included somewhat hesitantly and mainly as a concession to those who raised questions about the matter."

In essence, the leadership of the National Workshop was being asked to live a little more dangerously, to stop avoiding certain issues by dealing with them in a context that made them relatively safe and domesticated. For those in charge of designing conferences that is not a very difficult thing to do. But the problems keep on festering, from time to time exploding in ways that threaten to set back the progress that has been made in building bridges of understanding and mutual trust.

An example of that happened a few weeks after the "open letter" had been sent out. Cardinal John O'Connor of New York went on a post-Christmas visit to the Middle East. He very much wanted this to be a journey of reconciliation and, in the spirit of even-handedness, made arrangements to meet with King Hussein in Amman, Jordan, and with Israeli officials in Jerusalem. That seemed fair enough. But, as the good Cardinal learned just before he was to leave the U.S., such an arrangement was in conflict with Vatican policy. Once again, even-handedness turned out to be a weapon against Israel, or at least, an item on the ecclesiastical agenda where the principle of "moral equivalency" did not apply. For the Cardinal to meet with Israeli leaders in their offices located in the capital of their country would accord a recognition to the authority of the Jewish government that Rome was not prepared to concede. In the end, a compromise arrangement was negotiated and meetings took place. But instead of reconciliation the incident led to recriminations and renewed distrust. Frank Maria, the professional Antiochean-Orthodox Israel-hater within the National Council of Churches, mentioned before, wrote a letter congratulating the Vatican to the *New York Times* (1/23/87).

There is no argument about the fact that Jerusalem is very special, not only to Jews, but to Christians and Moslems as well. The real issue is what we say and do after we have cited the familiar formula that Jerusalem is a Holy City for the monotheistic religions: Judaism, Christianity and Islam. Having said that, are we as Christians willing to acknowledge that Jerusalem, the city where Jesus walked, ministered and died, the city of David, is essentially a Jewish city? And having said that, are we prepared to accept the legitimacy of Jewish sovereignty over the land of Israel and its capital, Jerusalem? The National Christian Leadership Conference for Israel letter to the National Workshop leadership was basically an invitation to have serious conversations on those issues.

The World Council of Churches issued a warning at its 1983 meeting in Vancouver, to the effect that "the tendency to minimize Jerusalem's importance for any of these three religions should be avoided." Fine! I, for one, have no desire to belittle the intensity of anyone's spiritual attachment to Jerusalem or anything else. But, it seems to me, that there is something else that ought to be avoided, namely a tendency to equalize the position of the three monotheistic faiths to the point of ignoring basic historical facts in order to deny the Jewish people sovereignty over their capital city.

Centuries before the birth of Christianity or Islam the Jewish people had established Jerusalem as the capital of its commonwealth. They have maintained a presence there ever since. It has been a "trimillenial love affair" (Lelyveld). Jerusalem is "home" to the Jewish people in a way that it is to no other people. Honesty requires that we not minimize such facts.

Christians and Moslems have genuine and legitimate concerns about open and free access to the sites that are holy to their faith. But for the Jewish people the very land of Israel lies at the heart of their covenant faith. That is the way it has been from time immemorial and it is something that ought not to be minimized. When the Vancouver Assembly of the WCC expressed an interest in becoming involved in a dialogue with Jews and Muslims that "can contribute towards political processes that would lead to a mutually acceptable agreement for sharing the city," one suspects that those political processes would be *à priori* designed to deny Jews sovereignty over Jerusalem and, therefore, the gesture would have to be considered basically insincere. A charade really.

At one time the Vatican favored internationalization of Jerusalem, which would also in effect deny the Jewish people sovereignty over their capital city. In recent years the Holy See has advocated "international guarantees" or "a special internationally guaranteed status" for Jerusalem assuring that there will be no discrimination against any faith. Only the most biased observers deny that there has been freedom of worship since Israel established its authority of the united city. Therefore, one becomes a little uncomfortable when Christians, who declare themselves to be pilgrims in the world, find it so hard to take chances with their Jewish brothers and sisters who have given no indication whatsoever that they wish to do to Christians and Moslems what the latter have done to them, in Jerusalem or anywhere else.

It seems to me that it ought to be stated candidly that Vatican diplomacy needs to catch up with Catholic theology, if the former is not to undermine the credibility of the latter. We Christians simply must come clean on the question of Jerusalem. A clear cut position in favor of full Israeli authority may well involve a certain sense of vulnerability. The Catholic Church, more than some other Christian communions, feels that there is much at stake in protecting its interests in the Holy Land. Furthermore, concerns about minority Catholic communities in Arab lands are quite real. There are no easy answers. But that was also true when Pope John XXIII, in "daring simplicity", ventured forth into the Second Vatican Council.

Once again a certain kind of "daring simplicity" is called for. The Servant Church is rightfully concerned about the requirements of spiritual devotion; it has a right to expect that in that respect its needs shall be met. But the Servant Church also dares to be vulnerable and is certainly not preoccupied with prestige or property claims. The Holy Sites, instead of serving as centers of reconciliation and common devotion, have often been the cause of the most unedifying intra-Christian conflicts. They must not now also become a stumbling block in Christian-Jewish relations.

In May 1983, the National Christian Leadership Conference for Israel issued a "Christian Affirmation on Jerusalem." It stated in part: "We believe that the essentially Jewish character of Jerusalem must be accepted by Christians, not grudgingly but gratefully. We see here a sign of God's providential grace in history and eternal faithfulness, a source of hope to all." It is not just a matter of the mystique of the Holy City, as real and alluring as that is; it is also very much a matter of the mystery of the divine covenant of grace.

Pressures on Vatican diplomacy vis-à-vis Israel and Jerusalem are bound to continue, because to a considerable degree they are being propelled by the expectations that have been raised by Catholic theology. In the words of Cardinal Roger Etchegary, the big and inevitable question with respect to the meaning of Israel has been raised within the Catholic community. Some daring answers have been evolving over the past decades.

But some big questions still remain. And one of them goes like this: "Will the Catholic Church be able to draw the political consequences from the theological truths it has been advocating about Jews and Judaism since Vatican II?" Or, referring back to the prayer by Pope John XXIII a few days before his death, will our conversion consist of a renewal so real and so concrete that it will encompass new Catholic attitudes and policies toward the State of Israel and Jerusalem?

VIII

Evangelical Activism

"We, representatives of Bible-believing Christianity, gather . . . to affirm the importance of the State of Israel, and to unite with the Jewish people against those who wickedly assail them and their beloved State." This we read in a proclamation issued during a National Prayer Breakfast in Honor of Israel in Washington, D.C. The question that arises (in addition to whether a Prayer Breakfast should not always be in honor of God) is this: "Who can legitimately be categorized as a representative of Bible-believing Christianity?"

There has been a lot of talk in recent years about THE evangelicals and, particularly in the Jewish community, there is a tendency to identify THE evangelicals with that segment of Christianity that sponsors events like the National Prayer Breakfast and is very vocal in its support for Israel. The impression is created, often with the active encouragement of certain evangelical spokespersons, that THE evangelicals constitute a clearly definable and identifiable group within the Christian community. But do they?

Merrill Simon, in his book *Jerry Falwell and the Jews,* distinguishes between two groups of Christians who each are supposed to have a distinct attitude toward Israel. "While the Evangelical Church has strengthened its ties with Israel," writes Mr. Simon, "the Liberal Church has taken an opposite stand" (p. 87). But such simplistic schemes hardly bear any semblance to reality. In the end their total lack of sophistication is bound to lead to more harm than good. Certainly Israel and its need for friends are poorly served by policy decisions based on that sort of fiction.

There is no such thing as "the Evangelical Church". There is however, an organization called the National Association of Evangelicals to which many denominations identifying themselves as "evangelical" belong. All of them hold a high view of the inspiration of the Holy Scriptures and in that sense are Bible-believing. But many would not endorse positions expressed in the proclamations issued by the organizers of National Prayer Breakfasts in Honor of Israel. That is one complicating factor. Another one is that millions of people who hold membership in so-called "mainline" churches also identify themselves as "evangelicals" because they represent the (often large) conservative wing within the more liberal denominations.

If the word "evangelical" proves to be less clear and simple than it at first may appear, would it help if we add the term "fundamentalist"? In other words, in order to be considered a Bible-believing Christian one must give assent to the theory of "biblical inerrancy", implying the infallibility not of the Scriptures as we have them, but of the original manuscripts. There are those who seem to believe that as long as a person is a biblical literalist, he or she will automatically join the pro-Israel forces who sponsor Prayer Breakfast type events. But that too is an overly simplistic way of looking at things.

First of all, not all people who agree on the theory of "Biblical inerrancy" reach the same conclusions as to what the message of a literally interpreted Bible is. That is especially true with respect to the question of Israel. There are extremely orthodox theological seminaries that require of everyone who is appointed to their faculties that they sign a statement declaring their strict adherence to a literal view of the Bible, but who do not accept the views on Israel embodied in various Prayer Breakfast proclamations.

What does the latter group affirm with respect to Israel? A central element in their beliefs is the conviction that the God of Abraham, Isaac and Jacob has never revoked the covenant once made with the Jewish people. They remain the chosen people. The term "Bible-believing" in this context implies, as a minimum, that one does not hold to a supersessionist theology, that one rejects the claim that the Church is the "true Israel" that has replaced the Jewish people.

Pre-millenialist and so-called dispensationalist theology tends to view the Christian Church as a "parenthesis in history," an emergency measure necessitated by the fact that Israel did not accept the kingdom as it was revealed and offered in Jesus the Messiah (or the Christ). Since a human

"No" can never cancel out the divine "Yes", the eternal covenant with Israel remains valid. For a while the divine plan may move on a side track, but eventually the detours of history will come to an end. Everything will return to the main track, which runs via the Jewish people and the city of Jerusalem.

Thus divine faithfulness to the promises made through the prophets of Israel is seen as the sure and firm foundation on which not only the future of Israel rests but the destiny of the world as well. According to most dispensationalist theology, history will soon come to its cataclysmic conclusion and in these endtime developments that, it is believed, we are witnessing today, Israel plays a key role. All this is happening according to the scenario foretold by the prophets.

The idea of the Church as parenthesis is, it seems to me, much to be preferred over the notion of the Church as replacement of Israel. It is, I believe, also much closer to the teachings of the Bible. Does that make me a Bible-believing Christian? On that particular point, yes, even though it has never secured me a seat on the dais during National Prayer Breakfasts in Honor of Israel held in the ballroom of the Sheraton Hotel in Washington, D.C. The reason, of course, is that, among the Prayer Breakfast sponsors, to be a non-supersessionist is not considered adequate ground to be counted among the Bible-believers. To be accepted as "one of them", a believer would have to buy into a good deal of added theological as well as cultural baggage.

For instance, to mention only one item, I am not comfortable with the view of "biblical boundaries" so glibly propounded in certain Christian pro-Israel circles. One of the dangerous implications of such a view is that, since the Bible is supposed to have set forth in clear terms where the boundaries in the end are to be established, any Israeli government that does not take this into account in its negotiating position concerning the West Bank and Gaza *ipso facto* is seen as unfaithful to the Word of the Lord. Not only "mainline" Christians, but millions of evangelicals simply do not fit within the narrow parameters of what is frequently presented as Bible-believing Christianity.

The sponsors of the National Prayer Breakfast and similar events are in fact a minority group even within the evangelical world. But, let me hasten to add, in our day they have become a much more vocal, visible, and probably influential group in the country, even though the verdict on their political effectiveness may still be out.

Much of the recent prominence of pro-Israel Christian millenialists is due to the fact that their views are held by such famous TV preachers as Jerry Falwell, Pat Robertson and Jimmy Swaggart. It is, therefore, not surprising that the Prayer Breakfasts have been held in conjunction with the annual meetings of the National Religious Broadcasters, an organization that for many years has been headed by Dr. Ben Armstrong, a kindly and capable gentleman who is also a fervent "lover of Zion".

The Christian Right's hegemony over the air waves contains one of the truly ironic stories of recent church history. It is so ironic because it is at least in part the result of attitudes prevalent some decades ago among the more liberal Protestant establishment, which did everything in its power to keep the views of conservative evangelicals off the radio. The control liberal Christians exercised over such matters had come to them without any cost or great effort on their part.

The Communications Act of 1934 sought to bring a measure of order to the rapidly growing broadcasting industry. Since the airwaves belong to the public at large, and since only certain people are licensed to use them, fairness seems to dictate that some time be allocated to serve "the public convenience, interest and necessity." And who would make the decision for the religious or, more specifically, the Protestant community? In order to take advantage of this opportunity, mainstream denominations formed broadcasting units as part of existing Councils of Churches. Stations were quite happy to keep their noses out of the hornet's nest of inter-church rivalries. They were more than willing to leave the decision about which Christian voices were to be heard free of charge to such Councils, even though the more conservative churches were not represented in them, partly because they could not join in good conscience, partly because they were not welcome.

Those who were locked out were left only one choice: buy time whenever possible, put on a show that will attract listeners and develop fundraising techniques to secure the money to pay the bills. By and large this was a business for mavericks, entrepreneurs in the Lord's business.

Step by step these people built what today is known as the Electronic Church. If the liberal establishment had shown a greater spirit of generosity toward their more conservative brothers and sisters, the latter might never have moved so far ahead of them in the use of media. The mainline churches got a free ride, but they also became lazy and their programs often lacked imagination. In the end they were poorly prepared for the age of new media technology.

I have already hinted at the fact that most Christian mission projects were started by mavericks, often without the blessing of or even in opposition to the wishes of the church establishment, who feared competition with their own fundraising efforts. Eventually many of such independent ventures were co-opted by the denominational bureaucracies, but sometimes it was too late for such a takeover to succeed.

One day during my tenure as director of communications of the Reformed Church in America, a proposal for the funding of a TV program arrived in our office. Accompanied by an appropriate memo, the package was sent off to the Rev. Peter Paulsen, the media expert on my staff. After a few months he rendered his considered opinion that the kind of program suggested was not feasible and simply would not do. The man submitting the idea was a somewhat maverick preacher in our denomination by the name of Robert H. Schuller. The proposed program is known today as The Hour of Power, one of the top-rated religious programs on the air.

Beware of the experts! I don't want to be too hard on my ex-colleague. Paulsen may well have been right in the sense that the program might have been a flop if it had become a bureaucratic effort. Committees rarely produce the creativity that makes such ventures succeed. I am not suggesting that expert advice should be dismissed offhand, only that it should be treated with a healthy dose of skepticism.

In this connection I cannot resist sharing a story I read the other day. A would-be farmer bought 4000 chickens, but by the end of the first week, 1000 of them had died. In a mood of desperation the farmer called his rabbi for advice. "Feed them rye," the rabbi said, "and all will be well."

During the following week another 1000 chickens died and once again the unfortunate farmer called his rabbi. "Feed them wheat," was the advice received this time. After another 1000 chickens had died, the farmer was told to feed them rice.

Finally, the farmer found himself without any chickens left. "What shall I do now," he lamented to the rabbi. "I have lost all my chickens and don't know what to do next."

"That's a pity," the rabbi replied, "for I have a lot more excellent advice to give."

The story of the National Prayer Breakfasts is a bit more upbeat. They have become something of a growth industry. The way this movement has developed over the past six or so years gives some interesting insights into dynamics at work within certain pro-Israel evangelical circles. In the beginning the two key players were E. "Ed" McAteer, former marketing executive for Colgate Palmolive and president of The Religious Roundtable, and the Rev. Mike Evans, a one-time leader in the mission-to-the-Jews movement who in recent years has preferred to be known as Middle East expert. McAteer's Roundtable was one of the organizations Evans served as Middle East consultant. Together they started the prayer breakfasts during the annual convention of the National Religious Broadcasters. The tie-in has turned out to be a very smart move, which, I suspect, originally was Evans' idea.

Soon things turned a trifle sour between them, however, especially when Evans invited Harry Hurwitz, an official at the Israeli Embassy, to be the featured speaker and then arranged for Sandra Sheskin, advertised as a "Messianic Jewish recording artist", to do the musical part of the program. With Hurwitz letting it be known that this sort of arrangement put him in an awkward position, the situation became painful for all concerned and, in the end, Ms. Sheskin was dropped from the program. Not long thereafter Evans was removed from the Roundtable as well as from the list of breakfast organizers.

However, another candidate was eagerly waiting in the wings, namely Douglas Krieger of TAV Evangelical Ministries. A one-time hot tub salesman, Krieger had recently appeared as a lightening star in the firmament of pro-Israel fundamentalist activities. He and his partner Douglas

Shearer were the moving forces behind TAV Evangelical Ministries. The "two Dougs", as some Jewish leaders fondly called them, were ready to engage in a major mobilization of evangelical support for Israel. After a meeting with Rabbi Marc Tanenbaum of the American Jewish Committee in New York, Krieger called my office one day to explain that while they appreciated the efforts of my organization, their specialty would be Jerry Fawell and other fundamentalist Christians who would feel uncomfortable dealing with the likes of me or an ecumenical network like National Christian Leadership Conference for Israel. My own experience with Falwell has been that he is less worried about contamination by association than some of his disciples.

However that may be, for a short while TAV produced a flurry of activities, accompanied by a good deal of newspaper publicity. The TAV people issued a position paper in which they openly challenged Jewish leaders to a reappraisal of their historic ties to liberal Christians, while at the same time pointing out quite candidly that "the Jews must not expect the Evangelical to set aside his frank and sometimes abrasive mannerisms." As a matter of fact, states the document, "the reappraisal which we are recommending will not be easy for the Jewish community. It will require that Jews look beyond the effrontery which Evangelical militancy generates to the unflinching support of evangelicals for both the State of Israel and the 'personhood' of Jews."

Alas, the alliance between "the two Dougs" did not last very long. Mailings from TAV began to focus increasingly on what to many people must seem a somewhat esoteric concern, namely the identity of "the Beast" or the "Antichrist" referred to in the Book of Revelation. Throughout the centuries several candidates have been suggested, including the Pope of Rome. Leading nominees in recent "endtime" prophecy literature have been Syria, the Common Market Nations of Europe, Russia, or a combination of these. The TAV people, in a publication called "The Antipas Papers," passionately defend the view that an alliance between religious and political forces within the United States will prove to be the true Antichrist. This view obviously gives some discomfort to those in the Christian Right who have been teaching that the U.S. is extra blessed because of its righteousness, particularly as manifested in its support for Israel.

Soon after his split from TAV, Krieger jubilantly announced that he had discovered a goldmine in the person of Terry J. Risenhoover, a promoter of speculative land sales in Alaska. This new alliance led to a brief flirtation with the Temple Mount Foundation, including an ill-conceived ad in the *Jerusalem Post* attacking government policies with respect to this most explosive of all holy places. Angry reactions from the Begin government led to a hasty retreat on that issue.

Risenhoover, as the new benefactor of the Prayer Breakfast, achieved instant stature in his role as chairman of the event. Unfortunately, soon thereafter this relationship ended when the Justice Department started an investigation of his operations and he had to declare bankruptcy. I have not heard his name mentioned since.

While Krieger's ex-colleagues at TAV issued the "Antipas Papers," setting forth the intricacies of endtime prophetic schemes, he himself moved to Denver as the promoter of a new magazine, *The Catalyst*, advertised as "perhaps America's only periodical galvanizing leading Jewish and Christian scholarship in addressing the major political, social, religious and economic issues of the day." In the first issue he stated: "The Jewish/Bible-believing Christian 'exchange' (preferred in place of the hackneyed liberal term 'dialogue') is central to the reason for the being of CATALYST." The magazine's first edition certainly was an impressive-looking production.

It is too early to tell whether the semantic change from "dialogue" to "exchange" will prove to be significant. Since there has never been a second issue of *The Catalyst*, it may be too late to find out. Krieger recently was listed as the editor of a new publishing venture, *Christian and Jewish Thought*, but I have not been able to find anyone who has seen a copy.

Terry L. Burrus, president of Catalyst Corporation, followed Terry Risenhoover as chairman of the 1985 National Breakfast. In 1986, A. Ari Marshall, president of The Lord's Airline, a one-plane business venture operating from Florida, succeeded him. The Lord's Airline advertised as a "chapel in the sky" that will be "void of girlie magazines" and will have the Ten Commandments in Hebrew and English imprinted on the craft's interior walls. The traveler is promised a "rich dose of Bible, as well as inspirational literature, music and fellowship on board." Marshall, who calls himself a "born-again Catholic," wanted his airline to be nondenominational. According to one ad, the Lord's Airline "recognized Jerusalem as the capital of Israel." That certainly is a nice thing to do, but may not have allayed all fears potential customers had about the safety of the aircraft. I have been told that the venture never got off the ground.

I am writing this shortly after returning from the Sixth National Breakfast in Honor of Israel, held on February 4, 1987. Krieger's name was no longer listed or mentioned. This time the event was sponsored "in association with The American Institute for the Study of Religious Cooperation," an organization founded and financed by Irvin J. Borowsky. This gentleman has singlehandedly produced The American Holy Bible, "dedicated in memory of Thomas Jefferson," and containing "Selections from The Scriptures of American Indians, Muslims, Hindus, Buddhists, Shintos, [and] Confucianists." The text is "adapted" from the Authorized Version of the Bible, which basically means that Mr. Borowsky has edited out or rewritten passages that he felt might give offense to someone. He wants this to be "a Bible for all Americans," but the fact that it was produced without any interfaith consultation to speak of may pose a few problems. At any rate, with its black and gold imprinted cover the volume looks very much like a good old trusted King James Bible.

The Prayer Breakfasts have had their tragi-comical moments. At one time a fundamentalist preacher named Stan Rittenhouse was pedalling his anti-Semitic book *For Fear of the Jews* in the lobby of the breakfast ballroom. An extra cause for embarrassment was the fact that the book's jacket contained an endorsement from Dr. N.A. Criswell, pastor of the huge First Baptist Church in Dallas, Texas. Poor Dr. Criswell was forced to admit in a hastily composed news release that, unfortunately, he had recommended the book without really checking out its content.

Evangelicals do indeed blunder at times. Because of their innate enthusiasm (one could almost characterize it as a quality of "bubbliness") and because of the maverick mentality that is often so strong among them, they tend to do their blundering in a big way. It certainly cannot be denied that evangelicals have come up with their share of quixotic ideas. There are, without a doubt, charlatans and opportunists among them.[5]

But, as far as I have been able to detect, a predilection for folly and fantasy has not inflicted them to any greater degree than some of the liberal groups I have worked with, particularly the radical wings of the latter. I am not unique in finding that people inclined toward extreme positions, be it on the Left or the Right, tend to be rather similar in psychological make-up.

Mainline leaders, in my judgment, tend to underestimate the mavericks on the Christian Right and to write them off as an irrelevant factor in the larger social context. The latter, in the meantime, aided by sophisticated media technology and wise in the ways of computerized mass mailings, developed their brand of evangelicalism into an increasingly powerful voice both in the religious and political arenas.

In the words of Lionel Trilling, "Liberalism is always being surprised." Liberals tend to keep on hoping for the best, expecting that in the end the more noble impulses of human nature will yet prevail. They are

---

[5]The American Christian Trust did send me a special invitation to attend the 1990 National Christian Prayer Breakfast in Honor of Israel. I accepted, assuming that the fact that I was invited as a "Jewish leader" was a case of secretarial oversight. The word "Christian" had been inserted at the urging of Rabbi Yechiel Eckstein, who told me that some of the specifically evangelical overtones in the past had made the claims of an interfaith breakfast less than credible.

Once again, it proved to be a very well organized event and an impressive demonstration of Christian support among certain groups belonging to the Religious Right (among the heroes of the occasion were Ed McAteer, Howard Phillips, Phyllis Schlafley, Edwin Meese, and the main speaker, ex-congressman Jack Kemp, who delivered a superb speech).

As usual, this breakfast too offered a few ironic twists. Sr. Rose Thering, who had succeeded me as executive director of the NCLCI, was honored with an invitation to be seated on the dais, but felt compelled to decline because of opposition among members of her executive committee. Sandra Sheskin, dropped from the program in 1982, and now married to "Rabbi" Brotman, a messianic Jew, was once again featured as a singer. Finally, Presbyterian Jack Kemp, one of the rare "mainline" participants in such an event, probably expressed the sentiments of quite a few local Presbyterians, but hardly any of his denomination's leaders.

often not only surprised but angered when, instead of awakening to our utopian dreams, we are forced to deal with the world of hard and ugly realities. Furthermore, like most of us, liberals often find it difficult to remain true to that most basic ingredient of all genuine liberalism, namely openness to new directions as dictated by ongoing critical inquiry and historical experience.

In light of the pendulum principle so often operative in historical movements, one might have expected that mainline church leaders would be somewhat prepared for the new challenge. However, in many instances they themselves had become so solidly identified with the countercultural movements of the preceding decades, that they lacked the critical insight, which is such an indispensable tool for picking up signals about future developments.

Moral Majority became the central focus of the new Religious Right (more recently the name has been changed to Liberty Federation, a nomenclature that does not seem to have caught on very well). Moral Majority was in essence a reaction (revolt, we should perhaps call it) against the radical challenges being posed to what many Americans considered to be traditional religious and cultural values. My own guess is that millions of people, who did not have a fanatical bone in their bodies, but who feared a devaluation of all values, felt sympathetic towards certain Moral Majority thrusts without ever joining the organization.

There were people who were, perhaps, incapable of articulating their concerns but intuitively sensed that a moral-spiritual vacuum might eventually be filled by forces that were basically nihilistic in nature and might lead to a normless society. They looked upon the New Right, not as the inauguration of the Kingdom of Righteousness, but as a possible corrective toward values that seemed worth preserving. In short, they saw themselves as part of a traditionalist movement rather than as agents of a right wing revolution.

As James Neucherlain put it in a *Commentary* article (January, 1983): "One need not be crazy or a sectarian zealot to be unhappy with prevailing trends in our society: in the arts, family life, religion, or public morality. It does not require a true believer's mentality to conclude that moral decay is far advanced in our common social life; it requires only a normally developed awareness of the way things are." (p. 19). Within the mainline church bureaucracies, including within the National Council staff, there were a few individuals like Dean Kelley, director of the office on Religious and Civil Rights, who dared to state publicly that just possibly the New Right, with all its faults and foibles, might yet produce a positive plus as a counterforce to the continued atomization and deterioration of our culture. But theirs were minority voices.

In *Pensées*, Blaise Pascall wrote that "people never do evil so completely and cheerfully as when they do it from religious conviction." Since both the Christian Right and the Christian Left in their own selective ways feel quite free to appeal to divine authority, it would seem advisable that we maintain a measure of healthy skepticism toward both.

For many Jewish leaders, particularly in the United States, the emergence of the New Right posed somewhat of a dilemma, because some of the most prominent leaders of that movement were outspoken and unapologetic supporters of Israel. Some Israelis - for instance a politician like Menachem Begin or a scholar like David Flusser, who were less concerned about complexities concerning the social agenda on the American scene, had fewer qualms about establishing ties with the evangelical Right. Furthermore, they were inclined to feel that whatever moralizing on the part of Moral Majority might offend certain Jewish leaders in the U.S., they in Israel suffered much more from the sanctimonious moralizing by liberal religious and political figures.

The American Jewish Congress, on the other hand, issued a declaration on the New Right entitled "Where we Stand." It found the New Right a "deeply disquieting" development, and deplored the "violent rhetoric" and "imperious self-righteousness" which, we are told, seems determined to "straight-jacket our minds." In response the Congress called for an "aggressive advocacy of the classic agenda of democracy." But isn't that precisely the point at issue? What exactly is the classic agenda of democracy? Is it the American Jewish Congress' agenda? The National Council of Churches' agenda? The agenda of the U.S. Catholic Bishops? Or does the real agenda of democracy evolve out of the free and at times fiery debate between all those agendas plus many more, including the views of an organization that somewhat arrogantly called itself the Moral Majority?

Frankly, I found all the talk about a New Inquisition, the ominous threat to the Bill of Rights and Jerry Falwell aspiring to be America's Ayatollah Khomeini a bit overdone. True, the aim of the New Right is nothing less than the reshaping of American culture. There is no doubt in my mind that when religionists enter the social arena as activist reformers, the danger of the politics of self-righteousness lurks right around the corner. But, it seemed to me that the New Right was merely a latecomer in a game that some other religious leaders had been playing for a long time.

In trying to reshape the structure of society, religious reformers can either seek to dominate the ecclesiastical bureaucracies, as has happened in a number of mainline churches, or they can form volunteer associations, often done in the past. In the founding of Moral Majority, Jerry Falwell chose the second route, which was probably the only option open to him in the evangelical world. Evangelical churches tend to be less centralized and it is harder to control things from the top.

As I see it, Jerry Falwell wanted to revive the type of Fundamentalism that was quite prominent earlier in this century. But he also wanted to give it a new social conscience according to his understanding of the moral issues of our day. Falwell has promoted a new political activism within certain evangelical circles. The pro-Israel activism in those same circles must therefore be seen in the wider context of a political agenda with international dimensions. It has, therefore, always seemed quite silly to claim that Moral Majority is a one-issue organization. I know of quite a few things its leadership would like to change.

Social concern is hardly an innovation among revivalist Christians. Pietist movements in the 18th and 19th centuries frequently pioneered Christian social ministries: care for unwed mothers, prison work, programs to alleviate the sufferings caused by the industrial revolution. Evangelicals were in the forefront of the war against King Rum and in the defense of Prohibition. However, in their day they also played a significant role in the anti-slavery movement.

But Fundamentalism, as it developed during the first decades of this century, was a different story. These were days of bitter polemics and sharp polarization within Protestantism. Higher biblical criticism was in its heyday. Science, particularly the theory of evolution, reigned supreme and, in some church circles, became an inclusive principle of interpretation. Accommodation to modernity was the order of the day. In some extreme cases, theologians applied those new ideas to issues of faith in ways that led to a virtual naturalization and humanization of the biblical text.

The forces of orthodoxy fought back, organizing themselves under the banner of the fundamentalist Movement. Reacting to the relativism of the modernists, they often displayed a rigidity that bordered on obscurantism. Separatism became the watchword and protective shield against the wicked heresies prevalent in both the church and the world.

After the Scopes trial in 1925 and the repeal of the Prohibition Amendment in 1933, the fundamentalist movement became increasingly isolationist, anti-intellectualist and socially irrelevant. The movement also became basically a-political. The children and grandchildren of the first generation fundamentalists did not always feel comfortable in an environment that they found excessively confining. Instead of attending one of the proliferating Bible Colleges, where they felt education had taken the form of indoctrination, some of those young adults once again applied to major universities. They began to avoid the designation "fundamentalist," preferring to be called "evangelicals," which retained the warmth of a gospel movement but lacked the connotation of rigidity.

Eventually, in true pendulum swing fashion, a reaction movement set in again. More recently, questions have been raised about the evangelicalism of some evangelicals. Especially professors teaching in evangelical institutions have been accused of not being evangelical enough, of not sticking firmly to "the fundamentals," with the issue of accommodation to modernity being raised once again. The Southern Baptists, for instance, are engaged in a fierce "Battle for the Bible," which (not so incidentally!) is also a struggle for control of the national bureaucracy.

Jerry Falwell and others have returned to the banner of Fundamentalism. But they want to broaden the agenda. In addition to such old concerns as liquor, tobacco, theater and dance, they are raising the issues of abortion, prayer in the schools, pornography, the need for a strong defense to counter Soviet designs and support for Israel.

The Pietists of the past were heavily involved in charitable activities; Jerry Falwell believes that it is time for evangelicals to become involved in political activism. Moral Majority, unlike denominational offices in Washington, D.C., is organized as a non-tax exempt lobby. Like the "mainline" churches, they want to influence policies. According to Falwell, the old fundamentalists were so busy fighting the social gospel that they forgot the valid social implications of the biblical message.

Cal Thomas, at that time a close associate of Jerry Falwell, wrote an editorial for the first issue of the *Fundamentalist Journal*, entitled "Christianity IS Politics." Basing his views on the historic confession of the Lordship of Christ, Thomas rejected an either/or approach to the Christian faith and life: social action *versus* salvation of souls. He called for a broader vision and, in doing so, was reaching back to one of the main roots of Evangelicalism, namely Calvinist Puritanism. That wing of the evangelical movement, with its greater openness to a political theology, has often been neglected in revivalist circles. In the typology of Richard H. Niebuhr's book *Christ and Culture*, Calvinism is correctly categorized under the theme "Christ transforming culture."

When he announced the founding of the Liberty Federation in 1986, Falwell indicated a desire to deal with broader foreign policy issues. Off he went on missions to South Africa and the Philippines, eager, it seemed, to embrace the regimes of Pieter Botha and Ferdinand Marcos. Some Jewish leaders, who had welcomed his visits to Jerusalem (especially since he sometimes came with hundreds of his followers), were less enthusiastic about the new Falwell diplomatic initiatives. So, one suspects, were many sympathizers with what was once the basic Moral Majority agenda. The past few years do not seem to have been among the best in recent New Right history.

Jerry Falwell has gained new prominence since he has "taken over" the PTL empire after Jim and Tammy Baker's extravaganza of success turned into a lifestyle of the rich and famous script gone sour. One gains the impression that the ensuing battles with charismatic supporters of the ministry and cash shortages have preoccupied Falwell to the point of weakening his political involvements. Some Falwell associates have suggested that he had already decided to lower his profile on the political scene. It is too early to tell how the recent traumas of the TV evangelists will affect the influence of the Christian Right in society at large. I doubt that there will be a swift retreat to a non-political Fundamentalism.

Some of the harshest criticism against Falwell's political activism comes from within evangelical circles, mostly from people who share his militant millenialist/dispensationalist outlook and his views on the so-called moral agenda. Moderate evangelicals, like the leadership of the National Association of Evangelicals, usually speak in rather muted tones about their differences with Moral Majority, often describing them as differences more in style than in substance.

Some aggressive dispensationalists, however, make no secret of the fact that they consider the new evangelical activism a sell-out to secular ideas and a betrayal of the fundamental non-conformity, which they believe the gospel demands. Political action, they protest, has become a substitute for the lost power of holiness and those who think they can use the political system will soon discover that they are consumed by it.

The authors of the Antipas Papers do not tire of pointing out that politics and religion are "the twin pillars of Satan's strength". They speak in scathing terms of Falwell's ties to President Reagan, "a man who has never attended church regularly; has been divorced; has paid little personal attention, if any, to his children and grandchildren over the years; has been portrayed in the press as being involved in astrology; has broken all his promises to the Evangelical Church with regard to their "moral" agenda (other than giving lip service recently to the "Prayer Amendment"); has presided over the biggest arms build-up in the history of the world, this man is being portrayed to evangelicals as their champion . . . " (Antipas Update, Second Quarter, 1984).

In the meantime, evangelical supporters of Israel were extending their activities to the Holy Land itself. In 1981 a group of pre-millenial Christians with a strongly "charismatic" orientation established the International Christian Embassy, Jerusalem (I.C.E.J.) and initiated the annual Feast of Tabernacles, which has brought thousands of Christians from all over the world to Jerusalem. The 13 last remaining nations with embassies in Jerusalem had just moved their staffs to Tel Aviv and the I.C.E.J. was to be a concrete demonstration of continued and worldwide Christian solidarity with Israel.

"Getting high on prophecy is not enough," proclaimed the embassy organizers to their co-millenialists. "Just keeping busy with prophetic charts and theologizing about Israel" will not do. Isaiah 40:1 became the embassy's motto as well as call to action: "Comfort ye, comfort ye my people!" They realized that they were speaking to a community where there seems to be an insatiable hunger for new prophetic interpretations, sometimes of a highly sensational nature. Without sacrificing their eschatological beliefs, the embassy staff were determined not to let eschatology become an escape from history. No more paralysis through endless and speculative prophetic analysis. Some evangelicals are discovering Israel, not just as a theological idea or as a Holy Land where Christians go to walk where Jesus walked, but as a country inhabited by flesh and blood Jews, struggling with issues of economic survival and national security.

From early childhood many of these have been admonished to "love the Jewish people" and to pray daily "for the peace of Jerusalem". But by and large it tended to be a love affair with an abstraction or, at least, with eschatological visions. The International Christian Embassy is to be commended for its efforts to put some concreteness into the picture and to encourage Christians to become involved in activities that have practical implications: buy Israel bonds, travel to Jerusalem, write letters to Congress and the White House, etc.

Yet, preoccupation with theological purity is never far off. Take, for instance, a mailing I received from Christian Action for Israel, located in Cape Town, Africa. The very first paragraph of the newsletter declares in capital letters:

"Christian Action for Israel is committed to the time honored truth of the Christian faith such as the Trinity, Deity of Christ, Virgin Birth, Blood Atonement, Bodily resurrection and Ascension, Second Coming, Final Judgment, Justification by faith alone, Sanctification through the cleansing power of the Holy Spirit, and Glorification at Christ's soon Return."

It wasn't until I came to page 9 that I learned that "the aim of C.A.I. is to give succor and assistance to Israel in every possible way." Why this eagerness to give a detailed account of one's orthodoxy? I suspect that it is motivated at least in part by a desire to fend off any possible criticism that activism implies that one has moved into the orbit of liberalism.

During August of 1982, when the Israeli action in Lebanon had led to a no-holds-barred media blitz against Israel, I helped lead a delegation of Christians to that tragic land in order that at least some people could report back what they themselves had seen and heard. I remember that as we stood on a hill outside of Beirut, and as the booming sound of mortar blasts were being heard all around us, a fundamentalist pastor was interrogating me about the doctrine of "blood atonement". In short, my orthodoxy was being tested. The more narrowly "the fundamentals" become defined and refined, however, the more difficult it becomes to achieve a measure of cooperation in support of a cause, not only between fundamentalists and "mainline" Christians, but between fundamentalists among themselves as well.

The history of Evangelicalism has been marked by numerous splits. It soon became clear that the International Christian Embassy, united in support of Israel, would not be spared the same fate of dissension. In 1985, the Embassy sponsored the first International Christian Zionist Congress in Basel, Switzerland. The delegates met in the same hall where Theodor Herzl had convened the First World Zionist Congress some 88 years earlier. I was pleasantly surprised to see the rather broad spectrum of Christian participants listed on the program. It seemed to bode well for future cooperation.

My optimism turned out to be premature. I had hardly arrived home when news came that the embassy branches in Great Britain and the United States had broken away from the Jerusalem group, who were being accused of an "unspiritual, unbiblical and God-dishonoring stance." There were demands for the "unqualified resignation" of the Jerusalem leadership. I am still not sure what this fight of fundamentalist against fundamentalist was all about, but I know that such divisiveness raises troubling questions about the effectiveness of Christian support for Israel.

During the early 1980's, Jerry Falwell, accompanied by a delegation of Moral Majority leaders, paid a visit to then Prime Minister Menachem Begin. In his customary blunt manner Begin made the point that Howard Squadron, at that time President of the Conference of Presidents of Major

Jewish Organizations, had told him just a few days before that Falwell's friends in Congress had not preformed so well in the vote on the sale of AWACS to the Saudis. The Christian visitors agreed with the Prime Minister's assessment and assured him that they would do better next time.

Have they? The record is very mixed. It shows that on several occasions TV evangelists like Jerry Falwell and Jimmy Swaggert have publicly broken rank with Ronald Reagan, a president they admired so much. But that does not necessarily mean that their friends in Congress or their supporters in Main Street U.S.A. will follow suit. Still, TV evangelists who reach millions of people obviously do have a certain influence in helping to create a climate of friendliness toward Israel among certain segments of the population.

Evangelical statements, usually composed by lesser figures, by and large lack the drabness so characteristic of the United Nations English in which many ecumenical pronouncements are cast. But sometimes they seem to be overburdened with bombast and excessive claims, thus helping to create a reality-rhetoric gap which is not healthy for intergroup relationships. For instance, in 1982 the Jewish Telegraphic Agency quoted TAV President Doug Shearer to the effect that "millions of evangelicals who support Israel will demonstrate this through meetings and demonstrations in order to change the shift in American foreign policy away from support of Israel back to the support Israel enjoyed in the past." If there has been a strengthening of U.S.-Israeli ties, it has surely not come about because millions of evangelical Christians have been bombarding the powers-that-be in Washington with letters, telegrams and telephone calls.

Mr. Shearer's statement, it seems to me, contained a number of flaws. It was premised on a romantic notion about a past that never was. Arabists have been entrenched in the State Department for many years, seeking (sometimes with more, sometimes with less success) to steer U.S. Middle East policy towards less of a pro-Israel stance. His statement also overlooked the fact that evangelicals simply are not organized well enough to sustain an effort of the magnitude he suggests. Furthermore, he exaggerates the intensity of feelings on this issue among evangelicals. For the vast majority of them, Israel is at best a secondary agenda item. The priorities lie clearly with the moral agenda of the New Right: abortion, prayer in the schools, homosexuality, etc. Mobilization of evangelicals on a policy dealing with such matters is much easier and can be pulled off much faster than marshalling the forces in defense of Israel's security when our government proposes to sell arms to Israel's enemies.[6]

In no way am I suggesting that evangelical activism is irrelevant to the cause of Christian support for Israel. Far from it! I would submit, however, that flurries of enthusiasm from time to time and an occasional inspirational mass meeting to honor Israel will have very little of a lasting effect.

Evangelical eschatologists tend to be people in a hurry. They also, in somewhat paradoxical fashion, frequently lack a sense of history. This can lead to impatience, which, in turn, sometimes produces the kind of *resentment* which Nietzsche claimed to be a key element in much religion.

For instance, during the Spring of 1987, the two Dougs (Krieger and Shearer) teamed up again, this time in an effort to mobilize evangelical participation in the first Los Angeles parade commemorating Israel's Day of Independence. A roaring contingent of "Christian bikers" plus the messages on some banners carried by others recruited for the event raised a few eyebrows as well as a question or two among Jewish leaders. The next issue of the TAV Prayer Letter, taking note of the offense some Jews

---

[6]Since this book was written, two new evangelical initiatives have come to my attention. The first is called Christians' Israel Public Action Campaign (CIPAC), launched by Washington D. C. attorney Richard Hellman. This organization, in distinction from the National Christian Leadership Conference for Israel, is officially registered as a lobby. Hence, contributions to CIPAC are not tax deductible. On the other hand, the group is not a Political Action Committee (PAC) in the usual sense, as it does not support or oppose candidates.

The second new venture is Ted Beckett's Foundation for Israel, which has as one of its primary goals, the establishment of a Prophetic News Network (in competition, I gather from the literature, with CNN). I recall visits from Mr. Beckett in the past, when he was promoting other commercial ventures, such as a huge multi-media show in Jerusalem, that—as far as I know—have come to nought. Also, the pious references to "annointed real estate business deals," that are supposed to finance the Foundation for Israel, somehow failed to inspire me with confidence. My advice to TV viewers: Do not cancel your subscription to CNN—yet.

had felt, contained the following item of prayerful impatience: "All too often, we try our best to 'clean up our act' for the Jews to carefully eliminate from our witness any element which might tread upon Jewish sensitivities. And carried to an extreme, which occurs more often than we might care to confess, we lose our Christian witness. That mistake was certainly not made in this instance. The Jews 'got everything . . . . I believe this is a crucial juncture for us, we can either capitulate to their endless demands, or we can draw the line and pray earnestly that God will begin to press them to a point of greater acceptance." It all sounds so much like some of the old Christian tirades against "the obstinate Jew."

Still, it would be wrong to conclude that blunders on the part of some evangelicals mean that no progress is being made. Many evangelicals are establishing increasingly mature relationships with the Jewish community. Nevertheless, it is my impression that evangelical activism on behalf of Israel is not growing. I rather suspect that it is waning. A Pat Robertson bid for the presidency could introduce new dynamics into the situation. Whether that happens or not, we can be sure that the subject of Israel will keep on stirring the souls and the theologies of evangelical Christians. It is at the heart of their theology of history and at the center of their eternal hope.[7]

---

[7] As it turned out, Pat Robertson's showing in the 1988 presidential election was not very impressive. In the meantime, Jerry Falwell declared victory and disbanded *Moral Majority*. Jim Bakker, who in my opinion, deserved a taste of prison as a warning against others who might want to manipulate Christians of modest means, was sent to jail for 45 years, a sentence that strikes me as outrageously excessive, especially in light of much shorter sentences received by the likes of Ivan Boesky. All this no doubt has meant some weakening of the evangelical political cause. However, I would not count evangelicals out as a formative influence in contemporary American life.

IX

Apocalypse Now and Then Again

I have from time to time found a certain pleasure in pointing out that the National Christian Leadership Conference for Israel network is more ecumenical than the National Council of Churches. Since 1978 a Methodist professor, an Assembly of God evangelist and a Roman Catholic priest have each served a term as the organization's president. The members of the executive committee represent a broad range of theological views and social-political orientations.

It seems to me that once ecumenicity has become a comfortable affair, it is time to open up new avenues of dialogue. For instance, Protestant-Catholic relationships have in the main become quite cozy, almost routine. Gone is the sense of excitement that was so intense only a few short decades ago when local church members gathered for Living Room Dialogues. I shall never forget when, as the first Protestant pastor ever, I was invited to preach at the St. James Catholic parish in Red Bank, New Jersey. Protestant and Catholic clergy became personally acquainted and opened up to each other in ways that most of us had never experienced before.

The fact that Catholic-Protestant relations have become rather comfortable can be considered a sign of progress. Myths on both sides have been dispelled; by the grace of God dialogue has helped to humanize us all. But when things become so comfortable, there is also a danger that a new spirit of provincialism will set in. There is no longer the vision to reach out to others in the fellowship of faith, no longer the desire or sense of adventure to cross the next boundary. It seems to me that very little dreaming is going on in the ecumenical movement today. In essence the movement has been turned into an establishment.

When Catholic-Protestant differences seemed virtually insuperable to most Christians, restless pioneers kept the vision of unity in Christ alive and created situations in which the dream could receive a certain preliminary but, nevertheless, concrete shape. Internal Christian divisions, or for that matter intra-Protestant divisions, still are immense. In many instances they are at least as great as those between devout Catholics and staunch Presbyterians a few decades ago. But there are not many pioneers of stature around who keep on exploring and probing at the ecumenical boundaries to see what common foundations of faith might be discovered despite substantial differences.

For many professional "ecumaniacs", fundamentalist/dispensationalist Christians really are people beyond the pale. On their part, many fundamentalists regard members of "mainline" churches as hopeless liberals with whom there is virtually no basis for fellowship or even conversation. I myself have often sensed the suspicion with which "outsiders", i.e. people who do not speak the language of a particular piety are approached. We tend to love the comfort of familiarity and easily confuse coziness with conviction and faith.

I do not wish to exaggerate the ecumenical quality of life among Christian supporters of Israel nor the number of people who find bonds of Christian unity through a common interest in demonstrating solidarity with the Jewish people and the state of Israel. Still, I have seen trust relationships develop among persons who would not likely have come to know one another had it not been for a common interest in "Jewish issues", some of which they recognized as rooted in Christian unfaithfulness to the basic tenets, not only of faith, but of common decency as well. In facing such issues together, Christians have sometimes been moved to reevaluate the importance of differences between them as well as the elements of faith they hold in common.

The sharpest differences among Christian supporters of Israel are to be found in the area of eschatology. People have come to very diverse interpretations of the biblical vision of the future, particularly the more apocalyptic passages in the Bible. But, as was often the case as well when Protestants and Catholics did not talk with each other, theological ideas are usually not the only or primary cause of separation. Cultural and educational factors tend to play an important role as well, as for example, different forms of spirituality or even a different ethos about such things as a glass of sherry before dinner.

At any rate, had it not been for a strong common interest in Israel-related issues, it is not very likely that I would have established a positive working relationship with someone like David Lewis, Assemblies of God pastor, prophecy teacher and all in all an entrepreneur for the Lord. Nor, I am inclined to think would I have developed a friendship with Gordon College professor Marvin Wilson, an evangelical scholar with a genuine desire to build bridges between people of diverse religious perspectives. Or take Frank Eiklor of Shalom Ministries, a born-again ex-marine, often childlike in his enthusiasm and his warm embrace of others, but at the same time a highly committed and courageous warrior against all forms of anti-Semitism. Finally, Dr. Arnold Olson, president-emeritus of the Evangelical Free Church and past president of the National Association of Evangelicals would not likely have become an associate and valued advisor of mine, had it not been for our common interest in Israel.

I owe a debt of gratitude to these and many other evangelicals who over the past years have broadened and deepened my sense of the catholicity of the Christian faith, even though they themselves might avoid that term. The Genesis story suggests that it is precisely through the otherness of the other that mutual enrichment is found (male and female the Lord created them!). But in daily life the fear of diversity can be very real, also among members of the various brands of Christianity. In the New Testament, on the other hand, variety is frequently mentioned as a major characteristic of the working of the Holy Spirit.

Before I sound overly romantic about my experiences within National Christian Leadership Conference for Israel, I should emphasize that I have never thought very highly of an ecumenicity of the backslapping kind. Honest disagreements and critiques should not be silenced for the sake of ecumenical alliances in support of Israel or any other cause. As I have become better acquainted with premillenialist/dispensationalist circles, there are elements in their life and faith that I have learned to appreciate. In some cases, however, I have also experienced a growing concern about possible excesses, especially among adherents of a highly apocalyptic theology.

A major source of criticism and controversy with respect to the premillenialist/dispensationalist movement has to do with its so-called

"Armageddon Theology". Many people were particularly concerned when President Reagan voiced a fascination with that subject during a 1985 telephone conversation with Thomas Dine, the executive director of the pro-Israel lobby AIPAC.

Many Jews distrust the apocalyptic scenarios of Christian dispensationalists because of the descriptions they contain of future destruction that will be visited upon Israel, even though divine intervention is expected to provide a last-minute victory of miraculous proportions. Furthermore, the fact that the final deliverance implies the conversion of a major "remnant" of the Jewish people to Jesus as Messiah makes the scheme even less attractive for most Jews.

Others are concerned that an apocalypticism, which proclaims that the "true believers" will be "raptured" out of this world before disaster strikes, is not conducive to developing a sense of social responsibility. This is a frequent charge against premillenialists, that they tend to encourage escapist attitudes. In some cases that is no doubt true. On the other hand, history shows that an intense futurism can also become the strong motivating drive to "redeem the time" that is still available and thus lead to activism.

For me personally the problem is not with millenialist views *per se*, nor with apocalyptic visions. These seem to be valid aspects of the biblical message, which deserve our consideration. Furthermore, apocalyptic imagery is the "in thing" nowadays, not only among the Religious Right but among the radical Christian Left as well. A glance through past issues of the radical evangelical magazine *Sojourners* yields plenty of examples of apocalyptic language, as will literature issued by certain anti-nuclear and ecology groups. Apocalypticism seems to fit well with the mood of our day and the Left as well as the Right, each in their own way, use the fear in the "politics of doom" as an important motivating force.

Premillenialists, it is sometimes claimed, lack a proper dose of fear because of their views on ultimate divine intervention. Ironically enough, on some topics certain liberal writers would like to see more effective hellfire preaching. "While it is right to ground peacemaking efforts on faith and Scripture," wrote Paul Johnson in the *Christian Century* (December 21, 1983), it seems highly inappropriate to minimize the fear that people do and should have over what nuclear weapons can do." In other words, faith is fine, but let's keep the fires of fear burning as well.

In the May 30, 1983 issue of *Christianity and Crisis*, James Nash suggested that Billy Graham might improve his standing as an ally of the antinuclear movement if only he would learn to use fear more effectively. "Graham as a crusader uses nuclear fears in a refined version of the standard operating procedure of fundamentalist revivalism. He recites the threats of impending holocaust, literally trying to scare the hell out of people, and then calls for personal regeneration before it is too late." For some liberal apocalypticists the problem with their evangelical counterparts seems to be that the latter do not focus adequately on the finality of doom. They sound too hopeful!

By their very nature, apocalyptic writings tend to have a "way-out" quality to them. They are written, if not out of a sense of panic, certainly from a sense of extremity and semi-finality, a feeling that the world, inflicted with a terminal illness, has fallen into a measure of decay that virtually puts it beyond human redemption. Direct and dramatic divine intervention is our only hope. Cataclysmic events lie ahead, and those who feel called upon to announce that kind of future are inclined to speak in high pitched voices. Hence the language of apocalypticism is usually not only very vivid and symbolic but often sensationalist as well.

It is easy to get carried away when one is enraptured by that sort of spirit. Some obviously do. I see a danger when Christians become too preoccupied with the apocalyptic segments of the Bible. How pervasive should that perspective be in Christian preaching and teaching? Some ignore it altogether; others seem to make it the sum total of the biblical message. I prefer to see the apocalyptical perspective balanced by other eschatological categories in the Bible, like the emphasis on the Kingdom of God found in all sections of the Hebrew and Christian scriptures. The hope of such a Kingdom perspective seems less in a hurry and tends to nurture greater openness to ongoing historical developments.

Karl Barth said that one should do theology with the Bible in one hand and the daily newspaper in the other. Premillenialists often seem to live like that. The headlines in the daily paper become incorporated into the message from the pulpit. But one can get carried away by current events. Enthusiasm sometimes leads to unfortunate carelessness.

My good friend David Lewis published a booklet entitled *Magog 1982 Canceled*, only a few months after we had returned from a factfinding trip to Lebanon. In it he presented what could be called a "delayed parousia theory". The gist of it was that, because of the Israeli action in Lebanon and the capture of massive supplies of Russian armaments, the Rapture and Armageddon may have been postponed by a very close margin. In other words, human action can and does affect "the count-down of prophecy" and, for some yet unknown reason, the Church was given an extended period of grace through the historical events that took place in 1982.

The book was rushed into print with such haste that a number of humorously unfortunate misprints were overlooked. For instance, the word "coaptation" became "copulation"; National Christian Leadership Conference for Israel's secretary-treasurer Dr. William Harter became the Rev. William Hater; and the organization Christian Bridges to Israel became Christian Brides to Israel. While such slips are not terribly serious, they unfortunately do not help gain a hearing in the broader Christian community.

Similar questions are being raised by people within premillenialist circles as well. For instance, Douglas Shearer, to whom I referred earlier, published a document entitled "The Messianic Scenario." He himself believes that "in all likelihood its consummation will occur during our lifetime." He objects, however, to an "emotional appeal that verges on an uncontrolled sensationalism", which is sometimes attached to basic premillenialist doctrine. He complains about the "paperback dilettantes" or "army of self-proclaimed decoders and Christian cryptologists" who hold their audiences in an atmosphere of endless hype and "frivolous debates, which seem to be forever centered upon the meaning of '666', the legitimacy of Israeli invasions, the reestablishment of blood sacrifices, the personality of Ariel Sharon, etc."

Shearer, as an insider, expresses sentiments here that are shared by many persons observing the movement from the outside. One wonders what to make of the excessive speculations, the forced and seemingly farfetched interpretations of biblical texts and the predictions about imminent end-time events which are revised or simply ignored and then soon replaced by new predictions as history refuses to follow the prescribed scenario. To some it appears like an endless script about Apocalypse Now, but no, not yet, but then again and again and again. True, some prophecy teachers carefully avoid the trap of date-setting. However, much of the literature in the field relates historical events and figures to biblical texts in ways that seem to feed on and then, in turn, further nurture a ferocious appetite for sensationalism and new prophecy thrills.

In the above quote, Shearer mentioned the name of Ariel Sharon. To the uninitiated it may have seemed somewhat startling to find this controversial Israeli general mentioned as a key player in "Armageddon Theology". But it is not uncommon. For instance, evangelist Harvey Smith, in his April 1984 Elisha Ministry Newsletter, inserted a "Prophetic News Bulletin" declaring that "Ariel Sharon, the hero of the wars of Israel, is the most likely candidate to precede the Anti-Christ to power (Daniel 11:19-36)." I know that there are people who have no problem picturing Sharon as an actor in a power play of apocalyptic proportions, but Smith's use of Scripture strikes me as pure sensationalism unworthy of the sacred text.

No text is quoted more frequently in pro-Israel fundamentalist circles than Genesis 12:3: "I will bless them that bless thee, and curse him that curseth thee. . ." I personally do not find it farfetched when people hold the view that those words have found repeated confirmation in Israel's history. But the way some people apply the text in the context of contemporary events can surely tax one's credulity.

One of the wilder illustrations of how Genesis 12:3 can be pressed into the straightjacket of human speculative schemes can be found in a small newsletter, *The Healing*, an occasional publication from Denver, Colorado. The story turns around events that occurred early in June 1982, when the Israeli airforce destroyed a nearly completed nuclear reactor close to Baghdad in Iraq. In response, the U.S. government temporarily froze shipments of F-16 fighter bombers and F-15 interceptors to Israel. As a result, claimed the editor of *The Healing*, the logic of the second half of Genesis 12:3 had to come into play: i.e. an unfriendly gesture toward Israel demands a correspondingly negative development in the U.S. "I believe," the editor wrote, "if the U.S. had not held up the planes to Israel, the air controllers would have chosen a different approach to their grievances."

Jumping from Genesis 12:3 to the 1982 air controllers strike seems quite a feat. But there is more to come. Eventually the freeze was lifted. Therefore, a pay-off is called for. And indeed, once again the "Genesis 12:3 rule" worked. On August 19, two Libyan SU-22 jets fired guided missiles at two U.S. F-14 Tomcats and, lo and behold, they missed! Once people get hooked on this sort of hype, they tend to need a stronger dose all the time in order to reach the same spiritual high.

In some Christian circles one also senses a strange intrigue with military matters and undercover operations. In advertising his TV prime time special "Israel, America's Key to Survival," evangelist Mike Evans claimed that the film would "expose top secret intelligence information, confirming dozens of prophecies never revealed to the American people before." Of course, it did not. But the hype was obviously included because there was reason to believe that it would have an appeal among the viewers Evans was trying to reach.

Evans has been a grand master at the game of using "prophecy" and support of Israel as an effective means for profitable fundraising efforts. I first met him in May 1981 during a pro-Israel rally at the governor's mansion in Montgomery, Alabama. Then Governor Fob James and his wife were staunch supporters of fundamentalist causes. Prior to the gala occasion in the garden of the Governor's Mansion, I had received mail from Mr. Evans on Messianic Life Ministries letterheads. At that time he still dreamed of establishing a major center for the training of missionaries to the Jews on Long Island, New York. By 1981, however, he had moved to Dallas, Texas, where a good deal of money was available for that kind of ministry at the time. While some mail still came of Messianic Life Ministries letterheads, other communications were now sent under the name of Lovers of Israel. Eventually Mike Evans Ministries became the common designation.

In December 1985, Mr. Evans caused a minor splash in the Israeli media when, during a visit to Jerusalem with a delegation of Lovers of Israel, he called a press conference to attack the Mormons and their plan to build a university complex on Mt. Scopus. He suggested that this choice site instead be given to Christian Zionists so that they could build a world center there. There is little evidence, as far as I have been able to discern, that Evans' suggested alternative to a Mormon center was considered an improvement in Jerusalem.

It can be troubling to see pious hype used in the cause of high finance. On that score few Christians can out-perform George Otis, founder of High Adventure Ministries, with broadcasting operations in Lebanon. His fundraising literature always has a truly high adventure flavor about it. Artillery fire, corpses and threats to George's life are described in graphic detail. So are the mighty acts performed in Jesus' name. For instance, after the 1982 Israeli invasion into Lebanon and the storming of Beaufort Castle, the PLO stronghold, Otis sent the following communique to this supporters: "Chuck Pollack and I issued a decree in Jesus' mighty name that death be forever bound over Beaufort Castle, and that the Holy Spirit of Jesus would evermore permeate its walls."

But, hold on. The clincher is yet to come. "I need you, oh, how I need you to pray about rushing an extra $1,000 to us right away. . ." he continued. In a later Western Union Mailgram, Otis' word for the tired contributor was "I will be so glad when our Jesus comes, for then you will never need an appeal for intercession and financial support. . . " However, in the meantime, "I am going to ask you to try to send an extra $1,000 this month." Apparently, $1,000 checks have become an integral part of this man's millenialism.

But, say the fundraising letters, you must keep in mind what your $1,000 investment will produce. It will make angels sing and cause the Devil to tremble. Take, for instance, the miracle Mr. Otis announced some years ago when the Israeli government gave him permission to build a Chapel of Prayer at the Lebanon border. "Now, there is a new opportunity," gushed George, "a new strategy from God. . . a sign of the first stirrings of the coming revival." This project, the potential contributor is assured, will do nothing less than "spiritually prepare the way of revival [in Israel], the rebuilding of the Temple, and the second coming of our Lord and King, Jesus Christ." In the meantime, the very gates of hell are being stormed! "This new strategy is one that will go right to the jugular vein of Satan. It will crush him under our heel. . ." That, one would think, is giving people their money's worth. But, as far as I know, the Chapel has never been built.

Evangelist Harvey Smith, whom I have mentioned, advertised a truly ingenious scheme some time ago. "I have just returned from the Middle East, and the Lord took me on a tour of Northern Israel and showed me the surprises He has in store for anti-God Russia," he told those on his mailing list. Then follows the announcement of a Telephonathon. Mr. Smith is eager to share what God has revealed to him, if people call in a pledge. Everyone who calls is assured of a personal prayer plus a prophecy about "the most recent update on Russia's invasion of Israel," plus, as an extra bonus, a special tape "on the most recent prophetic teaching out on Gog and the land of Magog." In this kind of literature there is no lack of claims about direct communications from God.

Now, one does not need to be a dispensationalist to believe that the Holy Spirit is very much alive and operative in history today. I too believe in the divine presence and guidance. Far be it from me to deny *ipso facto* the validity of mystical urgings or the fact that the power of God moves people to respond in faithful obedience. What makes me suspicious, however, is all that cheerful chuminess in the walk of mortals with the Sovereign Lord of history, the familiarity that seems to lack a sense of mystery, the manipulative potentials when people too easily claim to have received instructions from the Lord. For instance, the fact that presidential candidate Pat Robertson no longer mentions his claim in an earlier biography that God told him not to enter politics must make people wonder whose mind was changed.

Again, when someone tells me "God has led me to do so and so," I am quite willing to listen. There is a simplicity and lack of self-consciousness in some people's walk with God that strikes me as genuine, sometimes even enchanting. I have little desire to show hyper-sophistication and skepticism in the presence of those who seek with intensity to be instruments of the Spirit. But my attitude changes when people write letters assuring me and many others that they have received a mandate from the Lord that they are prepared to obey if only the person receiving the mailing will pay. As the Roman saying goes, "corruption of the best is the worst." It is not one of the worst corruptions of the best impulses of human spirituality when pious language is used for purposes that have at least the appearance of exploitation about them?

During the past few years I have received a number of appeals from people who felt the urgings of the Holy Spirit to visit the Soviet Union. States one of those letters: "In the past year several believers, both men and women, have witnessed a need to make some direct contact within the Soviet Union. For more than two years the Lord has been speaking to me to take His message of hope to those behind the Iron Curtain. A trip to Russia is serious business and one should not go just to be going. However, if God has need of servants to prepare the way for those in Russia to hear His call of deliverance, then we dare not refuse to go! Again, this is a project for those believers in the body of Christ who have a heart of compassion for Jews and Christians imprisoned for their faith."

In the case of this particular letter, it is important that one read between the lines. The urgency some evangelicals have recently felt to visit Russia is related to the belief that a Great Fourth Exodus is imminent, a movement that will bring about a massive emigration of Jews from the Soviet Union. All kinds of special revelations have been reported among certain Christian groups confirming that words spoken by Isaiah and Jeremiah are about to be fulfilled.

"Fear not," we read in Isaiah 43:5, "for I am with thee. I will bring thy seed from the East, and gather thee from the West; I will say to the North, Give up . . ." Or take the prophecy of Jeremiah 3:18: "In those days the house of Judah shall walk with the house of Israel, and they shall come together out of the land of the north to the land that I have given for an inheritance unto your fathers."

Predictions that such prophecies are about to be realized have created considerable excitement in certain millenialist circles. Many stories are circulating about what people are doing in different parts of the world in order to assist the expected flood of Jewish emigrees, including reports about the establishment of way stations in Germany. It is claimed that storage spaces have been filled with food, clothing and Russian Bibles. A businessman in Sweden is said to have purchased a fleet of buses to help transport Jews who are leaving the Soviet Union. All of this is fitted into an eschatological scenario that invokes the imminent Return of Christ.

But belief in the Fourth Great Exodus also has its implications for positions these Christians take on the question of "biblical boundaries". Israel's retention of the West Bank is considered crucial for prophetic reasons. In order for scripture to be fulfilled, no part of the Kingdom Land promised to the Jews may be surrendered. The Great Fourth Exodus now provides an extra motive for holding this position. Those multitude of people must all be settled somewhere, and without Judea and Samaria there will simply not be enough room to accomodate them all.[8]

---

[8] In light of recent developments, millenialist visions of a Fourth Great Exodus are a good deal less farfetched than when I wrote this chapter, even though the preparatory measures on the part of some Christians still seem far removed from reality. Glasnost and perestroika in the Soviet Union are having manifold repercussions everywhere, including in the Jewish community worldwide and in the Arab states.

a) A resurgent anti-Semitism, caused partly be economic chaos in Russia and the ancient practice of making Jews the scapegoats, plus a more liberal emigration policy have led to projections that as many as 1 million Jews may settle in Israel during the next 3 - 5 years.

b) Stricter U.S. immigration policies with respect to Russian Jews, while welcomed by most Israeli leaders who want to see increased immigration into Israel, still causes discomfort among others who fear a repeat of past experiences, when U.S. borders were closed to the victims of pogroms.

c) The Arab world perceives a double threat: loss of support among Soviet satellite states who have used their newly gained freedom to re-establish ties with Israel, and the prospect of perhaps 1 million additional Jewish neighbors. As some Arab leaders have candidly pointed out, this is not just a matter of potential settlements in the West Bank and Gaza; it is a matter of opposition to any Jewish immigration in principle, and Arab position that goes back to even before the establishment of the State of Israel. In short, the immigration issue cannot be separated from the question of the balance of power.

d) The new waves of immigrants pose an immense challenge to Israel's internal economic and political structures. The influx of new immigrants, many of them highly skilled and well-educated, is a definite plus. At the same time, during the transition period it will not be easy to provide housing and jobs to so many new people, especially since both those markets are already under pressure. U.S. Jews have been asked to raise $420 million during 1990 in "Operation Exodus," with a total projected need of 1 billion. There will also be appeals for U.S. government assistance, but budget deficits, as well as concerns about Israeli settlement policies, could make the response of the U.S. Congress less sympathetic than in the past.

Finally, what will be the role of this large new constituency in the dynamic of Israeli politics? Most Russian immigrants know little about Judaism and few are

Sometimes it is hard to sort out the elements of an almost disarming sincerity and the suspicion that one is dealing with people who have a shrewd sense of business interests. All our lives are marked by a mixture of motives and I am certainly not suggesting that a touch of skepticism should in every instance lead to the conclusion that we are witnessing the corruption of the best. Sometimes the mixture of piety and business produces perhaps somewhat strange but, nevertheless, charming or even humorous results.

Take, for instance, the mailings from the House of David in Lakewood, New York, combining a call for "prayer warriors" with a salespitch for "Hallelujah perfume." One letter from the House of David contained the following item: "In March I received a word from the Lord that is for all Believers who have their hearts circumcised with a love for the nation of Israel and Jewish people everywhere. This word, when acted upon by God's people, will prepare the way for the return of the Messiah." What then follows is a call for 15 million "prayer warriors", one for each Jewish person alive today.

Another mailing from the same source advertising the Israeli import Hallelujah perfume closes with these words: "One of the things that we have wanted to do for some time at House of David is to put feet to our prayers by physically helping the people of Israel. Long ago we saw that they desperately need help in exporting their products at reasonable prices." Hallelujah perfume seemed to provide the answer, a product, they assure us, with special wholesomeness, "not like a 'My Sin' or a seductive 'Worldly Pleasure'." There were no connotations of a temptress but rather a "soft, pure, clean, feminine touch." A product that keeps one's conscience pure and the Israeli economy sound should appeal to some customers who are looking for win-win items.

---

committed Zionists. Will they become a voting block, possibly with strong anti-Socialist sentiments?

In a world filled with geo-political shifts and uncertainties, the Middle East may become less of a priority on the East-West agenda, but still could provide the international community with some major surprises, both positive and negative.

I was also struck by the way Sandra Sheskin advertised a tour to Israel that she was leading. "Though God had prophesied to me that He was taking me back to Israel for Yom Kippur . . .," she wrote, "I was amazed as He led me to host what appeared to be the most economical and yet complete tour of Israel." Sometimes God moves in mysterious *and* economical ways! But also note the postscript: "This entire tour can be 100 percent tax deductible to any tour participant."

Another concern I have about the God-told-me-so approach is that it can easily lead to a kind of "cop-out Christianity." Instead of assuming responsibility for our frailties and follies, there is a tendency to ascribe it all to the sovereign dealings of the Lord.

As an example, the International Christian Embassy announced some time ago that, as they were planning the next Feast of Tabernacles, it became clear that "the Lord was calling for a new direction concerning the worship emphasis" during that mass gathering in Jerusalem. Translated from Christian piety, this simply means that some criticisms had been voiced about the kind of dancing in praise of the Lord that has been part of the celebrations. Everybody knew that Merv and Merla Watson had been responsible for that aspect of the festival. The ICEJ newsletter reported that simultaneously with the Lord's new instructions about music and dance, the Watsons were receiving "a number of prophetic words indicating an exciting new phase of ministry which is now beginning to open to them. . ." What was the simple fact? Disagreements about the worship aspect of the festival were leading to friction.

When a year or so later a major split occurred in the Embassy ranks, the Watsons left no doubt which side they were on: they joined the rebels. In cooperation with Embassy rivals, they were planning competition to Embassy programs by announcing that they were scheduling four major celebrations in Jerusalem every year. Now, these are petty fights, hardly of ultimate consequence in the advance of God's Kingdom. But I see no reason whatsoever to cover up the reality of the situation with elaborate claims about the sovereign dealings of the Lord. There are some messes for which we should take responsibility our selves. Not only is it a more honest way of doing things, but it is also much better for our mental health than all the pious talk about mystical guidance.

Finally, the God-told-me-so game can be played by both sides in a dispute. And that is precisely what is happening in fundamentalist circles today. For example, Bishop Earl Paulk, a leading figure in the International Communion of Charismatic Churches and a fundamentalist foe of all evangelical talk about the eternal covenant with Israel, preaches supersessionism with a vengeance. He describes TV evangelists who urge their audiences to "bless Israel" as deceivers of Christ's flock. As a matter of fact, claims the Bishop, their corrupting influence in the Church is a major cause for the delay of Christ's return, since they are preparing an unworthy Bride for the Glorified Lord. How does he know? The Lord Jesus told his sister.

In a booklet entitled *To Whom is God Betrothed: Examining the Biblical Basis for the Support of National Israel,* the Rev. Paulk claims to have received a direct mandate from Jesus via his sister. "When Jesus visited my sister Joan Paulk Harris in the hospital room shortly before her death," he writes, "He told her that He is lonely and longing for His Bride. As she looked into the eyes of Jesus, she said that she could see His disappointment at the Church's lack of understanding His covenant." (p. 2). Until the Church is firmly convinced that she is "Israel restored," Jesus will be "kept hostage in the heavenlies".

According to this view, Christians have no business blessing Israel, "a nation that has rejected Christ"; our only task is to preach salvation to the Jews. So the Bishop sadly concluded that some of the greatest evangelists of our day have apparently "never been dealt with by the Holy Spirit to comprehend the real truth of Israel's identity in the last days."

We talked earlier about theological reconstructionists in liberal church circles. It is not generally recognized that a Reconstructionist Movement is going on within fundamentalist circles as well. But the goal here is to restore supersessionism, not to overcome it. We hear about "new wave theologies". One aspect of the movement is so-called "dominion theology", which is not only supersessionist vis-à-vis Jews and Judaism, but also triumphalistic in the social-political realm. These people reject premillenialism as escapist and as lacking a social agenda. In its stead they advocate a postmillenialist position; i.e. the view that Christ will return after the millenium, brought about by the progressive triumph of

Christ's people in the areas of politics, law, education and culture in general.

What we see here is an alliance between Christian supersessionism and cultural progressivism, which is really a form of triumphalism. These people do indeed believe in the Christianization of America. Ed Dobson and Ed Hinson, both allies of Jerry Falwell, describe this position in a *Policy Review* (Fall 1986) article as "a scary vision for the majority of evangelicals and fundamentalists. . .". As a Pat Robertson presidential campaign unfolds, this may become one of the hotly debated issues. Some Robertson statements would seem to indicate a certain sympathy with this kind of "dominion theology", while other remarks imply a rejection of that position. In the Jewish community the combination of supersessionism and political triumphalism will obviously be seen as a major threat. Of course, they are joined in that concern by large segments of the Christian community, including the vast majority of evangelicals and premillenialist dispensationalists.

In conclusion I return to a point I have made in the preceding pages: that both the Jewish and Christian communities are extremely complex, filled with internal dynamics that must be understood by those who wish to engage in interfaith activities. Generalizations are not very helpful in dealing with the issues. Alliances based on naive stereotypes that are devoid of a sense of nuances usually end in disillusion. On the other hand, a refusal to cooperate on issues that involve common interests because of disagreements on other matters, while appearing noble, can involve a naiveté of its own.

It is, of course, true that Israel is only one item on the agenda of interfaith relationships. Most alliances that involve interfaith issues are of a somewhat limited scope, and both the potentials and the problems that such ventures entail will vary from group to group. I have attended meetings between orthodox rabbis and fundamentalist Christians.They found common interests in such areas as homosexuality, government subsidies to private schools and, of course, Israel. I have also attended meetings between evangelical Christians and Reform rabbis. They talked about the clear distinction that is made in dispensationalist theology between the Church and Israel, about the eternally valid covenant between God and Jewish people and, or course, Israel. I have been part of National and

World Council of Churches dialogues with Jewish leaders and in that case the dynamic was different again: considerable agreement on social and church-state issues and considerably more discomfort when questions pertaining to Israel come up.

In the background is always the politics that is part of the life of all faith communities, often fierce and filled with righteous passions. As I am concluding this chapter, the media are absorbed with the take-over struggles within the Christian Right, involving Jim and Tammy Bakker's PTL Television and resort empire and the power struggles between top figures among Christian media stars.

In the midst of all the soap operas and side shows going on in the religious communities, it may be easy to shrug one's shoulders and forget about it all, including the fact that Israel's future security may well in large measure depend on the broadest possible support among various constituency groups in the United States. Certainly in that context the various Christian groups are not a minor factor.[9]

So, my own feeling is that a healthy dose of skepticism in all such interfaith efforts will do no harm. That is, unless it leads to a kind of isolationism which, I believe, none of us can afford. Least of all, Israel, whose enemies have always put great hope in the idea that in a world full of gruesome tyrannies they might yet succeed in singling out Israel as the one country that should be declared an outcast among what is euphemistically called the "family of nations." To friends of Israel that ought to be a con-

---

[9]As I come to the close of this chapter, I want to mention with special appreciation an organization called *Bridges for Peace*. Founded years ago by the highly respected evangelical leader, Dr. G. Douglas Young, the organization is now headed by Mr. Clarence H. Wagner. With offices in Tulsa, Oklahoma as well as in Jerusalem, this mostly volunteer organization has conducted programs in support of Israel that are so balanced in general approach, so lacking of hype and sensationalism in their appeals for funds, so quietly effective in their educational quality, that one might easily neglect to mention them—as I have done in the preceding pages. This is a mistake I wish to correct in this footnote. *Bridges for Peace*, in my judgment, represents some of the best in the evangelical tradition, including the fact that they are not afraid to maintain ties with persons in the broader ecumenical community.

cern of perhaps not apocalyptic, but, nevertheless, frightening proportions.

The road of interfaith alliances will never be easy. It requires a good deal of patience, understanding, honest confrontation and, hopefully, a touch of humor. As the Brazilian theologian Rubem Alves once wrote, "humor keeps hope alive." Even, I would say, in an apocalyptic age and in a world where we religious people do some strange things.

X

The Mission Dilemma

The mission issue impinges on Christian-Jewish relations in a variety of ways. First, there is the fact that a number of denominations have had mission programs in the Arab world for many decades. Several references have already been made to ways in which church policies have been affected by that reality. It is a complex situation, often influenced by a mixture of motivations and perceived missionary interests.

One force at work in the dynamic is love, affection and often admiration for Arab peoples and their culture. The Arab world, too, has its mystique and its own kind of seductiveness. Arab culture, with its ancient traditions and customs, can get hold of people who open their minds and hearts to what it has to offer. Arab hospitality is a lovely thing to behold.

I shall never forget traveling in a four-wheel drive Jeep with my son through the desert in Oman. When we approached a small oasis he suggested that we pay a visit to the owner of the fruit orchard there. After the two of them had exchanged the customary Arab greetings, this man became our host in a way that cannot help to touch one's heart. I think about that Omani every time I might be tempted to conclude that terrorism is deeply embedded in every Arab soul.

Most Middle East missionaries I have known have developed a love affair with the region. In some missionary families those sentiments have been transmitted from one generation to the next, making them in effect like "leading families" in the land, in some cases with close ties to the ruling elite. Of course, less of that is happening in the more nationalistic climate of today.

But love is not the exclusive force at work here. There are other powerful factors, among them fear, guilt and frustration. Christian denominations are constantly reminded that their missionaries operate in basically closed societies. Visas for their personnel are issued, refused or revoked at the pleasure of the local ruler. When a missionary presence is permitted, it is done so as a favor or because the church workers perform a function in education, medicine, agriculture, etc. that is seen as serving the national interests of the country. Expulsions of personnel and expropriations of facilities have occurred. Hence, there is a good deal of self-censorship in what churches say publicly about conditions in Arab countries. A more open society like Israel, where one can criticize the government in the full assurance that one can return later for a repeat performance, tends to be somewhat at a disadvantage in the propaganda war, which is never absent from Middle East politics, including church politics.

The guilt and frustration factors can be traced to a variety of sources. It seems to me that they are engendered partly by the belief that U.S. foreign policy has by and large been unfair to Arab interests, or at least, tilted in an unbalanced fashion toward Israel. U.S. missionaries in the Middle East feel a constant need to be apologetic about their own country. The situation is aggravated by the fact that missionaries to the Moslem world can rarely report dramatic conversions as a result of their work. Samuel Zwemer, the great pioneer in mission to the Arab world, is reported to have said that, after a lifetime of work, he could count the converts on the fingers of one hand. And he did not face the restrictions that are placed on Christian outreach in the Arab world today.

When these missionaries return home on furlough and pay visits to their supporting churches for fundraising purposes, they do not have the right stories to tell. Their audiences wish to be inspired, which means above all that they want to hear about the "souls" that have been saved. At the very least, that is true in the churches that contribute most of the money for mission.

In their talks or "Dear Friends" letters sent from the field, many Middle East missionaries make attempts to present foreign policy issues or even mild defenses of terrorist activities. But in most cases, their efforts to convert the folk at home prove to be as frustrating as their evangelizing activities abroad. Nevertheless, some have come to see advocacy of Palestinian rights as the *raison d'être* of their missionary calling.

A few years ago, Basheer K. Nijim edited a book entitled *American*

Church Politics and the Middle East. It was basically designed as a hand-book to help those who seek to promote goodwill toward the Arab cause among church constituencies. Peter Johnson, in an essay entitled "Mainline Churches and United States Middle East Policy," makes some interesting observations. He believes that "for at least some time in the future, the WASP churches of the establishment grouped in the National Council of Churches will continue to play the most important organized religious role in influencing the formulation of foreign policy." (p. 65). Of missionaries he says that they were "increasingly to become 'more Arab than thou' as the Palestine question became a central issue in Arab national politics." He then continues: "The missionaries were intent upon protecting their own position as Americans in the Arab world... What we have here is what might even be called the religious face of the State Department, which is noted for its pro-Arab cast" (p. 73).

As Peter Grose pointed out in his book *Israel in the Mind of America*, long before the founding of the state of Israel the missionary establishment had voiced its opposition to the idea of Jewish restoration, seeing it as a clear threat to the Christian presence, not only in the Holy Land, but in the Arab world at large as well. He quotes an elderly Presbyterian veteran of the faculty at the American University of Beirut as writing (shortly before Israel's independence was achieved): "Everyone zealous for Christian missions must feel a veritable heartbreak for the way in which the hasty and ill-advised endorsement of the Zionist program by Congress has nullified the sacrificial labors of generations of missionaries and educators." (p. 214).

When, during the Fall of 1985, Shiite militants decided to release one of the hostages they were holding at that time, Presbyterian missionary Benjamin Weir became their candidate. He performed according to what I believe their expectations were. He returned home pleading for understanding of the reasons why terrorists engage in desperate murderous acts. When, after the seajacking of the Achille Lauro and the brutal murder of Leon Klinghoffer, the U.S. intercepted an Egyptian plane that was carrying the killers plus Abul Abbas, the architect of this despicable affair, the Rev. Weir did what many Middle East missionaries would do as an almost automatic reaction: express outrage at U.S. aggression. The Presbyterian Church later elected him to serve a term as its Moderator, thus, for a season at least, making him the major denominational spokesperson.

But, as we have seen, in conservative churches, like the Southern Baptist Convention, the mission establishment, too, plays a central role in molding the denomination's position toward Middle East issues. It should not be forgotten either that, at least in many Protestant churches, mission boards are where a good deal of the churches' income is to be found.

But there is another side to the mission question that is relevant to our story, and that is what this chapter is really about. I am referring to that very controversial issue, mission to the Jews.

I have entitled this chapter "the mission dilemma," because, as defined by Webster's Unabridged Dictionary, "dilemma" involves among other things "a perplexing and awkward situation." To multitudes of Christians, the question of mission when dealing with our Jewish neighbors has a special dimension of perplexity and awkwardness about it that does not apply to what might be called "mission in general."

Some of my friends would disagree with the word choice. For them the issue does not involve a dilemma at all. They pronounce an unequivocal 'no' to the very notion of Christian mission to the Jewish people, or, putting it a bit more mildly, a Christian "witness" to Jews. Paul van Buren, by many considered to be the leading "Israel-theologian" in Protestantism today, states frequently and bluntly in speeches that are often widely quoted (see *Religious News Service*, November 26, 1985) that Christians who try to convert Jews are "working against the will of God and the expressed command of Jesus." He argues that, if Jews had said 'yes' to the Church's message, the Jewish people, as a people with a Jewish identity and as a people set apart for a divinely appointed mission in the world, would cease to exist. But God wills that there be a Jewish people. And, more than ever since the Holocaust, we too should see the survival of that people with their own corporate identity as a moral mandate.

According to van Buren and other scholars, Christians must accept the Jewish 'no' to the Church and appreciate that 'no' as a positive. "If there were no more Jewish people," van Buren never tires of emphasizing, "we would have lost the single most concrete and enduring sign in the world of God's faithfulness."

In Romans 11:25-26, Paul admonishes gentiles not to "be wise in your own conceits," but rather to understand the mystery of Israel, which will remain a mystery until the divine destiny for both Jews and gentiles will be fulfilled. Referring to this, Krister Stendahl, in his book *Paul among Jews and Gentiles*, speaks of "an affirmation of a God-willed coexistence between Judaism and Christianity in which the missionary urge to convert Israel is held in check" (p. 4).

In some instances local or state councils of churches have taken up this theme in their assemblies. For instance, in 1983 the Texas Council of Churches by unanimous vote passed a resolution condemning efforts to bring a witness about Jesus to Jews because "the Jewish people today possess their own unique call and mission before God." The council specifically singled out for criticism the establishment of organizations that target the Jewish people as a special "object" for mission. My own hunch is that such unanimity on very controversial issues usually says more about group dynamics during church meetings than about the quality of theological debate that took place there. But even if the resolution may not speak for the majority of Texan Christians, it does reflect the strong conviction of at least a minority of them.

There seem to be a growing number of Christians who are prepared to accept some kind of dual-covenant theology, positing that there are two parallel roads to approach the God of the Bible, the road of Christ and the road of Torah. All this is reminiscent of Franz Rosenzweig's view that both faiths are to be seen as manifestations of the same Truth. In other words, they represent equally true and valid views of reality and each must honor the other as a servant of God. Sometimes, I think, Jewish listeners have a tendency to hear the sounds of a two-covenant theology when a non-supersessionist position is presented that may actually be very far removed from the Rosenzweig view.

At any rate, some Christian theologians who are strong advocates of dialogue with Jews and who are also profoundly aware of the churches' history of anti-Judaism, seem to feel that historic Christianity is in fact not a valid view of reality as understood in faith. They, therefore, propose a process of *radical reconstruction.*

Convinced that anti-Judaism goes to the very heart of New Testament teachings and is inherent in historic Christian doctrines, scholars like Rosemary Ruether and Roy Eckardt, to mention two of the more prominent authors in the field, call for changes in the Church's teaching about the centrality of Christ and his resurrection that to many other Christians sound like extreme positions or even apostasy.

"I am the Way, the Truth and the Life;" "there is no other name under heaven given among men by which we must be saved": these and other New Testament statements signify to some Christians the element of uniqueness expressed in the gospel of Christ's saving work. However, to other Christians they represent a claim to absolutism and exclusiveness that simply has to go because it inevitably leads to intolerance and missionary triumphalism.

To most Jewish scholars the radical theological reconstructionists in the Christian community represent a true sign of hope. They make no secret of the fact that they wished that all Christians would think like that. But they are sophisticated enough to know that the voice of a few individual scholars, influential as they may be in certain intellectual circles, is quite a different matter from the voice of the Church as it expresses itself through synods and councils.

In the mind of Jewish leaders, the mission issue is intimately tied up with the question of survival. To some it may seem that such an attitude is part of a Holocaust syndrome. Well, the Holocaust is indeed a very important part of the picture, but not as an isolated interval in history. Rather the Holocaust is experienced as the culmination of a long history of persecution in which Christian anti-Judaism has played a key role. The 'No' to Christian mission has, as it were, been engraved upon the psyche of the Jewish people.

In line with most Jewish leaders, Irving Greenberg, an Orthodox rabbi and president of the National Jewish Resource Center, sees the work of radical Christian scholars as "the most powerful proof of the vitality and the ongoing relevance of Christianity. . ." (*Quarterly Review*, Winter 1984). But by the same token, he and his wife Blu Greenberg continue to pursue dialogue with Christians who come to a diametrically opposite conclusion about what constitutes the vitality of Christianity. As far as they are concerned, Greenberg is recommending an essentially reductionist theology, which the church at large will continue to reject. Their interest perks up, however, when, in his *Quarterly Review* article Greenberg poses this question: "Should not Jewish theology seek to be open to Christian self-understanding, including the remarkable, unbelievable claim of resurrection, Incarnation, etc.?" And Blu Greenberg, in her contribution to the book *Evangelicals and Jews in an Age of Pluralism*, shows great sensitivity for the kind of dilemma many Christians experience with respect to the issue of mission. But more on that later.

In the meantime, mission to the Jews is a reality, because on the opposite pole of those who pronounce an unequivocal 'no' to such mission stand people who voice an unqualified 'yes.' They, too, see it as a clearcut case. As a matter of fact, they believe that "Jewish mission" is not just one aspect of the overall mission of the Church, but ought to be a priority concern: first and foremost to the Jews (Romans 1:16). Once again, it must be pointed out that the picture is rather complex. Those who think immediately in this context of Jews for Jesus and right wing fundamentalists, have, I fear, a somewhat distorted image of the situation.

Nevertheless, it is true that the most aggressive "Jewish mission" enterprises are usually sponsored by independent agencies of a conservative theological persuasion and often with a millenialist-dispensationalist orientation. One example is The Elisha Ministry, located in St. Louis, Missouri, and headed by the Rev. Harvey A. Smith. I mention this particular mission, not because it is necessarily typical of such ministries, but because it presents in a rather pronounced form some of the problematics inherent in such ventures.

Elisha Ministry letterheads used to feature the American flag in red, white and blue interposed with the white and blue of the Israeli flag. Underneath the two flags is printed the motto "Together We Stand." More recently, I suspect because of budgetary considerations, the mailings are printed in black and white. Also, the letterhead now features two Israeli flags. But the motto is still "Together We Stand."

The flags say something about the theological orientation of this mission. Israel is seen as at the center of today's prophetic happenings.

But the flags are also an indication of the dilemma such ministries face. These people are very eager to be counted among the staunchest supporters of the state of Israel, but because of their theological stance, they encounter much suspicion, both in the American Jewish community and in Israel. For many of these people this is very painful.

Support for Israel sometimes takes rather extreme forms. For instance, a sample letter published in the Elisha Ministry newsletter and recommended for mailing to government officials reads in part:

"Dear Mr. President, Senator, Congressman: I wish to express my full support for the nation of Israel. I believe that the Bible gives to God's chosen people all the land of Israel, West Bank, Golan Heights, east bank of Jordan and all of southern Lebanon to Tyre and Sidon as well as southern Syria to Damascus."

Another appeal letter by Mr. Smith offers "a new ministry for our partners," namely "a limited genealogical service free for our partners to find out if they have any Jewish ancestry or roots in their family." I am no longer easily surprised by various fundraising gimmicks, but I must confess that this one struck me as a somewhat startling novelty.

Sometimes the fundraising letters from pro-Israel Christian ministries do not come straight out stating that they seek the Conversion of Jews, but they nevertheless want to assure the donor that they are involved in the Real Thing. So, they use "hint language" in order to convey to the prospective contributor that great things are happening, while avoiding coming into conflict with Jewish leaders, either in this country or in Israel.

Many donors want to know that true mission is being done with their money. I am not suggesting that conservative Christians don't care about human suffering and don't contribute to programs that feed the hungry or heal the sick. They indeed do. But, by the same token they want to know that the true inspiration behind the mission, the ultimate goal is the "salvation of souls".

But how does an evangelist, let us say after a meeting with then Prime Minister Begin, get people so excited about what has happened that they will generously contribute to this ministry? "Hint language" is the answer.

My files contain numerous examples of this. The reader is told that prophetic scriptures were discussed (Begin loved quoting the prophets of Israel as much as his Christian visitors). Then the letter goes on to describe how there was sense of the mighty power of the Holy Spirit in the room. That's often enough to raise the level of expectation and excitement. Who knows what may grow from the seed that has been sown?

But some evangelists, including the Rev. Harvey Smith, do not beat around the bush. They are quite open and honest about their intentions, even if one may sometimes have doubts about their statistics. For instance, the January 1984 Elisha Ministry mailing contained the claim that "in the past two months fifty dear Jewish souls were won to the Lord". The June 1986 newsletter reported that Smith had witnessed to several rabbis in Buffalo, New York. Since it does not say that fifty Jews were baptized or what "witness" the rabbis gave in the encounter, the language of the newsletter leaves much room for interpretation.

But, as I stated earlier, fundamentalist-dispensationalist Christians are not the only ones advocating and practicing mission to Jews. There are evangelicals within the so-called mainstream churches who feel a strong commitment to a witness that has as its aim the conversion of Jews. For instance, the Episcopal Church, a communion about as mainstream as one can get, has within its fellowship a Christian Ministry Among Jewish People (CMJ/USA). It is advertised as "an authorized agent in the Anglican Communion founded in 1809 to work in loving service among the Jewish people." This ministry and similar projects tend to adopt a less aggressive approach than those who operate with a more apocalyptic sense of urgency.

While CMJ/USA is not officially sponsored by the Episcopal Church, it does have a semi-official status within the Anglican communion. Its board of advisors includes a number of bishops. The leadership of this ministry is well aware that the past Christian record vis-à-vis Jews and Judaism may not recommend it to its intended audience. The Rev. Philip Bottomley, CMJ/USA's director, wrote in one of the ministry's newsletters that "two thousand years of bad history requires us to be very sensitive in our witness in order that Jewish people may actually hear what we are saying." One folder defines the organization's purpose as follows: "CMJ/USA is an Episcopal organization offering teaching on the Jewish

Roots of our Faith and how to witness for Jesus among Jewish people in the United States."

Over against Episcopalian Paul van Buren's position, the Rev. Bottomley quotes Scripture: "there is no scriptual basis for saying that a Jew who believes in Jesus ceases to be a Jew. Peter and the Apostles would have been amazed at such a statement. On the day of Pentecost, Peter addressed the crowd as 'my fellow Jews' (Acts 2:14). Paul stated emphatically 'I *am* a Jew' (Acts 21:39), not 'I *was* a Jew.'" (*SHALOM*, March 1986).

It is because of this biblical position that CMJ/USA supporters are often referred to as "a fundamentalist group" by other Episcopalians, who find their presence at General Conventions of the Episcopal Church somewhat of an embarrassment (*New York Times Magazine*, September 1985). But in fact their broadly evangelical views are shared by millions of Christians who, while perhaps not involved in mission to Jews, defend its legitimacy if they do not actually advocate its practice.

The results of a poll, commissioned by the Anti-Defamation League of B'Nai B'rith and made public in January 1987, show some interesting facts about evangelicals. By and large Jewish leaders reacted quite positively to the data the poll yielded (cf. *New York Times*, January 8, 1987). For example, ninety percent of those interviewed disagreed with the statement that "Christians are justified in holding negative attitudes towards Jews since the Jews killed Christ."

Two statistics, however, were found to be disturbing: the fact that fifty nine percent of those surveyed agreed that "Jews can never be forgiven for what they did to Jesus until they accept him as the true Savior" and that fifty percent said Christians should "actively help lead Jews to accept Jesus Christ as the Savior."

As to the first point, the way the question is posed creates, it seems to me, a few problems of its own. The question did not ask: "Do you believe that the Jewish people today are to be held responsible for the death of Jesus?" I wonder whether fifty nine percent of the respondents would have answered that question in the affirmative. Instead, however, the question as posed simply implied that certain Jews did something to Jesus and then wants to know whether there is forgiveness without faith in Christ. Since, as far as evangelicals are concerned, the source of forgiveness for any misdeed done by anyone is to be found in the atoning sacrifice of Christ, the fifty nine percent may reflect more their view on forgiveness than their feelings about Jewish cupability. It seems to me that mixed questions like that produce as much confusion as enlightenment.

As to the second point, I was surprised that the percentage was not higher. It is hard to say how the person questioned interpreted the qualifying word "actively" when asked whether one should "help lead Jews to accept Jesus Christ as the Savior." Perhaps it raised in their minds images of an aggressive kind of evangelism that singles out Jews as special targets, an approach they may not feel comfortable with. During August 1986, the Lausanne Committee for World Evangelization sponsored a Consultation on Jewish Evangelism in Great Britain, attended by one hundred and sixty delegates from 17 nations. They issued a declaration in which they expressed grief "over the discrimination and suffering that have been inflicted upon the Jewish people in the name of Jesus the Messiah," adding that "these deeds constituted a denial of God's love for his people and a misrepresentation of the person and work of Jesus."

After a denunciation of all forms of anti-Semitism "as contrary to the gospel and to the content of the New Testament," the Lausanne declaration made the following point: "We must protest, however, when past history is used to silence the church in her witness to the Jewish people. To withhold the gospel from the Jewish people would be an act of gross discrimination." My guess is that, if this proposition were to be submitted to the same people surveyed in the A.D.L. poll, more than fifty percent would agree with it.

Past history makes it imperative that great sensitivity be shown, so the argument goes, but it does not excuse one from the missionary mandate. For many Christians, history, even the horrors of the Holocaust, cannot supersede Holy Writ. That point is made repeatedly in articles promoting "Jewish Evangelism." For instance, *The Banner*, a magazine sponsored by the Christian Reformed Church, published an article in its October 1, 1984 issue on courses taught at Westminster Theological Seminary in Philadelphia to help students witness to Jews. "Christians," we read there, "need to ask forgiveness for many wrongs committed against Jews." Further-more, "deep sensitivity to Jewish feelings must characterize all evangelis-tic witness to Jews." But this can never mean that Jews are to be excluded from Christian witness.

It is important to keep in mind that from the very beginning the Church saw itself as an *apostolic* community, which means that mission was not regarded as an elective, but rather as a divine imperative. Or, to put it differently, mission was not seen as one of the many activities with which Christians keep themselves busy. Rather, it was the Church's *raison d'être*. Mission is not done for the sake of the Church's wellbeing; it belongs to her *being*. That notion, in my view, rather than being a Chris-tian invention, grows out of a perspective that is deeply rooted in the Hebrew scriptures. Furthermore, as some Jewish scholars have pointed out, there were periods in their people's history when that perspective was translated into proselytizing practices.

But here we are talking about the Christian dilemma. Between the "Mission, yes!" proponents on the one side and the "Mission, no!" people on the other, there are multitudes of church members for whom the issue has become a matter of profound moral-spiritual struggle, a genuine dilemma. There are elements in both the 'yes' and the 'no' positions to which they ascribe a degree of validity, and their sympathies tend to sway back and forth as the debate goes on. For instance, taking the New Testa-ment as a whole, it would seem very difficult, if not impossible, to defend the position that the conversion of a Jew is a bad thing. Such a view would seem to undercut the very foundation of the Church's origins. Therefore, Christian adherence to both the New Testament message and its practice would seem to require that the gospel of Christ be shared with all people, none excluded.

Blu Greenberg, in her contribution to the book *Evangelicals and Jews in an Age of Pluralism*, shows great sensitivity in her understanding of the dilemma many Christians face on this issue. "Now I know the dilemma that evangelical Christians face, and I am not trying for the jugular. . . Scripture says, go convert the Jews. What is a decent Christian to do? I know how it feels. As an orthodox Jew, as one who believes in revelation, who loves torah, and who tries to live her life according to *Halakah* yet also as a woman of the 20th century who is committed to the new values for women I have experienced the dilemma in my own life many, many times: the tension one feels between faithfulness to Scripture and the need to respond to unfolding religious realities, the conflict one feels about Biblical authority and infallibility when it clashes with historical and social necessity, the tension between absolute and pluralist models, the anxious feeling one has at times that by chipping away a tiny piece, one begins to weaken the whole structure. Yes, I understand the dilemma a well-meaning evangelical faces" (p. 231).

Once again, "evangelical" here has to be taken in a very broad sense, because I meet Christians representing a wide range of Christian theological opinion who feel the tension described here very personally. They have to be honest to their understanding of Scripture. At the same time, they have to be honest to a deeper understanding of history as well. To claim, as some Christians still do, that anti-Judaism and persecution represented the activities of some bad individuals who were not truly reborn Christians, is clearly a dishonest or, at least, a willfully ignorant response to the truth.

Furthermore, Scripture itself contains elements of ambiguity, or of high paradox, if that term is preferred. It is enough to give one pause for reflection. For instance, the mission mandate of Matthew 28:18 tells us to go and make disciples of all nations (*ta ethna* in Greek). But the Jewish people are not to be counted as a nation among the nations. There is a very important difference, because they are the people of the covenant, the people of the promise, the people of the Book *par excellence*. Even the fact that some Jews may not be very familiar with their own heritage does not gainsay the truth that in addressing them we are dealing with people whose souls has been stamped, so to speak, by the history of Israel. I have the impression that of all people it is perhaps the most difficult for a Jew to become a hundred percent secular person; someone who has lost all sense of Jewish history and heritage; a person totally out of touch with Torah.

At any rate, some Christian statements have sought to deal with the element of uniqueness with respect to the Jewish people while at the same time talking about witness. In a policy document developed in the Presbyterian Church, U. S. before its union with the United Presbyterian Church as few years ago, we read this: "In witnessing to the Jews. . .we encounter a unique reality, namely, that they already worship and serve the One True

God. Like the apostle Paul, we are eager to share with them what we believe to be the saving grace of Jesus Christ for us and for all humanity. But at the same time, like Paul in Romans 9:11, we too live with the mystery that God's election of the Jews for salvation is irrevocable."

But what does it mean to recognize this mystery and to acknowledge the horrors of past Christian history? What form of Christian witness remains valid in light of those truths? How does one maintain the integrity of one's faith, the integrity of one's relationship to Jewish neighbors with whom one seeks to engage in dialogue, and the integrity of one's support for Israel? For many Christians these have become profoundly perplexing questions.

As a starter it may be helpful to distinguish between witness and proselytizing, but in the end that does not really resolve the issue. Take, for instance, the two essays by Vernon Grounds and Blu Greenberg, an orthodox Christian and an orthodox Jew, in the book *Evangelicals and Jews in an Age of Pluralism*. "I draw a sharp distinction between proselytizing and witnessing," writes Dr. Grounds (p. 220). Ms. Greenberg suggests a distinction between "mission-proselytism" and "mission-witness" (p. 232). So, they seem to agree in substance. But what happens when one turns to specifics?

In his rejection of proselytizing, Dr. Grounds appeals to a World Council of Churches report, as well as the writings of the Catholic scholar Tommaso Federici. In both cases proselytism is defined in terms of illegitimate pressures, coercive actions and the violation of another human being's personhood. He recognizes potential abuses and the need to let a person make decisions in freedom. Nevertheless, he maintains, none of those considerations would warrant declaring a moratorium on Christian mission, nor the watering down of what we believe about Jesus as the Christ.

Blu Greenberg, on the other hand, holds that "the idea that only through Christ will Jews be saved is out of order. . .It is obscene!" (p. 230). In order to appreciate the case she makes for this conclusion I would urge the reader to turn to the full text of her essay. She writes with passion about her people and their history, but also with a profound understanding of her dialogue partners.

Can Christians meaningfully share their faith in Christ without implying that their Jewish neighbors are separated from the God of redemption? How does a Christian convey his or her convictions and feelings about Jesus, his uniqueness as understood in faith, his ministry of reconciliation, without implying that Jews live in darkness without him?

Witness, at best, is a sharing of one's faith in an atmosphere of love. At worst it is a drive for mental and spiritual conquest, usually born much more out of the insecurity of the zealous evangelizer than his or her inner peace about personal decisions that have been made. The failure to clearly distinguish between scoring points or pushing another person against the wall with clever arguments and a loving witness to one's faith has frequently led to a spiritual imperialism that has alienated countless people from the Christian community.

The apostle Paul suggested that a basic mission strategy as far as his Jewish brothers and sisters were concerned was to provoke them to jealousy. Love, lived out in joy, more than anything else will make others wonder what internal resources produce such results. But in light of the past two thousand years, Paul's advice, at least to many serious people, sounds like a sick joke. Instead of following the road of love, the Church pursued the path of polemics. When that did not work, it applied power and turned to persecution. No wonder Jews pick up negative signals whenever they are made the "object" of Christian witness.

On the other hand, Christians often feel that they are being pushed toward a minimalist position in order to maintain friendship with the Jewish community. Must they deny or leave unmentioned what Jesus means to them in order not to be accused of proselytism? How low-key must Christian witness be in order to be considered legitimate? A take-it-or-leave-it approach or a hyper-intellectual approach that does not seem to care about commitment are for many Christians hard to accept as valid witness. And so the arguments, or perhaps it would be better to say the probings, move back and forth.

At its first meeting in Amsterdam in 1948, the World Council of Churches reaffirmed its commitment to the missionary mandate, including mission to Jews, but rejected the idea of singling out Jews as special targets for Christian outreach. Rather, witness to Jewish neighbors should, according to the Council, be done "as a normal part of parish work." At that time, Christian-Jewish dialogue was still a function of the Commission on World Mission and Evangelism.

Eventually, as the dialogue proceeded, Christian-Jewish relations became the concern of the Division for Dialogue with People of Living Faiths and Ideologies. Some have suggested that it would signal a further advance if conversations with Israel were conducted in the framework of the Commission on Faith and Order, i.e. as part of the ecumenical rather than the interfaith dialogue. Thus it would indicate the common roots of Judaism and Christianity plus the idea that the alienation between Church and Synagogue is to be seen as the original schism.

Obviously, such a move would eliminate the notion of mission altogether, because one does not missionize people with whom one entertains ecumenical relations, although within an ecumenical context one could still speak of a mutual witness to one another. But others, both in the Jewish and Christian communities, hold that to structure the dialogue on the principle that Christianity and Judaism are in essence "one faith", is going a bit too far. Some also see a danger that Christians who urge this approach in effect seek to define for Jews how they should understand the dialogue relationship, even though there are leading Jewish scholars as well, like David Flusser, who defend the "one-faith" thesis.

Since 1973, however, the WCC office on Christian-Jewish Relations has been called the "Consultation on the Church and the Jewish People," thus correctly suggesting that dialogue is a matter of mutual exchange, a two-way street. Also, mutual consultation seems very far removed from mission or evangelism. But, on the other hand, consultation sounds so safe, so businesslike, so devoid of deep engagement or even passion.

What is dialogue really all about? Surely, it involves more than the exchange of information. After all, such a function could eventually be handled by a computerized data bank with an "800" number. Because, above all, dialogue has something to do with person-to-person encounter, it belongs in Martin Buber's world of I-thou. As such it involves risk, on both sides. Without the element of risk, or exposing oneself to the possibility of fundamental change and mutual transformation, dialogue will end up in sheer boredom, or at least in interminable meetings attended by "official" representative who love consultations as long as their travel expense accounts hold out.

Some Christians become visibly upset, if not actually annoyed, whenever a Jew is grasped by the figure of Jesus to the point of a radical life commitment. Why don't those Jews understand what seems as clear as light of day to the Christian dialogue expert, namely that they don't need "it". The implication, of course, is that Jesus is for the gentiles and has no redemptive relevance for Jews. A similar argument can be heard from the Jewish side when certain rabbis assure the world that they discourage people from becoming converts to Judaism because they don't need "it" either, i.e. by simply leading a good life one can gain a place in the world to come without "it".

These assurances sound very well-meaning. But it strikes me as somewhat arrogant, even triumphalistic, when people are so confident telling another person what he or she needs. Who are we really to pontificate on such matters, except in a general and abstract way? Theoretically, people may not need this or that, but life has its own needs and the heart its own reasons. What do we know about the searchings of another's soul, about the hungers of the heart, about the passionate inner struggles?

It is my contention that an honest-to-God encounter with Judaism and Israel could have radical consequences for the life and theology of the Church, and that, in the main, that would be a good thing. But it is risky business. And what is true of the corporate entities engaged in dialogue is also true of the individual participants. Dialogue that is totally safe is never very serious, and certainly not very interesting. The same can be said of dialogue that has smoothed out all rough edges and, with the aid of neat phrases, resolved all ambiguities.

Take the 1985 Vatican document, "Notes on the correct way to present the Jews and Judaism in preaching and catechesis in the Roman Catholic Church." It contains some very obvious ambiguities. On the one hand, as we have seen earlier, the document reaffirms the words of Pope John Paul II to the effect that the Jewish people are "the people of God of the Old Covenant, which has never been revoked. . ." and refers to the "witness-often heroic" which this people has made to the whole world throughout their history.

On the other hand, "Notes" observes "the sad fact that the majority of the Jewish people and its authorities did not believe in Jesus. . ." In other words, the Vatican does not seem to agree that the Jewish 'no' to the Church's message should in every respect be appreciated as a positive. Furthermore, the mission of the Church is defined in terms of "the all-embracing means of salvation" that leads through Jesus to the Father. It seems an almost explicit rejection of a dual-covenant theology when the document adds: "Church and Judaism cannot then be seen as two parallel ways of salvation and the Church must witness to Christ as the Redeemer for all . . ."

Dr. Eugene Fisher does not read it that way. He still argues that there is a basis in teachings of the Holy See and the popes since Vatican II for the view that "the Jews, in not becoming Christians, were and are following God's will." He maintains that this Jewish response is part of the mystery with which the apostle Paul struggles in Romans 9:11. And he, too, has a point.

Apparently, the "Notes" wish to present a clear claim of the salvific and universal significance of the Catholic Church without denying that Jews can and should draw salvific gifts from their own traditions (cf. *Midstream*, January 1987, p. 61), but also without denying the apostolic mandate of the Church. How to put all of this in a nice, neat formula? Personally, I doubt that this can be done. The paradoxes of faith and life cannot be packaged that easily. I am not plugging for obscurantism; clarity of language is a good and virtuous thing. And as a tool for educators the "Notes" could definitely be improved upon. But even under the best of formulations, the Catholic Church (as well as many other churches) would still be saying both that the Jewish people continue to be the people of the covenant, that throughout history they have given a witness to divine faithfulness (in a sense their very survival is such a witness!) *and* that the Church is called to share the message of Christ with all people, including Jews.

Some will insist that this is not a satisfactory arrangement. But ambiguities and inner tensions are part of all historical existence. Geoffrey Wigoder, in commenting on the "Notes", complained that "despite the dis-

continuation of mission, an implied conversionist hope is manifest."
(*Midstream*, June/July 1986, p. 12) Absolutely! There is no denying the
fact that a certain sense of satisfaction will stir the souls of many Christians, even Christian advocates of dialogue, when someone from another
faith or no-faith decides to join their fellowship. The more prominent the
convert, the bigger the catch. And I dare say that precisely the same sentiments prevail among Jews when the person turns out to be a convert to
Judaism.

How pure are the motives of the various parties involved in such situations? One can only guess or try to play God. But to start complaining
about "implied hope" seems to me to ask for interfaith relationships that
transcend the boundaries of historical existence. Past history fully justifies
Jewish suspicion about Christian witness. It is, therefore, right that Christians should be needled and pushed to clarify their positions. Do you
advocate mission to Jews? That is a fair question. Do you practice such
mission and, if yes, what form does it take? Another fair question. Can
you guarantee me that you have abandoned, not only advocacy of mission,
not only the practice of such mission, but all "implied hope" that someone
of my community might become committed to the faith of your community? For some Christians the answer will be 'yes'. But most Christians, I
believe, would hope that such a promise would not be made the condition
for dialogue or friendly relationships.

Suspicions within the Jewish community usually are especially strong
with respect to evangelicals, because after all, that is where the strongest
missionary drive often is to be found. And on their part, many evangelicals who have become sensitized to Jewish concerns are struggling with
the mission issue. As we noted before, the International Christian Embassy in Jerusalem has chosen the words of Isaiah 40:1 as its motto:
"Comfort ye, comfort ye my people." That, say the Embassy leaders, represents their calling and they remind all who will listen that the text does
not say "Preach ye, preach ye to my people." Perhaps others are called to
do that. As Jim Jackson, past director of the U.S./I.C.E.J. branch put it in
his newsletter, "the purpose, goals and sovereign call of God upon the
Embassy is to awaken the Christian community the world over to our responsibility to stand with the Jewish people as God's ancient covenant
people. It is not our purpose to evangelize."

Nevertheless, it cannot be taken for granted that those fine distinctions will be accepted and observed by all supporters of the International Christian Embassy or all those who participate in events sponsored by it. When I.C.E.J. spokesman Jan Willem van der Hoeven was quoted in *The Jerusalem Post* (International Edition), as stating that "Christianity is for the gentiles" (implying that God himself will take care of his people the Jews, i.e. open their eyes at his appointed time), many I.C.E.J. supporters did more than display a frown. There is little doubt that the Embassy's non-missionary position has cost them in terms of finances and has been a contributing factor to the internal fights that led to the split with the British and American branches a few years ago.

Still, it is my impression that a growing number of evangelicals are prepared—while not denying the missionary mandate, which they in good conscience cannot—to adopt a position "in which the missionary urge to convert Israel is held in check," as Krister Stendahl words it. For some this means that the resolution of the dilemma is simply pushed to the eschaton, when God himself will intervene in the history of Israel in such a way that, as Paul stated it, "all Israel will be saved" (Romans 11:26).

In the meantime, I hear some evangelical leaders say that our calling towards the Jewish people is to repent of past sins and to show unconditional love, which includes that one stands in solidarity with the always beleaguered nation of Israel. To others in the evangelical community this sounds like compromise, if not outright deception. To them the priority can never lie in Israel's security, important as that is. It must always be that the gospel be preached to all nations.

For those who cannot in good conscience write off the universal claims of the gospel's message, the question of the *form* that Christian witness should take vis-à-vis the Jewish people become crucial. In light of what the scriptures teach us about the eternal covenant and in light of what history teaches us about Christian conduct over almost 2000 years, what can be considered a valid witness to our Jewish neighbors?

Furthermore, how well have we listened to the witness of Israel before we issue our urgent calls to conversion? As J. Coert Rylaarsdam wrote in *Face to Face* (III/IV, 1977, p. 18): "For the foreseeable future the primary concern of Christian mission to the Jews must be the redemption of Christians, specifically with respect to their understanding of their relation to the faith of Israel." Markus Barth, in his booklet *Israel and the Church in Ephesians*, makes the point that "Israel is God's chosen missionary to the Gentiles" (p. 109). Hence, he adds, such designations as "Christian mission to the Jews had better be dropped. The way in which it often is carried out alienates more Jews than it wins" (p. 110). The younger brother owes a testimony to the older brother, says Barth, but it must be characterized by modesty, "by his asking for forgiveness" (p. 113).

Then, what shall we still say and do after we have truly listened and confessed? It seems to me that whatever form gentile witness to Jews takes after that, it will lack all characteristics of ambitious campaigns and triumphalistic "crusades". There is evidence that some of this is already happening. Gentile mission to the Jewish people in the old style is being practiced on a lesser scale than ever before. On the other hand, "Jewish mission" in the sense of aggressive outreach by converts from Judaism to their own people is probably on the increase. Such mission has dimensions all its own. Some thoughts on the phenomenon of "Hebrew Christians" or "Messianic Jews" will follow in the next chapter.

I would like to sum up this one with a quote from an article John S. Conway wrote for the first issue of the journal *Holocaust and Genocide Studies* (vol. 1, no. 1, pp. 127-146, 1986). Toward the conclusion of the article "Protestant Missions to the Jews 1810-1980: Ecclesiastical Imperialism or Theological Aberration?" Conway writes:

"By its essence the Christian Church is mission-oriented and committed to the person of Jesus Christ as the Saviour of the World. For Christians, mission is the sharing of the Good News about God's action in history through Jesus Christ. The Church may renounce all claim to exclusive truth or absolute authority, or it may reject the methods of persecution, coercion and enforced proselytism of earlier years. But it cannot deny or obliterate its duty to witness in one way or another. The task for Christians is to attempt to find appropriate forms which will reflect neither the repellent aspects of triumphalist mission, nor the inadmissible relativism of a conscious or unconscious syncretism. The task for Jews is to be aware that the church's terrible and tragic involvement in the genocidal missions of the past need not represent the only possible pattern of relations between the followers of the Jew, Jesus and the people of his original family."

XI

Messianic Jews: Conspiracy or Tragedy?

There is an old joke, about three Jews who had converted to Christianity. While the details differ from one narrator to the next, the basic point the humor seeks to convey is always the same, with the underlying question: Why does any Jew decide to become a Christian?

"I did it, because it improved my chances in my professional career," said the first one. "I converted," stated number two, "because I wanted to save my children from the persecutions that are always the fate of the Jewish people."

The attention turned to him, number three said: "I became a Christian out of conviction," a remark met with gleeful hilarity and the response: "Go tell that to the goyim!"

In Charles Silberman's version of the story, the first Jew says that he converted out of love, not for Christianity, but for a Christian girl. The second person asserts that becoming an Episcopalian greatly enhanced his chances of getting a judgeship. The punch line reads: "What do you take us for—a couple of goyim?" (*A Certain People*, p. 69) The implication is clear: converted Jews may fool Christians, but their own people know the score.

The basic sentiments expressed in this story find their roots deep down in the soil of Jewish history. That does not mean, however, that the story is not also based on a good deal of mythology. Like all generalizations, it contains a mixture of fact and fiction. To say that every Jew who converts to Christianity is motivated by desire for security, social standing or material gain is an obvious absurdity. But bittersweet humor, a prominent feature in both Jewish and Black history, does not aim for dialectical balance; it is a way of dealing with historical experience, particularly a history of oppression and persecution.

During much of Christian history it did indeed pay for a Jew to convert to Christianity. And so it is not surprising that Christian prejudice has sometimes produced Jewish opportunism. "The baptismal certificate is the ticket of admission to Western culture," said Heinrich Heine. Joining a church, especially if a person picked the right one, could certainly be a help in getting ahead. Consequently in the era of emancipation, many Jews—some famous, many of them Mr. and Mrs. Middle Class, but all longing for social acceptance—followed the path of least resistance and converted.

To the vast majority of Jews such conversions have always seemed a betrayal of one's own people. In pre-emancipation history, during periods of harsh anti-Jewish measures and pressures to forsake the faith of one's fathers and mothers, multitudes of Jews chose martyrdom over accommodation and misery over a life of dishonesty. Against that background it should not be difficult to understand the sense of betrayal that is felt by Jews when some of their people convert. To many of them it seemed synonymous with "going over to the enemy".

The question of "rice Christians" has been long and widely debated in Christian missiological literature. All across the globe Christian missionaries have established charitable programs and institutions—agricultural, medical, educational, etc. In most cases those missionaries were basically good people, motivated by the best of intentions. Many were genuinely interested in improving the lot of those who lived in destitute circumstances. But motivations always come in mixed bags. Christian good works often became the means for cultural imperialism; the salvation of one's soul, interest in one's physical well-being and the Westernization of one's lifestyle frequently had a way of getting bundled together.

Anyone who has ever visited mission fields has had to confront the phenomenon of "rice Christians", people who, one suspects, bought into the package with at least some material motives. To even consider that possibility makes one feel uncomfortable. I remember a trip to the Reformed Church's mission in Oman and my discovery that the handful of converts who had been gained from Islam after many years of witness all worked for the mission. I realize that in many cases a convert has a hard time finding employment elsewhere. Some people suffer for their faith.

173

But the temptation to join the mission because it might offer a higher standard of living is also very real.

Similar situations are to found in the history of Christian missions to the Jews. As I look back at the mission in which my father was involved in Rotterdam, Holland, I find it hard to avoid a sense of discomfort. I know, I am judging things from the perspective of a different era. The masses of Jews who passed through that harbor on their way to the United States were often poor people, many of them confused in a strange environment. They could use a helping hand.

The people in Elim, as the mission was called, were no doubt well-meaning and often loving individuals. But they were dealing with foreigners who were experiencing a high degree of vulnerability. It is hard to recognize the delicacy of such a situation when one is also eager to convey a Christian witness.

I do not deny that moments of crisis can become the occasion when a person is most prepared to engage in a radical evaluation of one's life and thought and that this sometimes does lead to renewal. But, on the other had, one hates to think of a mission approach that goes by the principle of "get 'em while they're down!" A Hebrew-Christian clergyman, the only missionary to the Jews who, as far as I am aware, was ever employed by my own denomination, once told me that he looked in the local paper for accident victims with Jewish names whom he would then contact in the hospital. That struck me as a form of spiritual ambulance chasing that will give all witness a bad name.

I have often admired the work of inner city missions. The dedication displayed by some of the workers there can be impressive indeed. But again, when the soup is dished up with a little sermon—as used to be quite common and, perhaps, still is—one cannot help but wonder whether witness is not in danger of getting mixed up with pressure, something quite contrary to the dimension of free choice, which must be at the heart of every conversion. On the other hand, recognizing the inherent ambiguity in all missionary work doesn't go far in helping us to understand the convert's life, be it the dynamic of his or her inner life or that of the convert's position in social context.

174

The picture is complex and the problematics vary according to the cultural environment and different historical experiences of communities. In the case of Messianic Jews, the focus of this chapter, we are confronted with a number of dilemmas. Some of them are unique to their particular situation, others representative of the problems and ambiguities that most Jewish converts must face.

First, there is the personal dilemma, especially the sense of "homelessness" that so often accompanies conversion. Where does one really belong? In many cases conversion involves rejection by one's own people, a rejection not always compensated for by acceptance in the churches. In many local congregations Jews tend to be viewed as "different", and this can put the family members in somewhat delicate and often uncomfortable positions.

It is precisely this sense of being "twice exiled" that is put forth by some Messianic Jews as a rationale for their claim that separate Hebrew Christian congregations are a necessity. Bruce Joffe writing in *Christianity Today* (July 13, 1984) quotes a certain Mr. Elliot Klayman as follows: "Traditional Jews separate from us because we are 'Christian' and many Christians remove us from their fellowship rolls because we are Jewish. No wonder God has seen fit to raise up Messianic congregations where we can worship as led by the Holy Spirit, fellowship with those who are like-minded, and live a cultural existence that identifies us as we perceived ourselves to be—Jews!" (p. 21).

When Messianic Jews say that they seek to worship as led by the Holy Spirit, they imply, among other things, that the churches have developed a wide variety of worship forms, except an Hebraic one. Why is it all right to have a Catholic-sacramental form of worship in the Episcopal Church and a much more freewheeling kind of worship in Baptist churches, but not an approach to worship that has deep biblical roots and has a special meaning to Hebrew Christians? Does our discomfort about such worship perhaps have to do with what the U.S. Catholic Bishops have called the "de-Judaization" of Christian theology, which began very early in the Church's history?

Personal dilemmas have a way of spilling over into family situations.

175

Parents, even though they do not necessarily practice Judaism themselves or have exposed their children to a Jewish education beyond a bare minimum, can feel quite passionate about the conversion of their son or daughter to Christianity. It is not necessarily that they don't get along with their Christian neighbors or that they have hostile feelings toward Christian associates at work. Quite the contrary; their relationship to Christian individuals may be very friendly. But the Church as a collective is something else again. It is somehow perceived as another world, not as a friend but as an antagonist. Consequently any faith—or no faith at all—seems better than for a convert to join that world. In light of history such feelings seem quite understandable to me. Many Jewish converts make a concerted effort to explain that they have not joined Christendom with its history of corruption, but that they have become followers of Jesus who, it is believed, had something quite different in mind.

I am writing this a few days after Edith Stein, a Jewish convert to Christianity who was among the multitudes murdered in Auschwitz, was beatified by Pope John Paul II during a visit to Germany. Family members had been invited to attend the ceremony but were divided on how to respond. There obviously was an immense sense of ambivalence among them. No matter how often it may be claimed that one cannot be a Jew and a Christian at the same time, some family members were almost passionate in their claim (with a good deal of validity, I would say) that Edith Stein had not been killed because of her Christian beliefs, but because of her Jewish background. "To be a Jew is an indelible status from which there is no exit, writes Charles Silberman. How come? "Because Judaism defines itself not as a voluntary community of faith but as an involuntary community of fate." (*A Certain People*, p. 70). Edith Stein and other Jewish converts could not escape that fate during the days of Nazi persecution.

Beyond the families, both the Jewish and the Christian communities as well as their interrelationships are affected by the reality of conversion. A particular church's mission philosophy and practice vis-à-vis Jews is always a point at issue. But there are other dynamics at work as well. Take, for instance the situation (on which I shall comment further a little later) that arises when Jewish leaders seek support from Christian leaders in their opposition to Hebrew Christian groups. Is there a danger at times that Christians will attack other Christians mainly as a gesture of goodwill toward Jewish dialogue partners? And wouldn't that be in essence a betrayal of dialogue vis-à-vis those (Hebrew) Christian brothers and sisters?

Finally, many Jewish converts to Christianity feel a strong affinity with the state of Israel and in one way or another want to lend their support to that country. Some of them want to settle there and claim citizenship. I have met Hebrew Christians who come across as more Zionist than the Zionists. But that in turn has led to dilemmas for both the Israel High Court and the Knesset.

Take the case of the Carmelite monk Daniel Rufeisen or "Brother Daniel" as he came to be known. A resident of Israel, in his pre-Christian days he had been recognized as a courageous member of the Jewish resistance against the Nazis in Poland. As the son of a Jewish mother, he sought Israeli citizenship according to the provisions of the Law of Return. In the end the decision of the High Court was to deny his request. At this juncture in history, the Court said in effect, a confession of Jesus as Messiah inescapably means that one ceases to be a Jew. It is important to observe that the case was decided on the basis of historical, *not* halachic arguments.

Simon Schoon, in his important study, *Christelijke Presentie in de Joodse Staat* ("Christian Presence in the Jewish State"), quotes Judge Silberg, who read the majority opinion for the Court, as stating: "the healthy instinct of the Jewish people, and its thirst for survival are responsible for this general axiomatic belief" (p. 86). At one time it could conceivably have been different; halachic law might have prevailed. But too much has happened in history. The Holocaust had happened just a few short years ago, and the issues of mission and conversion have in recent years increasingly been dealt with in terms of survival.

After the Holocaust, more than ever before, each Jew who converts is portrayed by at least some as representing a step along the road toward extinction of that part of the community that survived Hitler's gas chambers. Mission consequently is described in terms of spiritual liquidation. After all, wouldn't successful mission to the Jews in the end mean a world without Judaism?

Michael Cook, writing in the *Union Seminary Quarterly Review* (Vol.

XXXVIII, No. 2, 1983), clearly follows the historical perspective on the issue of Hebrew Christians referred to above. "In the first century," he stated, "a Jew could become a Christian and still remain a Jew. . .Today, however, from the Jewish point of view, there can be no such person as a Christian-Jew or a Jewish Christian. After nineteen centuries of a parting of the ways, the theological distinctions between Jews and Christians are so formidable that no one can genuinely be both a Jew and a Christian" (p. 135).

Paul Van Buren, writing from his particular Christian point of view, treats the subject in terms of an "impossible possibility". In his book *Discerning the Way*, he strongly advocates the validity of both the way of Israel and the way of the Church. But then he raises the question: Is it necessarily disobedience to God's purpose if a Jew becomes a Christian?" (p. 63). After raising a number of issues that do not need to be repeated here, he posits as one of his conclusions the thesis that surely one way to be a Jew is to be a (Christian) Jew," adding, "This possibility, however, flies in the face of the history of the past nineteen centuries." (p. 64) It is history that has made it an "impossible possibility", while contemporary life, namely the empirical phenomenon of Hebrew Christians, makes it a reality that cannot be ignored.

The Knesset became involved in the issue of conversion in 1977 when one of its members, Rabbi Yehuda Abramowitz, introduced legislation making it illegal to induce people to conversion by offering them some sort of material benefit. The Abramowitz Bill, sometimes referred to as the anti-bribery law and also known as the "Enticement to Change of Religion Law", was railroaded through the Knesset (for instance, the requirement of three readings was fulfilled by doing two readings on the same day when few Knesset members were present). It seems to me that this law reflects more the mentality of the Shtetl of yesteryear than the realities in the independent and pluralistic state of Israel today.

Someday a court case may be conducted on the basis of this law, but I dare say that in order to win, one would have to prove quite outrageous behavior on the part of the accused individual. In the meantime the law would seem to be more of a nuisance measure and mild form of intimidation in a basically free and democratic society than a social necessity. Conversions for cash are, one suspects, not a common phenomenon in

Israel.

The Brother Daniel case officially reaffirmed a position held with virtual unanimity among world Jewry, namely that anyone who confesses Jesus as Messiah *ipso facto* ceases to be a Jew. The Abramowitz Bill, on the other hand, in a way made official a longstanding and widespread suspicion among Jews that anyone who converts to Christianity quite likely has done so out of ulterior motives. At the present time Messianic Jews have become a major focus of concern. By and large they seem to bear the brunt of those two arguments.

One suspects that one reason this is the case is that they make themselves so visible. They are not the type to crawl into a dark corner or, in a chameleon like fashion, try to blend in with their environment. In the Middle Ages, a Jewish convert to Christianity was literally forced to go through a formal procedure of total renunciation of his or her tradition: "I do here and now renounce every rite and observance of the Jewish religion, detesting all its solemn ceremonies and tenets that in former days I kept and held".

In the modern era of emancipation and assimilation, many Jews voluntarily sought to hide their Jewish heritage, although it must be admitted that the social pressures to abandon distinctiveness as the price of acceptance remained very strong indeed. So the philosopher Heinrich Heine sought to look and act like a good Lutheran, the logical choice in the Germany of that day. On today's U.S. scene one may prefer to look and act like a Presbyterian or, perhaps better yet, an Episcopalian.

But now come the Messianic Jews, many of them children of middle class families whose parents by the usual measures of success have "made it" in America. If *they* decide to change their names, it is frequently for the purpose of Judaizing them. Rather than being ashamed of their Jewishness, they seem to flaunt it, wearing yarmulkas and being determined to practice some of the things Jews in previous ages were forced to pronounce detestable as the price of church membership. Furthermore, most of the young Messianic Jews, rather than identifying with the respectable historical mainline churches, seem to have a greater affinity with evangelical [and in many cases, fundamentalist] Christianity.

Why do they do it? To advance their careers? To be better accepted in the churches or society at large? To feel more secure, better protected against ridicule and criticism? Not very likely. Charles Silberman may have been a bit over-optimistic in some of his analyses and conclusions about the status of Jews in the United States today, but I have not seen any credible arguments disputing the central thesis in this book *A Certain People*, namely that numerous opportunities have opened up to Jews during the past decades. That, of course, does not mean that prejudice has been totally banned from corporation board rooms, country clubs and other places where narrow-minded elites hang out.

So, how to explain the phenomenon of those young Messianic Jews? Stanley Rosenbaum, writing in *Midstream* (December, 1985), says that in his experience they "exhibit a high degree of sociopathology along with their sincerity" (p. 11). A few sentences later we read that he had discovered that "many Jews for Jesus are a species of mental masochist: they expect and even want insult." Now, it is true that Moishe Rosen, the founder and still the leader of Jews for Jesus, has often stressed to those who join the movement that any kind of specifically Christian witness to their own people, no matter how sensitively they may try to go about it, will mean risking the displeasure of Jewish community leaders. Hence, for anyone who wishes to go that route, disapproval and rejection must be accepted as a normal consequence of such a choice. It seems to me that such an argument can be attributed at least as much to realism as to masochism.

I have encountered some strange and very insecure characters among members of Hebrew Christian fellowships. True, many of those people never had a strong sense of self-identity as Jews and, as already mentioned, many had grown up in homes where they were deprived of few things except perhaps a basic education in their Jewish heritage. It is hard to find meaning in a religion one misunderstands. But to suggest that Messianic Jews are mostly social misfits and masochists, or ignoramuses with respect to Jewish tradition, strikes me as an argument so obviously unbalanced that it is bound to be ignored.

Much more common than the sociopathology argument is the claim that the messianic Jewish movement is controlled by deceitful people. Some time ago one of the Presbyterian churches in the town where I live had a member of Jews for Jesus as a guest speaker. It should be pointed out that Jews for Jesus, with their very aggressive missionary tactics, are one element in a movement that is much broader and quite diverse. While there appears to be a growing network of Hebrew Christian groups across the country, I see little chance that this will at any time soon develop into a centrally controlled organization in which a few leaders can claim to speak for the whole. These groups tend to share a good deal of the fragmentation that afflicts much of the evangelical movement with which they have such a close affinity.

But, at any rate, the visit of a Jews for Jesus member to our local Presbyterian church produced the usual kind of letter to the editor in our weekly newspaper. The writer expressed surprise that an "established (read "respectable mainline") Christian church" would sponsor such a group. Leaving aside for now the point that inviting someone to speak does not necessarily imply that one sponsors the group that person represents, I want to focus on the language many such letters contain. I find a striking similarity in the terms used when Messianic Jews are referred to. They are called "renegade Jews" whose avowed purpose is to "seduce other Jews away from their faith." Words like "subterfuge", "dishonesty", "ensnaring", "brainwashing" and the like recur time and again in the polemical literature about these people. It almost begins to sound like the cultic incantation of phrases by people who are opposed to cults and their practices.

In general one gets the feeling that what is conveyed here is the existence of a sinister Jewish-Christian plot, a conspiracy to undermine Judaism itself. From the Jewish point of view the accusation of alleged deceit becomes understandable to some degree in light of the fact that the very claim that one is Hebrew Christian, a Messianic Jew or a Jew for Jesus is considered a contradiction in terms. To hold the opposite view as a Jew, contrary to the consensus of the community at large, and thus to reject what is viewed as simple logic, can easily become interpreted as willful ignorance, and thus dishonesty.

To go further and embellish on the claim with elements from the traditional Jewish milieu in order to communicate one's Christian beliefs to other Jews makes things even worse; it evokes anger and recriminations in the community these people are felt to have left. I once heard the complaint that Jews for Jesus won't hesitate to use "Jewish humor", an observation that struck me as rather funny. Can one really expect that conversion will cure a human being of a characteristic like a sense of humor that has been nurtured by the culture in which that person has been raised?

But, what is essentially an internal Jewish debate soon becomes expanded to involve the Christian community as well. The churches too, it is said, should be offended by the views of Messianic Jews. Why? Well, it is claimed, by blurring the distinctions between Judaism and Christianity these people negate the uniqueness of both faiths and in essence make a mockery of them. Therefore, Christians are urged to join Jewish leaders in condemning any person who holds and propagates such views. He or she ought to be made a *persona non grata* in both communities. Some Christian groups, like the Long Island Council of Churches for instance (partly, I'm sure, out of a sense of loyalty and solidarity with Jewish leaders), have gone on record publicly condemning Messianic Jews and accusing them of dishonesty. At least, they came very close to doing that. Their statement actually mentioned "alleged dishonest conversionary tactics employed by such groups as Jews for Jesus, B'Nai Yeshuah and the Unification Church."

It seems to me that two points need to be raised here. First of all, the use of the word "alleged" makes one wonder whether those Christian leaders had made any attempt to enter into dialogue with the Christians they were condemning. After all, the Long Island Council of Churches is an organization dedicated to ecumenicity.

Secondly, what was the purpose of mentioning Messianic Jews in one breath, so to say, with the Moonies? I can see that adherents of another faith community may feel justified in suggesting such a forced marriage, but it seems to me basically unfair, and even somewhat dishonest, for the Long Island Council of Churches to do so.

I realize that the Long Island situation was aggravated at the time by the activities of evangelist Mike Evans, who was busily raising funds to complete the building of a center in the region specifically designed for the training of missionaries to the Jews. Obviously, this became a highly emotional issue in the Jewish community and, understandably, Jewish leaders looked to Christian dialogue partners for support in their resistance to this venture. But I am concerned that some of my friends in the Christian-Jewish dialogue movement may show excessive eagerness to demonstrate their good faith as dialogue partners by issuing blanket condemnations and leveling accusations of bad faith against other Christians without making an honest effort to engage in dialogue or to distinguish between various groups. No good is to be served if the much needed internal Christian debate on these issues is aborted prematurely.

In the meantime, to the vast majority of Christians all this looks like a rather baffling affair. Most, unfortunately, do not know very much about history, particularly the history of Christian anti-Judaism, and, therefore, are not attuned very well to Jewish sensitivities. But some of them do read their Bibles and begin to wonder whether they are being asked to agree with the proposition that the apostle Paul and the early (Hebrew) Christians were all imposters. After all, their message and behavior were by and large rather similar to that of Messianic Jews today.

A conspiracy mentality and all the pressures that tend to accompany it, are not very conducive to the development of a historical consciousness and the insights as well as sympathies such a consciousness can provide to deal with today's dilemmas. Not all young adults who join Hebrew-Christian groups are hopelessly neurotic; many of them are honestly searching for something that will give meaning to their lives and "answers" to the inner struggles of their souls. Furthermore, all the talk about seduction and subterfuge seems to ignore the fact that in the main we are dealing with one of the better educated groups in the nation and that quite a few members of these Messianic communities have been recruited on the campuses of some of the best colleges and universities in the country.

True, in a sense they are vulnerable, as is every person who ventures forth on a spiritual/intellectual journey. There are problems we ought to look at. But they will not be resolved by attacking those who are engaged in the battle of people's minds, be they Christian, Jewish or adherents of some sort of ideology. I find profound irony in a commentary by Carl Alpert, published in *The Jewish Week* (May 11, 1984), which deals with a story about a group of parents who had organized themselves to combat missionary activities among Israeli youths. There were allegations of compulsion, kidnappings and even hypnosis. "They have brainwashed my daughter, and she is now estranged from our family," one parent is quoted as saying. But the "culprits" in this story were not Christians or cultists who were trying to get Jewish youths in their clutches; the attack was conducted by angry parents against "Jewish missionaries" who had even persuaded some of these young adults to join a yeshiva.

I realize, of course, that the issue of Messianic Judaism has dimensions and dilemmas all its own. Those dilemmas are rooted in a long and bitter history. Hence, the issue ought to be approached more in terms of tragedy than in terms of conspiracy. In this position I am basically aligning myself with views I found expressed in Simon Schoon's book entitled *Christian Presence in the Jewish State*, mentioned before. Schoon, for a number of years pastor of the Christian Moshav Nes Ammim in the Haifa region, received his doctorate in theology on the basis of this dissertation. His non-missionary stance as well as that of the Nes Ammim community are widely recognized in both Jewish and Christian circles.

His discussions of some Hebrew Christian groups are certainly not uncritical. Nonetheless, in light of history he sees their lot basically in terms of tragedy. He makes the point that "the Jewish Christians may not become the victims of the growing desire for dialogue with the Jewish community" (p. 232), maintaining that as churches we must respect their right to define their own identity both inside and outside of the Church. Reflecting on those sentiments, I came to the conclusion that they expressed concern that was developing in my own mind. Schoon's study is mentioned without suggesting that anyone but myself bear responsibility for what is being said in this chapter.

Personally, I do not share many of the views and practices of the groups under discussion. As pointed out earlier, all witness needs to be handled with a good deal of honest self-appraisal. Our motives tend to be mixed, most of all when we are engaged in such noble activities as the saving of souls or the raising of funds for good causes. What could possibly tempt us more to pious self-righteousness than the claims that we are giving testimony to the Lord, especially when we do so to those whom we consider his chosen people. The end so easily comes to justify questionable means.

But the same is true when we fight those whom we consider to be heterodox. As a church member my main concern is with Christian responses to Messianic Jews. Have we ever tried to engage in honest dialogue with them, really listening to them and attempting to understand their experiences? Is it a valid Christian position to say that they blur the distinctions between Christianity and Judaism and thus make a mockery out of both? From a Christian point of view and from the perspective of Christian origins, that strikes me as at least debatable. They do indeed deny the absolute incompatibility of the two faiths and they do affirm the legitimacy of a Hebrew-Christian lifestyle and worship form. One may disagree with these positions, but is that enough ground for declaring them to be heretics along the lines of the ancient Judaizers or for questioning their integrity? I do not think so.

All the talk about dishonesty and conspiracy strikes me as too simple. Isn't it at least partly true that those Messianic Jews are caught in a trap and ought we not admit that the trap was set by gentile Christian history? In the previous paragraph I referred to Christian origins, which seems right to do. At the same time I believe that it should always be done with great reluctance. After all we ought to know what has happened since. Still, I would hate to see certain believers, Jews who, perhaps mistakenly, but, in many cases, honestly seek to make the early Hebrew-Christian community a model for today, be made to pay the price for the sins of Christian history. I am afraid some of that is going on in the drive to discredit all Messianic Jews.

They are a reality in our midst. I note some disagreements among Jewish commentators as to the threat they pose to the community. Some Jewish leaders speak in terms of a crisis situation and seem to view the expansion of the Hebrew-Christian movement as an explosive one. Others claim that evangelizing efforts directed at Jews continue to be an unsuccessful venture; what has really exploded is counter-missionary activities and hence anti-missionary publicity. The truth probably lies somewhere in between. My observations lead me to believe that we are witnessing a persistent albeit gradual growth of the Messianic Jewish movement, both in Israel and in other parts of the world.

If that is correct, we can expect continued repercussions in the Christian-Jewish dialogue movement. Are there ways of handling the situation more creatively than we have often done in the past? It is not going to be easy. There is both anguish and anger in the Jewish rejection of other

Jews who, they feel, have forsaken the faith and broken the covenant relationship. In the background, I repeat, is the burden that the Jewish people bear of a long history of persecution, sometimes not only permitted but even perpetrated by Christians. Centuries of agony are not wiped out by a few years of more or less friendly dialogue sessions.

The situation is not helped by the fact that converts frequently come across as hypercritical and condescending toward the traditions of their people by advertising themselves as "fulfilled" or "completed" Jews. No matter what they are trying to say, it must surely be clear to them what other Jews hear them say. It all sounds so terribly like the old Christian triumphalism which, it would appear to many listeners, those converts have swallowed hook, line and sinker. There must be better and less offensive ways of expressing whatever blessings one has found in the Christian faith. True, the New Testament speaks of the "scandal of the cross", but that is not to suggest that we can add our own self-righteous offensiveness in the name of Christian witness.

On the other hand, there is also anguish in the position of many Messianic Jews who often see themselves as entrapped in a no-win situation; the harder they try to retain elements of their Jewish heritage, the harsher become the criticisms and accusations of dishonesty. Add to that the suspicions that are often aroused by such attempts in the Christian community, and one can understand why these people may come to see themselves as condemned to a spiritual no-man's land.

Historically one of the great problems for Jewish converts to Christianity has been that they became absorbed in a basically Hellenised church. They may originally have been attracted by the figure of the Jew Jesus and by the message of salvation that the New Testament presents as rooted in his cross and resurrection. But in the end, church membership has meant that converts and their families have become assimilated into a de-Judaized movement, a church which in most cases is hardly aware of the Hebraic characteristics of the New Testament. Once, very early in Christian history, things may have been different, but that past is hidden behind many centuries of bad history.

Messianic Jews say in effect, "Let's try to start all over". They want to integrate their encounter with Jesus and the message of the gospel as they have come to understand it with the heritage of their forebears. In seeking to initiate new beginnings, they open old wounds. For the Jewish community there is too much remembrance. In the churches there has been far too little remembrance and hence a sad lack of genuine repentance. And so the experiment with the "impossible possibility" ends up in pain, a pain for which this moment in history seems to be able to provide little healing.

And what about the future? I would not wish to hazard a guess. However, both Judaism and Christianity are faiths that seek to keep hope alive. Hope, in essence, never says "never".[10]

---

[10]On Christmas Day, 1989, the Israeli Supreme Court once again ruled that Messianic Jews are not entitled to automatic Israeli citizenship. Belief in Jesus was adjudged to be tantamount to abandoning the Jewish faith and community. This case was decided on an appeal by Gary and Shirley Beresford, a couple from Zimbabwe, who were both born Jewish, had not been baptized or joined an established Christian denomination, but publicly affirmed their faith in Jesus as the Messiah of Israel. Justice Elon, in his 100-page decision, once again appealed to historic experience when he wrote that "messianic Jews attempt to reverse the wheels of history by 2000 years" (*New York Times* December 27, 1989). It is significant, however, that Justice Elon used the occasion to question the opinion of Justice Silberg in the Brother Daniel Rufeisen case, that, according to Halacha, one who is born a Jew is always a Jew. Apparently, this is still true for persons who renounce their faith by declaring themselves atheists, but not for those who continue to believe in the God of Abraham, Isaac and Jacob, but also affirm their faith in Jesus.

XII

History: Horror and the Challenge of Hope

Is the glass of Christian-Jewish dialogue half full or half empty? Sometimes I am inclined to answer one way, sometimes the other. One thing can be said with certainty: our cup is far from running over.[11]

---

[11]Events that occurred during Holy Week 1990, once again showed how political gamesmanship by both Christians and Jews can adversely affect constructive dialogue. On the one hand, the Middle East Council of Churches, in a blatant attempt to politicize Holy Week observances across the world, distributed a "Prayer from Jerusalem" to denominations in many countries, requesting that it be read from the pulpit on Palm Sunday. The document was so patently partisan in its pro-Palestinian stance, that leaders of a number of European churches rejected this shameless attempt to use the most sacred week of the Christian calendar for propaganda purposes out of hand. In the United States, the National Council of Christians and Jews also issued a protest. Sad to say, however, several church bureaucracies, my own denomination's included, mindlessly followed the suggestions of the Middle East Council of Churches, and sent the "Prayer" to all local congregations.

On the other hand, an armed group of settlers in Israel moved into St. John's Hospice, near the Church of the Holy Sepulchre, on Good Friday eve, after obtaining a lease from an Armenian businessman. The fact that Israeli government funds were involved in this transaction was particularly troubling to many Christians as well as Jews. Equally troubling were the reactions of some members of the Greek Orthodox hierarchy, who suddenly treated this neglected and abandoned building, which had been advertised as being for sale in several church newsletters, as a Holy Site that had been invaded by Jews.

The St. John's Hospice transaction is now subject to litigation in the Israeli courts, and in the interim most of the Jewish residents have been evacuated. In the end, the key issue is not whether Jews have a right to live in that section of Jerusalem, just as the key issue with the Auschwitz convent was not whether nuns had the right to pray there. The basic question is one of sensitivity to the delicate balances that must be maintained if interreligious relationships are to contribute to world harmony, rather than hateful tensions.

But nevertheless, some historical dynamics have been set into motion. More people are engaged in a more honest quest for open dialogue. An increasing number of Christians are raising a growing number of questions about missionary practices. Some education curricula have been revised for the better. Christians join with Jews for Yom Hashoah services, and so forth and so on.

What has all this accomplished? I agree with Howard Singer's conclusion in his (May 1987) *Commentary* article, "The Rise and Fall of Interfaith Dialogue," that the movement has achieved more than was conceivable 50 years ago but less than many people had hoped for. However, when he then adds that "there seems little prospect that their hopes will be more fully realized in the future" (p. 55), one has to wonder how long or how short a view of the future he holds. After all, the dialogue as we know it today can be measured only in decades.

Some will no doubt say that I myself, while pointing to positive development, have put the emphasis too heavily on the side of pessimism. Well, I hardly consider myself an optimist about human nature or about historical movements. But I am basically a hopeful person. I agree with Pierre Teilhard de Chardin that people of faith are "pilgrims of the future". There is a biblical futurism that cannot be captured by such categories as optimism or pessimism. So, I conclude this book with a few reflections on history, memory and human responsibility.

Martin Buber stated in his book *Prophetic Faith* that "the world of prophetic faith is, in fact, historic reality seen in the bold and penetrating glance of the man who dares to believe." (p. 135) People who live in this world as those who dare to believe, as for example prophets, cannot adequately be described either as optimists or pessimists. Their faith, however, does tend to have a quality about it that gives them courage to face today and hope to move toward tomorrow.

According to Thomas Carlyle, history is at bottom, "the biography of great men," the story of heroes. But recent history has taught us once again with unmistakable clarity that an Adolph Hitler, hailed by multitudes of people as a great and heroic deliverer, can inflict horror and death upon millions. In this connection we are reminded of the fact that in Christian tradition suffering rather than heroism has often been seen as the interpretive principle of history. Therefore, the symbol of the cross has become central to many Christian philosophies of history.

To someone like Nicolas Berdyaev, with little interest in theology in the traditional sense, the historical process itself became a basic source of suffering. His constant complaint was that man is nailed to the cross of time. To him, time as measured by the clock and the calendar represented transitoriness, tragedy and failure. What he called "common time", as distinguished from the creative existential moment, condemns people to live in what he considered to be an unreal world. History must be transcended and the way that is done is through ecstasy. Thus we can be saved for the real world and touch eternity in the midst of fallen time.

For most Christian theologians the problem is not history as such, but human sin. Not "fallen time" but "fallen humanity" has distorted the reality of the good creation. The cross of Christ. became the central symbol of human sin, but also of divine love. In his 1949 study *Meaning in History* (note, not the meaning *of* history), Karl Löwith wrote that "nothing else than the life and death of Jesus Christ, the 'Suffering Servant', who was deserted and crucified, can be the standard of a Christian understanding of the world's history." The scandal of the cross becomes a central interpretive principle of "the way things are".

Others do not wish to focus so exclusively on the cross in their interpretation of history. They emphasize a message of the cross and the resurrection. The cross is not only the symbol of human sin and the horrors of history; it is also the source of healing and a new kind of power. The power of the cross lies in the triumph of love. In such a context we are introduced to a new kind of hero, the person who (in analogy to the Divine Being) enters into the suffering of others.

After attending a preview of the film "The Courage to Care," which is a movie about people who risked their own lives in order to rescue Jews from the horror of the Holocaust, I mentioned to a guest from Holland that the film featured a Dutch woman. When asked for her name and I told him, he replied, "I can tell you that she is a big unknown." But that, it seems to me, is precisely the point. Here we are talking about the heroism of the non-famous, the non-celebrities. I like to call it "the heroism of the common life", of men and women who in the midst of a grabbing and greedy world have the courage to do the decent thing. They do not achieve high standing, like General Secretary of the United Nations for example; nor do they worry too much about their *curricula vitae*, neither to hide their past nor to be honored. These people, in a not very conscious fashion, live lives that are a true expression of a theology of the cross and the resurrection.

But now we face a new horror, one that is closely related to the horrors of the Holocaust. Because the simple fact is that in the course of Christian history the norm (certainly as far as the Jews were concerned) has been the exact opposite of such demonstrations of love. The cross, rather than becoming the symbol of Christian identification with the sufferings of others, became a weapon to hurt others, a symbol of hatred against those accused of being "Christ-killers". It all sounds so incredible, almost like the ultimate absurdity, but such is the truth. When people tell us from personal experience how, in certain countries during their childhood years, they would cross the street rather than pass in front of a church because Jewish children often were beaten up, they are not making up a story. They are telling us the crazy truth about certain aspects of Christian history. The most incredible thing about it all is that the beatings usually increased during the Christmas and Lenten seasons.

Let me quote somewhat extensively from an article I wrote some years ago for the *Reformed Journal* (May 1982).

> ". . .when it came to their relationship with God, Christians have usually interpreted the cross in terms of reconciliation, unmerited love for sinful human beings, and divine identification with the needs of the world. Its message became one of comfort to people who knew themselves to be unworthy. But, what happened when it came to Christians' encounters with Jews? In that case, in a spirit of incredible self-righteousness and cruel malice, the cross was frequently turned into a crusader's sword—a curse against the people who were called 'Christ-killers,' an instrument of scapegoating that has set the stage for persecutions, pogroms, and holocausts. "In the novel *The Last of the Just*, by Andre Schwartz-Bart, Golda asks Ernie, 'Tell me why do Christians hate

191

us the way they do? They seem so nice when I can look at them without my star.' ' "It's very mysterious,' replies Ernie. 'They don't know exactly why themselves. . .Do you know who Christ was? A simple Jew like your father. A kind of Hasid. . .'He was really a good Jew, you know sort of like the Baal Shem Tov—a merciful man, and gentle. The Christians say they love him, but I think they hate him without knowing it. So they take the cross by the other end and make a sword out of it and strike us with it! You understand, Golda', he cried suddenly, strangely excited, 'they take the cross and they turn it around, they turn it around, my God. . .'

"Sholem Asch, who is best known for his books *The Nazarene, The Apostle* and *Mary*, wrote a booklet entitled *One Destiny: an Epistle to Christians*. There he presents his spiritual credo that Judaism and Christianity are two parts of a single whole. Referring to the crucifixion, he states: "The legend about the Jewish crucifixion of the Messiah has cost millions of Jewish lives. It carries a long streak of blood after it, right down to our own time. It has become the microbe of hate in the spiritual body of Christianity. It has caused and still causes daily trouble for the Jews. It brings tears to mothers, anxieties and terrors to children. I myself suffered throughout my childhood from the accusation of blood guilt. Every Christian holiday was transformed by the legend into a day of fear and sorrow for Jews."

"'That cross makes me shudder,' said a Jewish woman to Father Edward H. Flannery as they passed by a cross displayed in New York City at Christmas time. 'It is like an evil presence.'"

Still, it took me a long time to discover the true dimensions of Christian culpability with respect to anti-Jewish measure throughout the centuries. It is not the kind of thing most students are taught in theological seminaries. Some have heard about the fourth century church father John Chrysostom, who was known as "the golden tongued preacher," but whose mouth spewed venom when he spoke about the Jews. There is in general vague familiarity with the fact that Luther in his later years said some vicious things about Jews. But, by and large, there is little awareness that we are not dealing with unfortunate "incidents" in Christian history, aberrations from the norm, but rather with a continuous saga that goes from generation to generation, from century to century. The moments of respite and tolerance, not persecution, were the exception.

Even for a person with my background it takes a profound reeducation to discover what the true story is. The lack is not historical data, nor is the problem a shortage of sound and solid research. The crisis of the Christian community lies much deeper than that. It has to do with our refusal to deal with memory as a moral issue. In Christian theological terms, the problem lies in our reluctance to engage in genuine confession, our resistance to repentance, and hence our failure to find new freedom though forgiveness.

Alan Ecclestone is right when he observes in his book *The Night Sky of the Lord* that "the Holocaust has not been felt in the marrow bones of contemporary Christian life." (p. 99) True, what is being asked of us is a very hard thing to do. Father Edward H. Flannery has described his well-known study *The Anguish of the Jews* as "an invitation to Christian heritage, to undergo what might be called a historical psychoanalysis. . .". (p. 3) That means that we are being asked to enter into an experience that is bound to be extremely painful.

Remembrance is a moral, even a divine, imperative. Abraham Joshua Heschel has taught us that what the Bible requires can be compressed into one word: REMEMBER. Even if that might be considered an overstatement, that would not invalidate the central truth that this remark contains. For instance, the repeated and urgent admonitions in Deuteronomy that the people should not forget are rooted in the view that forgetfulness can be a form of unfaithfulness; memory is not just a matter of the mind but a moral issue.

There is such a thing as a slip of the mind. But, that is a wholly different matter from what concerns us here. When the one-time General Secretary of the United Nations, Kurt Waldheim, has a hard time getting his bio together, then we are not dealing with a problem of recollection, but rather with a flaw of character, a failure of moral nerve.

In George Orwell's book *1984* we find described a world in which three basic principles prevail: newspeak, doublethink and the mutability of the past. Whenever the past does not suit the purposes of the powers that be, they simply discard it, declare it inoperative and a non-happening. There is no memory in that world. Statues, inscriptions, memorial stones and monuments—anything that might shed light on the past—have been systematically altered. Such a world is every dictator's dream. Sometimes such dictators receive support from professors who have degrees from highly respectable academic institutions. They are in fact propagandists who disguise themselves as educators. For instance, the work of pseudo-scholars, like the historical revisionists in our day who deny that the Holocaust ever happened, is so dangerous because it has a basically totalitarian impulse behind it.

The burden of memory is at heart the burden of our humanity. There is something glorious about our ability to come to terms with the past— our national, church and family histories. By facing history, we face ourselves. But this is precisely the freedom of the human spirit from which we all too frequently seek to escape.

In the words of the poet Shelley, "the world is weary of the past, oh might it die or rest at last!" It is that sentiment that causes people to say they are tired of hearing about the Holocaust. Let bygones be bygones! Some people anxiously warn that no good will come from rehashing past history; it will provoke annoyance and anger among those who do not wish to hear. But as Elie Wiesel has pointed out with never ceasing passion: If this generation does not remember, will there be a next generation? After all, in the final analysis, it is not the past but the future that is at stake.

For the sake of the future it is so crucial that we cultivate a sense of history. It is troublesome when Johnny cannot read or if Mary doesn't know how to count. But equally troublesome is how many of our young people lack a sense of historical consciousness and context. I recall a letter to the *New York Times* a few years ago, written by Jean Mayer, the President of Tuft University, in which he claimed that a lack of a sense of history is the single biggest deficiency in otherwise bright high school students who apply to our top colleges.[12]

---

[12]The Palestinian uprising, which is usually referred to as the *intifada*, started in December 1988, shortly after I had finished writing this book. Thus, what in broader context is clearly an Arab-Israel conflict, has become ever more sharply focused on "the Palestinian question." For several decades after the re-birth of the State of Israel in 1948, the Arab states had no inclination whatsoever to promote the idea of a Palestinian identity. Hence, no effort was made to establish a Palestinian state in the region west of the Jordan and in Gaza before Israel took control of those territories during the 1967 war.

Critics of Israel love to quote the now famous remark by Golda Meir to the effect that there was no such thing as a Palestinian people in Palestine, who claimed a Palestinian identity separate from their Arab brothers and sisters. In fact, Ms. Meir had a good deal of historical evidence on her side. The very name Palestine lay dormant for almost 2000 years, until the post-World War I era. At that time Arab sources generally contested the use of the designation "Palestinian," while Jewish pioneers adopted it with alacrity, attaching the name to many of the earliest institutions they established.

While one can quarrel with details in Joan Peters' historical research on the Palestinian issue (*From Time Immemorial*, Harper & Row, 1984), her basic thesis that Palestinian nationalism is a relatively late development seems to me indisputable.

By the same token, over the past few decades a growing Palestinian identity has developed as a powerful historical reality. There is no sense denying that, or to expect that it will just die off. It seems more likely that it will gain in intensity, and friends of Israel in the Christian community might do well to face these historical realities more frankly than has often been done in the past.

Rosemary and Herman Ruether, in their book *The Wrath of Jonah* (Harper & Row, 1989), call for a re-consideration of certain Christian positions, and they provide a good deal of historical data that could be helpful in a renewed dialogue on these issues. Unfortunately, however, their book is so permeated with an anti-Zionist animus and so unbalanced in its treatment of Christian positions with which the authors disagree, that it will probably contribute more to further polarization than to reconciliation.

There are those who suggest that, in order for a rapprochement to take place, both Jews and Arabs must stop marshalling historical arguments, since they will lead only to dead-end roads. I disagree. Historical amnesia is never helpful in the solving of conflicts. The question it seems to me, is whether an historical perspective can be part of the discussions while at the same time the parties refuse to be captives of the past. Anwar Sadat and Menachem Begin were capable of the dramatic and daring gesture that could lead to a breakthrough. Unfortunately, at

This is an age of immediacy. We live in the era of the TV image. Every day millions of people view the world through the eye of a camera lens, controlled in many instances by people who are more interested in emotional impact than in historical context. Complex situations like the Middle East are dealt with in 30-second commentaries by celebrities for whom ratings, rather than remembrance, are a survival issue.

My point is not that the emotional dimensions of life should be ignored or that the media are to be blamed for all our problems. Modern technology simply tends to expose our weaknesses on a larger scale. Historical amnesia was a well-known phenomenon before the invention of television. It is as old as our natural tendency toward intellectual laziness, reinforced at times by ulterior motives and a nastiness of spirit.

Henry Ford I, who did not achieve fame because of his philosophical insights, is known to have pontificated on the subject of history. His views can be summed up in his somewhat philistine conclusion that history is "mostly bunk". Now let us remember that this same man, who held such a low view of history, used the *Dearborn Independent*, a paper totally dependent on the Ford fortunes, to propagate anti-Semitic forgeries like the *Protocols of the Learned Elders of Zion* as historical fact. Thus we have a classic illustration of George Santayana's dictum that those who will not remember the past may well be condemned to repeat it. Unfortunately, when we repeat the past, we tend to repeat its worst features.

In recent history the Bitburg incident has become a sad reminder of

---

present the predominant figures in the Middle East display little inclination to follow in their footsteps. Hence, the stalemate in peace negotiations, while the stockpile of the most poisonous and destructive weapons in the region is growing by the day. On the one hand, it is hard to see how a Palestinian state, dominated by Arafat's PLO as presently constituted, would contribute to peace in the region. On the other hand, it is hard to see how the *status quo* or Yitzhak Shamir's talk about the need for a "big Israel" to accommodate a big immigration can lead to anything but further tension and bloodshed. Perhaps our best hope right now is for new leaders to emerge, who dare to try new approaches.

what happens when historical amnesia sets in. Here we saw a world leader, the President of the United States, demonstrate a tragic lack of sensitivity because he basically lacks a sense of history. In this case the blow came, not from an enemy, but from someone whose record toward the Jewish people and Israel had been a positive one. But this only goes to show that historical amnesia does not pose less of a danger to our future when it is manifested in the lives and actions of well-meaning people.

It seemed eminently appropriate that on the Bitburg issue President Reagan was personally confronted by Elie Wiesel, who has become one of the most authoritative voices against forgetfulness in the world today. With consuming passion he has become a witness to horror. Still, while he could hardly be described as an optimist, he is definitely not a prophet of despair. It is also clear that he is not a man without humor. That, I believe, is in large measure due to the fact that he is not a man without hope. His writings are much more than a witness to inhumanity; they are a call to a sense of responsibility rooted in a basic affirmation of life.

Elie Wiesel has played a key role in making the Holocaust a subject of conscious reflection and extensive research. He was one of the first to break the silence that had prevailed for some decades after World War II. I think this silent interval was needed, especially by the victims who were facing the task of rebuilding their lives. The silence did not mean that those people were not dealing with the experiences of the hell through which they had passed. It was precisely their daily struggles with the horrendous realities of the Holocaust that gave their daily decisions about starting anew, establishing families and assuming social-political responsibilities such a quality of courage.

But eventually the memories were vocalized more and more. The Holocaust became a central concern also in Christian circles, especially among those who recognized that this period of horrors was, in a very real sense, a chapter in Christian history. For some theologians the Holocaust was to be a preoccupation in their moral, spiritual and intellectual pursuits. Theirs was often a lonely journey, because there was an inclination among many scholars to give their research little serious consideration.

Nevertheless, because of the perseverance of the few, we now see a growing interest in Holocaust studies, the establishment of Holocaust institutes, the development of Holocaust curricula, annual Holocaust observances and the like.

   At first, I must confess, I felt ambivalent about this persistent emphasis upon the Holocaust and concerned that we might become captives of our preoccupations with the past. For many, especially those of us who lived under Nazi rule as young people, the experience had been one of intense immediacy and concreteness. We knew precisely who the enemy was and what needed to be done. They needed to be killed through acts of underground sabotage; their armies needed to be defeated by the allies and their reign of terror brought to an end. There was little reflection about it all.

   After the war, not least for the sake of our own emotional/spiritual health, we needed to come to terms with the hatreds that had been so unquestionably nurtured in our souls. When does the moment come that one concludes that enough is enough? When, in a world where new horrors were being perpetrated, did one make a commitment to work for the future? I wasn't sure that such a strong focus on the Holocaust would be helpful in the task humanity was facing.

   However, the more I learned to view the Holocaust in terms of a broader history, the more I became persuaded that the intense reflections and the persistent research on the Holocaust might indeed help us to work for a better future with new insights and wisdom. As Rabbi Nahman of Bratslav has said, "In remembering lies the secret of redemption." Without memory we will have a hard time discovering our destiny. Historical amnesia can so easily become a way of life, a way of living in dishonesty and thus an escape from responsibility.

   I have become convinced that Holocaust studies and Holocaust observances can indeed serve a redeeming purpose in our society. At the same time I have also developed new ambivalences. Holocaust concerns are themselves in danger of becoming poisoned by elements of commercialism or even hucksterism. The endless Holocaust conferences circuit, the never ending fundraising efforts, the grantmanship, the rivalries between Holocaust bureaucracies, the career seekers, the hunger for publicity: these and similar factors become the seeds of a Holocaust politics that is the more distasteful because it is done in the name of defending holy ground.

When I first heard a Jewish Federation executive use the phrase "there is no business like Shoah business," I was shocked. But the more sacred the cause, the greater is the need that we face up to the danger signals. The U.S. Holocaust Memorial Council, established by an act of Congress in order that a museum might be built in Washington, D.C. to keep alive the memory of the martyrs and to hold before future generations the lessons we have learned about the nature and consequences of bigotry, became itself the battlefield of clashing interests and egos in conflict. The January 16-22, 1987 issue of the *Jewish World* in New York carried the following headline: "Holocaust Museum tangled in its own barbed wire." The story that followed gave the unedifying account of bitter infighting among Council members and staff, a situation that had been the subject of rumors for months.

The theology department of the university featured in John Updike's novel *Roger's Version* has among its faculty members a specialist in "holocaustics". It is sad to see the Holocaust associated with tongue-in-cheek descriptions of vanity and pomposity. On the other hand, we need to recognize that we ourselves invite ridicule when we treat the Holocaust as if it were another fad to be manipulated for professional and financial interests.[13]

It is a sin to use the Holocaust in ways that will breed cynicism. It is a betrayal of the memory of those who have died, many of them hoping that humanity would yet come to its senses. Cynicism, like forgetfulness,

---

[13] A recent article by Judith Miller in the *New York Times Sunday Magazine* (April 22, 1990) presents further evidence of continued infighting among the Holocaust Memorial Council members. When President Reagan unveiled the museum's cornerstone in October 1988, one of the prime movers of this project, Elie Wiesel, chose not to attend, because he felt that the atmosphere surrounding the project had become too political. Wealthy real estate developers in Washington, D.C. had become the main players in the Council's leadership. Eventually, large donors succeeded in having their family names attached to major segments of the building, like the auditorium and the cinema-lecture hall. How trivial and vulgar does all this seem, especially when done in the name of the sacred memory of Hitler's victims!

poses a threat to our future. It undermines faith, dims the sparks of hope that are still aglow in the world and weakens people's motivation to engage in loving and responsible actions.

"Remembering for the Future" is the theme of a conference to be held in Great Britain during 1988. The folder announcing the events states that "the purpose of the International Conference on the Impact of the Holocaust and Genocide on Jews and Christians is twofold. It is intended to fix the memory of the past in unforgettable form. At the same time it aims to blaze a trail of hope for the future. The lessons of the Holocaust must be used to emphasize the virtues of understanding and respect for all faiths and all people." These are noble and hopeful goals. They represent a vision that can be kept alive only if we refuse to succumb to the kind of Holocaust politics referred to above.

The conference organizers speak about blazing a trail of hope, not about igniting the fires of guilt. But, are not those of us who are calling the churches to confront the past of Christian anti-Judaism really trying to put a guilt trip upon our co-believers? That question is raised with monotonous frequency. I would say that our aim is the exact opposite. What the world needs now is not more guilt-ridden Christians. Unresolved guilt is one of the worst forms of captivity to the past. Rather than turning people into "pilgrims of the future", it leads to paralysis and simmering resentment. We are calling for "creative memory", a facing of the past, a confession of Christian complicity in persecution that will lead to a sense of forgiveness and thus to a new freedom for the future.

Through memory we can shape destiny. "Life can only be understood backwards; but it must be lived forwards," wrote Sören Kierkegaard. Even in the darkest moments of history we can discover glimmers of hope. For instance, the Holocaust has its endless horror stories. They must be told. But there is are also stories of human decency and responsibility. They, too, must be told, because they constitute signposts of hope. They speak of character, courage and self-sacrifice.

What turns people into haters? We need to try and find out. On the other hand, what makes people do the humane thing, even in some instances when it endangers them and their families? We need to research that as well. Dr. Samuel P. Oliver, a sociologist at Humboldt University and himself a survivor who was helped by non-Jewish friends, apparently is doing precisely that in what he called the "Altruistic Personality Project".

We need memory and we need vision. Memory without vision can easily turn into a state of morbidity. Vision without memory will eventually either lead to utopian fantasies or to a nostalgia that pursues a past that never was. None of these can serve as a sound basis for moral-spiritual renewal. They are not motivating forces that give hope for the future.

One of the most inspiring stories of memory and vision is the history of the Jewish people and their love affair with the land of Israel. Few have written about that story with greater poetic fervor than the late Abraham Joshua Heschel in his book *Israel: an Echo of Eternity*. Let me cite a few passages:

> "Why did our hearts and minds throughout the ages turn to Erets Israel, to the Holy Land? Because of memory, because of hope, because of distress.

> Because of memory. There is a slow and silent stream, a stream not of oblivion but of memory, from which we must constantly drink before entering the realm of faith. To believe is to remember. The substance of our very being is memory, our way of living is retaining the reminders, articulating memory.

> Jewish memory, far from turning into a collection of stale reminiscences, was kept alive by the power of hope and imagination, transcending the limits of believing (p. 60/61) . . .

> Perhaps the most characteristic quality of Jewish existence is *bittahon* ("hope"). Believing and hoping are one. It is part of our very existence to be faithful to the future, to keep alive the beginning by nursing the vision of the end. Hope is the creative articulation of faith (p. 94) . . .

201

> What lends meaning to history? The promise of the future. If there is no promise, there is no meaningful history. Significance is contingent on vision and anticipation, on living the future in the present tense.
>
> This is one of the gifts of the Bible to the world: a promise, a vision, a hope." (p. 127)

The story of Zion is a story of repeated destruction, suffering and the shedding of tears in many strange lands. Is is also a story of hope kept alive through some of the darkest moments of history. Zionism represents a historical movement through which that hope was translated into actions that laid the foundation for a new future. The Zionist pioneers in the end convinced a people who might well have succumbed to a total sense of powerlessness that it is not the will of God that we be victims, but rather that we should be partners in fulfilling the divine plan for humanity.

And so Israel was re-born. It is not the ideal society. Far from it. But it is one of the great signs of hope in modern history. Israel represents a triumph of the human spirit in the post-Holocaust era.

Christians who seek dialogue with Jews but avoid the subject of Israel deprive the churches of one of the most hopeful potentials that such a dialogue can produce. On the other hand, Christians who romanticize Israel in the name of love for the Jewish people may also miss an opportunity to learn important lessons from the Jewish experience. Together we are "pilgrims of the future". In spite of horrendous disasters and failures, the future beckons us to dare to believe and, trusting in the faithfulness of God, to choose life and not death. L'Chayim!

Barth, Markus *Israel and the Church* Richmond: John Knox, 1969

Buber, Martin *Prophetic Faith* New York: Harper & Brothers, 1960

Croner, Helga (Ed.) *Stepping Stones to Further Jewish-Christian Relations* New York: Stimulus Books, 1977

Ecclestone, Alan *The Night Sky of the Lord* New York, Schocken Books, 1982

Flannery, Edward H. *The Anguish of the Jews* (Revised and Updated) New York: Stimulus Books, Paulist Press, 1985

Grose, Peter *Israel in the Mind of America* New York: Alfred A. Knopf, 1983

Halsell, Grace *Prophecy and Politics: Militant Evangelists on the Road to Nuclear War* Westport: Lawrence Hill and Company, 1986

Heschel, Abraham Joshua *Israel: An Echo of Eternity* New York: Farrar, Straus & Giroux, 1967

Kenen, I. L. *Israel's Defense Line: Her Friends and Foes in Washington* Buffalo: Prometheus Books, 1981

Kennedy, Moorhead *The Ayatollah in the Cathedral* New York: Hill and Wang, 1986

Metz, Johann Baptist *The Emergent Church* New York: Crossroad Publ., 1986

Morley, John F. *Vatican Diplomacy and Jews During the Holocaust—1939-1943* New York: KTAV, 1980

Nijim, Basheer K. (Ed.) *American Church Politics and the Middle East* Belmont, (Mass.): Association of Arab-American University Graduates, Inc., 1982

Paulk, Earl *To Whom is God Betrothed: Examining the Biblical Basis for Support of National Israel* Atlanta: K. Dimension Publ., N. D.

Pieters, Albertus *The Seed of Abraham* Grand Rapids:
Eerdmans Publishers Comp., 1950

Schoon, Simon *Christelijke Presentie in de Joodse Staat
Kampen* (Holland): J. H. Kok, 1982

Silberman, Charles *A Certain People* New York:
Summit books, 1985

Simon, Merrill *Jerry Falwell and the Jews* New York:
Jonathan David Publ., Inc., 1984

Stendahl, Krister *Paul among Jews and Gentiles*
Philadelphia: Fortress Press, 1976

Tanenbaum, M., Wilson, M., Rudin, A. j. (Eds.) *Evangelicals and Jews in an Age of Pluralism* Grand
Rapids: Baker Book House, 1984

Van Buren, Paul *Discerning the Way* New York:
Seabury Press, 1980

About the Author

Isaac C. Rottenberg was born in England and grew up in the Netherlands. During the Nazi occupation of Holland, several members of his family were imprisoned and he spent more than two years in hiding.

After the war, the author studied law at the University of Leiden. He later left Europe with his wife to make a new beginning in America.

Mr. Rottenberg was graduated from New Brunswick Theological Seminary and was ordained as a minister of the Reformed Church in America. He has served his denomination as pastor, national executive and as lecturer in theology. Among his many ecumenical activities, he served as the first chairman of the Office on Christian-Jewish Relations of the National Council of Churches.

From 1980-1988, Mr. Rottenberg served as the Executive Director of the NATIONAL CHRISTIAN LEADERSHIP CONFERENCE FOR ISRAEL.

Red Mountain Associates
Hemlock Farms
Box 2113
Hawley, PA 18428
717-775-0954